AF262755

Seurat
and the Sea

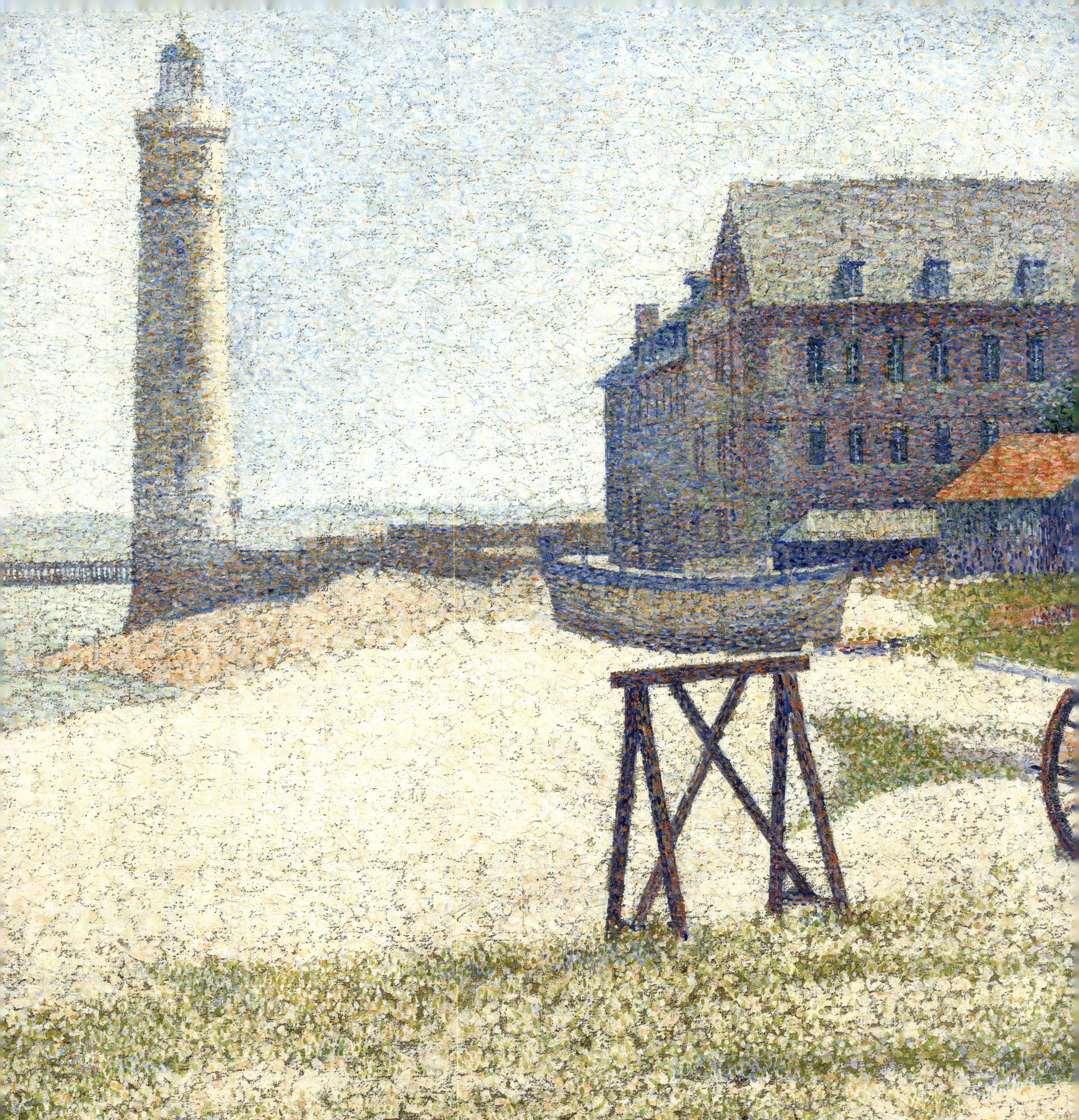

Seurat
and the Sea

Karen Serres

With contributions by
Paul Smith and Richard Thomson

COURTAULD
GALLERY

in association with
Paul Holberton Publishing

First published to accompany the exhibition

Seurat
and the Sea

The Courtauld Gallery, London
13 February – 17 May 2026

The Courtauld Gallery is supported by
Research England.

The exhibition is presented in the Denise
Coates Exhibition Galleries.

Dr Karen Serres is Senior Curator of Paintings
at the Courtauld Gallery, London, and curator
of the exhibition.

Professor Paul Smith is Professorial Research
Fellow in the History of Art, University of
Warwick.

Professor Richard Thomson is Emeritus
Professor in the History of Art, University of
Edinburgh.

Front cover: detail of cat. 16
Frontispiece: detail of cat. 5
Back cover: detail of cat. 22

ISBN 978-1-913645-90-8

British Library Catalogue in Publishing Data

A CIP record of this publication is available
from the British Library

Produced by Paul Holberton Publishing
paulholberton.com

Designed by Laura Parker

Distributed by Yale University Press, New
Haven and London

Authorized Representative in the EU: Easy
Access System Europe, Mustamäe tee 50, 10621
Tallinn, Estonia, gpsr.requests@easproject.
com

Printed by 4-Flying Srl trading as e-Graphic,
Verona, Italy

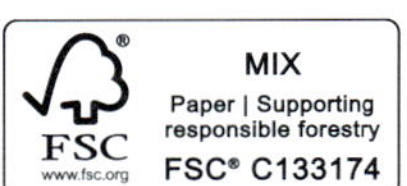

Contents

Exhibition Supporters

Title Supporter

Kenneth C. Griffin

GRIFFIN CATALYST

The Government Indemnity Scheme
This exhibition has been made possible by the provision of Government Indemnity. The Courtauld would like to thank HM Government for providing Government Indemnity and the Department for Culture, Media and Sport, and Arts Council England for arranging the indemnity.

Detail of cat. 22

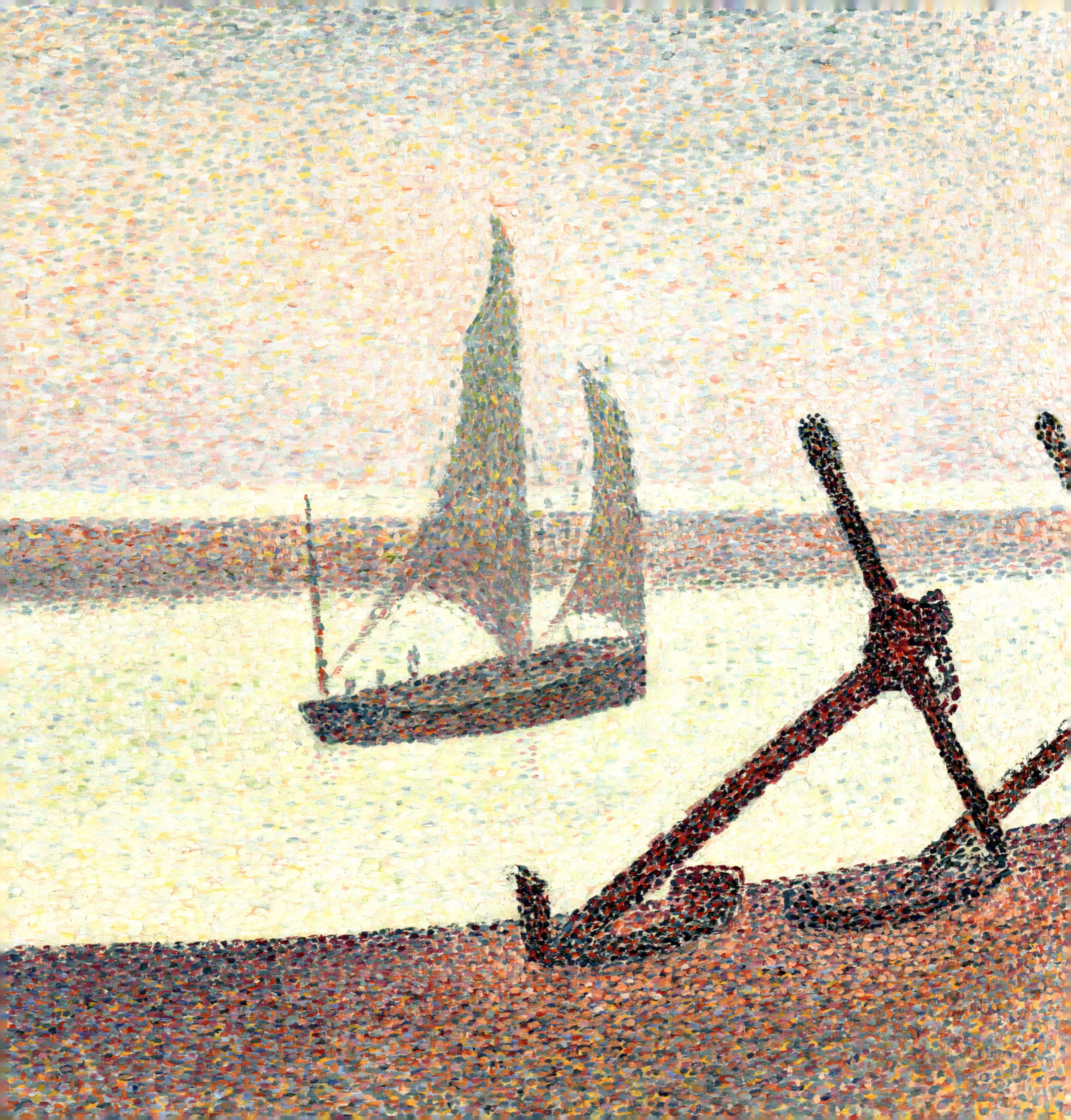

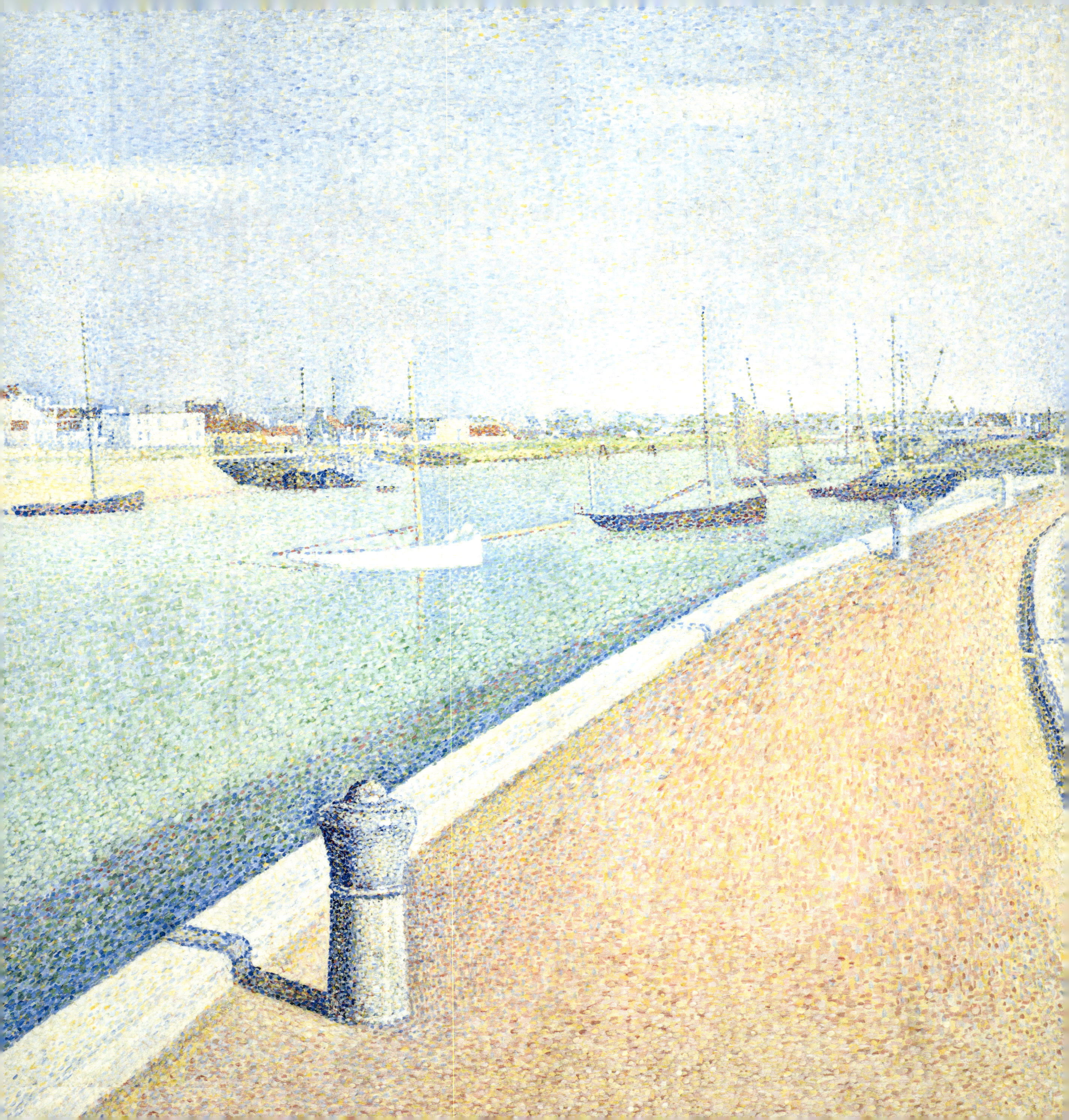

Director's Preface

MARK HALLETT

Märit Rausing Director,
Courtauld Institute of Art

At the Courtauld, we pride ourselves on putting together exhibitions that are distinguished by the clarity of their focus and the thoughtfulness of their curation. These are displays that invite considered interpretation, as well as offering a feast for the eye. More particularly, they encourage visitors not only to scrutinise individual works of art but to move purposefully between them, so as to enjoy these works' complex relationships with one another and to appreciate the broader stories they tell. The pleasures of close looking – one of the skills we aim to inculcate in our students and in all those who visit our galleries – include the appreciation, through sustained visual analysis, of the dialogue between objects as well as the richness of these objects in their own right. These pleasures, in turn, multiply when we start to recognise the forms of continuity and variation that emerge as we cast our eyes across longer sequences of interconnected works, carefully assembled across the exhibition space. At such moments, the rewards of a refined and reflective kind of curating, and of a similarly patient and concentrated form of looking, become ever more evident and satisfying.

Seurat and the Sea exemplifies this model of display and curatorship, and this invitation to rove slowly and attentively between interlocking sets of images. It is the first UK exhibition devoted to this great French artist in almost thirty years and the first to concentrate on his seascapes. Seurat produced more examples of this kind of picture than any other, on the back of a series of summer painting campaigns on the northern coast of France, undertaken between 1885 and 1890. Our display brings together the largest grouping of such works ever to have been assembled: 26 in total. These images include stunning preparatory drawings and oil sketches as well as a wealth of fully realised canvases. In bringing this particular set of objects together, *Seurat and the Sea* gives us a unique opportunity to track the subtle yet profound development of the artist's seascape practice across the six extraordinarily productive years that preceded his dreadfully untimely death at the age of 31 in 1891. In doing so, we come to realise the crucial role that these shimmering, limpid and highly experimental works played in Seurat's wider output, and in the development of French painting in this period.

For conceiving of this project, and for bringing all her formidable curatorial intelligence and creativity to bear on its realisation, I would like to thank the exhibition's curator, Dr Karen Serres. Karen, a much-admired Courtauld colleague of long standing, has done an extraordinary job, not least in securing a series of stellar loans from an international constellation of museums, galleries and private collectors.

I would also like to thank Griffin Catalyst for their continued support of our exhibition programme. Griffin Catalyst, the title supporter for *Seurat and the Sea*, as for a large number of our recent shows, is the civic engagement initiative of Citadel founder and CEO Kenneth C. Griffin, who has also personally supported the display. We would like to express our deepest appreciation to him for offering such an exemplary model of enlightened philanthropy.

Foreword

ERNST VEGELIN
VAN CLAERBERGEN

Head of the Courtauld Gallery

In the 1920s, a remarkably large proportion of Georges Seurat's painted œuvre came onto the international art market, including six of the seven celebrated major figure paintings that the artist produced during his brief but profoundly original and influential career. The industrialist and collector Samuel Courtauld recognised the opportunity. Buying both for his private collection, which now forms the core of the Courtauld Gallery, and for the nation through the Courtauld Fund, Courtauld acquired no less than thirteen works by Seurat, ensuring that the artist would be represented in depth and at high quality in UK collections. Courtauld's purchases included two of the artist's seascapes. The quiet and contemplative character of these works surely struck a chord with Courtauld's own private and poetic nature.

For an artist more commonly associated with modern Paris and its lively suburbs, it is surprising to learn that views of the Channel coast account for the largest single subject category in Seurat's oeuvre. These works were admired by his contemporaries, including in avant-garde circles, and they came to be regarded as particularly expressive of Seurat's unique sensibility. *Seurat and the Sea* is the first time that an exhibition has brought together a representative selection of these works. It features examples from each of Seurat's five summer campaigns between 1885 and 1890. A particular highlight is the presentation of the complete series of paintings made in Port-en-Bessin in 1888 and Gravelines in 1890.

Seurat and the Sea reflects the Courtauld Gallery's commitment to looking anew at aspects of Impressionism and Post-Impressionism, often through a highly focused approach. For this, we rely heavily on the generosity of colleagues and friends around the world, and I am immensely grateful to the museums and generous private collectors in the United Kingdom, France, the Netherlands, Belgium, Germany, Switzerland, the Czech Republic, the United States and Australia who have supported this exhibition with the loan of major works of art in their care. It is thanks to them that this exhibition has been realised at this exceptional level.

Seurat and the Sea is curated by Dr Karen Serres, the Courtauld Gallery's Senior Curator of Paintings and a leading museum scholar of Impressionism. Her research and her commitment to quality are evident throughout the exhibition and this publication. I am immensely grateful to her for leading what has been a highly ambitious and complex undertaking. I hope that this beautiful catalogue will be enjoyed by a wide audience as well as serving as a point of reference for scholars, and I want to thank Professor Paul Smith and Professor Richard Thomson for their valuable essays. Of the many colleagues in the Gallery who have contributed in various ways to the preparation of this project, it is a pleasure to thank in particular our Registrar of Exhibitions, Amy Graves, who has managed the logistics, as well as Dr Barnaby Wright and Dr Karin Kyburz. It is a privilege for the Courtauld Gallery to be able to conceive and present exhibitions such as this. *Seurat and the Sea* has been many years in the making and we are profoundly grateful to all those who have supported us along the way.

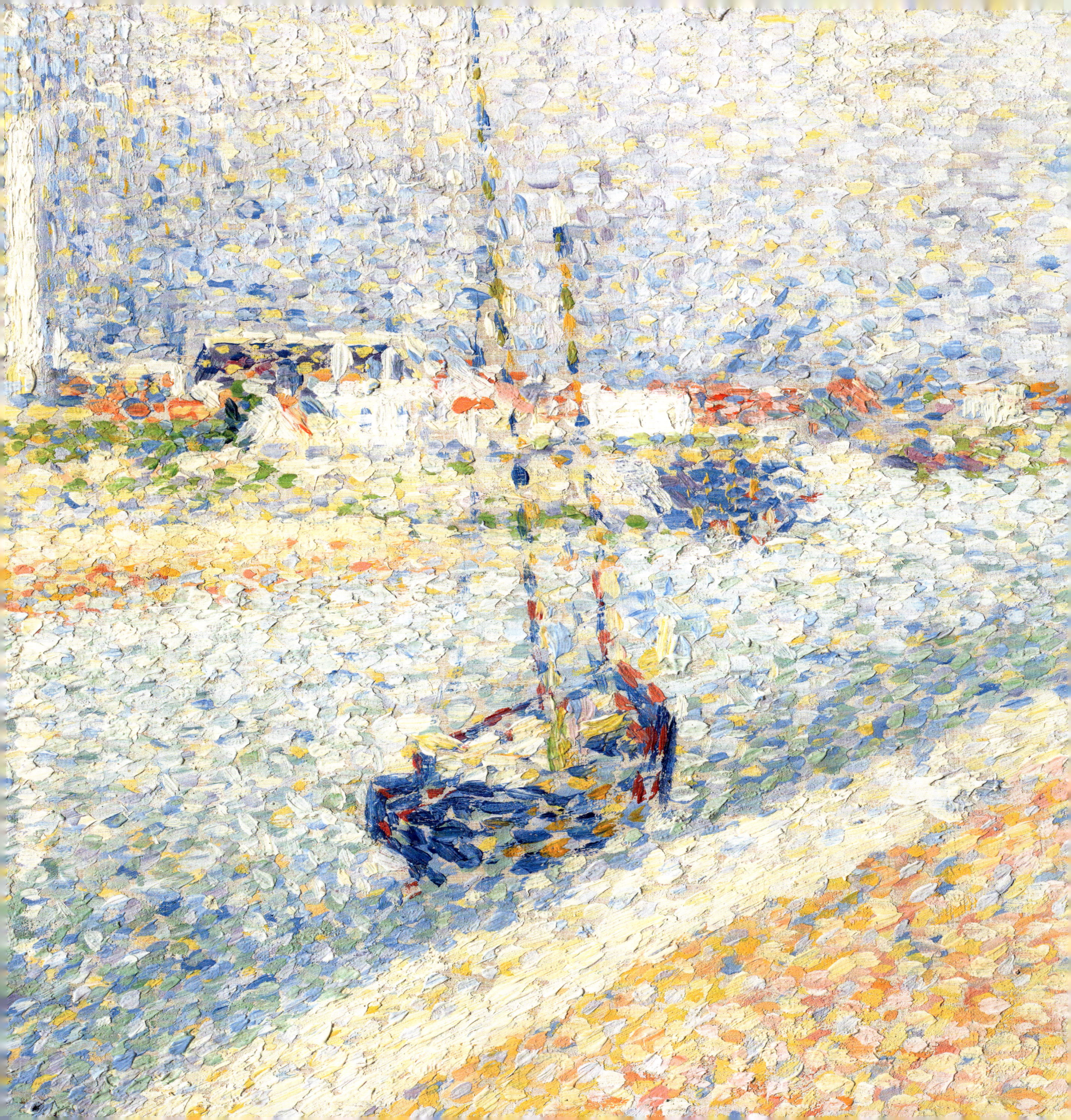

Acknowledgements

It is a pleasure to express our gratitude to the many individuals, museums and galleries that have made this exhibition and publication possible.

The project has benefitted from generous loans from numerous public institutions. We would like to thank the Baltimore Museum of Art (Asma Naeem, Lara Yeager-Crasselt, Katy Rothkopf and Jamiee Shim); The Barnes Foundation, Philadelphia (Thom Collins, Nancy Ireson and Andrea Cakars); the Centre Pompidou, Musée national d'art moderne/Centre de création industrielle, Paris and Musée de l'Annonciade, Saint-Tropez (Xavier Rey, Séverine Berger, Raphaële Bianchi, Kim Dang, Rania Moussa Morin, Noëlle Albert and Sophie Frouchart); the Indianapolis Museum of Art (Belinda Tate, Robin Cooper and Sherry Peglow); the Kröller-Müller Museum, Otterlo (Benno Tempel, Jannet De Goede and Wobke Hooites); the Minneapolis Institute of Art (Katie Luber, Matthew Welch, Rachel McGarry and Tanya Morrison); the Musée des Beaux-Arts de la Ville de Tournai (Julien Foucart, Magali Vangilbergen and Gwendoline Moran Debraine); the Musée d'Orsay, Paris (the late Sylvain Amic, Paul Perrin, Anne Robbins and Candice Brunerie); the Museum of Modern Art, New York (Glenn D. Lowry, Ann Temkin, Jodi Hauptman, Lily Goldberg and Eliza Frecon); the National Gallery, London (Gabriele Finaldi, Christopher Riopelle, Chiara di Stefano and Sam Dorman); the National Gallery, Prague (Alicja Knast, Veronika Hulíková, Anna Pravdová and Eva Klimtová); the National Gallery of Art, Washington, D.C. (Kaywin Feldman, Mary Morton, Kimberly A. Jones, Margaret Doyle and Rebecca Myles); the National Gallery of Australia, Canberra (Nick Mitzevich, Magda Keaney, Lucina Ward and Eliza Ormsby); The Nelson-Atkins Museum of Art, Kansas City (Julián Zugazagoitia, Aimee Marcereau DeGalan and Cailin Carter); the Saint Louis Art Museum (Min Jung Kim, Simon Kelly, Annie Chappell and Kimberly Broker); Tate (Maria Balshaw, Karin Hindsbo and Nikita Payne); and the Victoria and Albert Museum, London (Tristram Hunt, Rosalind McKever and Lucy Gray).

Equally important to this exhibition are loans of major works from private collections. We would like to thank most sincerely Rupert Burgess and Petra Ransom; Jack Shear and Allison Wucher; the Bailly Gallery, Geneva and Paris, especially Charly Bailly and Maureen Diziain; and those individuals who wish to remain anonymous.

We are also indebted to the many people who shared information and advice throughout the various stages of the exhibition's development. For help facilitating loans, we are hugely grateful to Keith Gill, Eric Widing and Gudrun Klemm at Christie's, London, New York and Düsseldorf, and Gary Tinterow, Carli van de Kerkhof and Tucker Garrison at the Museum of Fine Arts, Houston. We benefitted from the support of Her Excellency the Ambassador of France to the United Kingdom Hélène Duchène, Thomas Brégeon, Anissia Morel and the staff of the French Embassy.

For assistance in research for the exhibition and its catalogue, thank you to Any Allard; Sébastien Chauffour; Sophie Derrot at the Bibliothèque de l'Institut national d'histoire de l'art, Paris; and Juliette Parmentier-Correau at the Fondation Custodia, Paris.

For discussions on the technical examination of Seurat's paintings, heartfelt thanks go to Professor Aviva Burnstock from the Conservation

Department of the Courtauld Institute of Art, London; and Elizabeth Walmsley at the National Gallery of Art, Washington, D.C.

At the Courtauld, numerous colleagues have contributed to the project. Special thanks go to Amy Graves, as well as Graeme Barraclough, Kate Edmondson, Tanya Millard, Chloe Nahum, Matthew Thompson and Barnaby Wright. Karin Kyburz was incredibly helpful in researching and sourcing images for this publication; many thanks to her.

We are also grateful to Rob Baker (and his Marketing and Communications team), Caitlin Brooker, Morgan Brown, Leyla Bumbra, Fergus Carmichael, Aimee Clark, Savash Djemal, Ketty Gottardo, Helen Higgins (and her colleagues in the Learning Department), Hannah Kauffman, Camilla Knight, Beattrys John, Gerlind May, Siân Morris, Charlotte Newton, Dervla O'Shea, Jon Ping (and his Commercial and Visitor Services team), Abi Pole, Anne Puetz, Sarah-Lily Russ, Sandra Santos, Éléonore de Sibert (and her Advancement team), Margot Sprague-Davies, Ashleigh Toll, Anthony Tyrrell (and his Estates and Facilities team), Angela Wright and Charlotte Yates.

Thank you very much to Belinda Moore for her work on the exhibition interpretation graphics; to Zerlina Hughes and her team at ZNA for lighting the exhibition; and to Erica Bolton, Daisy Taylor, Ashleigh Chow and the team at Bolton & Quinn for press relations.

For their work on the production of this publication, warm thanks are due to Paul Holberton, Laura Parker, Katherine Bogden Bayard and Kristen Wenger at Paul Holberton Publishing, and Enrico Lenti and the team at E-Graphic, Verona.

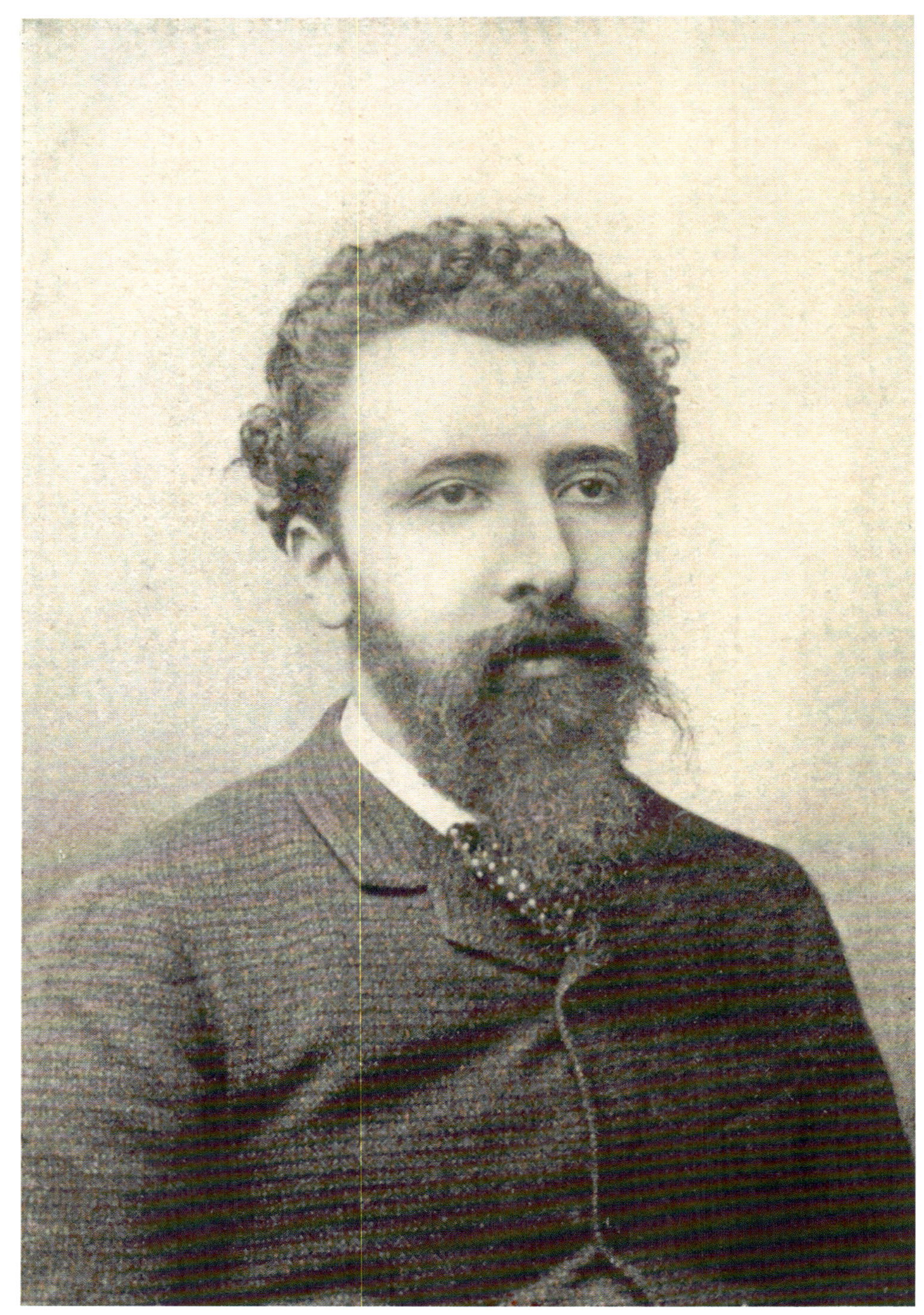

Seurat's Seascapes

KAREN SERRES

The French artist Georges Seurat (1859–1891, fig. 1) is best known today for developing a radical new technique of painting with dots of pure colour, which gave birth to Neo-Impressionism; for creating a handful of ambitious and controversial monumental paintings; and for dying at the age of 31, leaving behind a corpus of fewer than 50 canvases.

The fame of Seurat's seven large figural compositions – works now so iconic as *Bathing, Asnières* (fig. 2), *A Sunday on La Grande Jatte* (fig. 3), *Models* (*Poseuses*, 1886–88, The Barnes Foundation, Philadelphia) and *Circus Sideshow* (fig. 11)[1] – has often eclipsed the major group of paintings he created during five summer sojourns on the northern coast of France between 1885 and 1890. Depicting ports and the open sea, they offer a vital insight into the development of Seurat's highly original and innovative style over the course of his short career. In many ways, they represent a counterpoint to his better-known Parisian production, which examined modern life and places of leisure in and around the city. In contrast, his 'marines' are an exploration of light in open spaces devoid of people. They represent a return to nature that enabled him to test and refresh his technique at an elemental level. Widely present in exhibitions during his lifetime, these paintings were key to bolstering Seurat's reputation and remained highly influential for avant-garde painters after his death.

Remarkably, over half of Seurat's known painted production represents views of the Channel coast. Of the 38 canvases he exhibited in his lifetime, 24 were seascapes. In the past, this aspect of Seurat's work has most often been examined as part of a wider consideration of his oeuvre, most especially in publications by Richard Thomson, Michael F. Zimmermann, Paul Smith and Michelle Foa, which remain essential reading.[2] Insightful essays by Éric Darragon have shed light on particular sites.[3] Three exhibitions have also included a number of seascapes. The first was the exceptional retrospective of Seurat's work held in 1991–92 in Paris and New York, curated by Robert L. Herbert, long the foremost expert on Seurat.[4] A section of the exhibition and catalogue was devoted to Seurat's 'marines', as was the case in the 2014 exhibition on the extraordinary collection of Seurat's work in the Kröller-Müller Museum in Otterlo.[5] Finally, a focused exhibition in Indianapolis in 1990 reunited, for the first time in a century, Seurat's last four seascapes and shed light on his stay in Gravelines in 1890.[6]

Despite this previous interest, *Seurat and the Sea* is the first exhibition and publication exclusively devoted to this group. It brings together seventeen of these remarkable paintings to understand their place in Seurat's oeuvre and to chart the circumstances of their creation (the remaining seven seascapes are also illustrated in this publication). They are accompanied by a selection of the lively oil sketches and Conté crayon drawings made on those same sojourns, some in preparation for larger paintings and others as independent works. Together, they constitute the largest group ever assembled of the works created by Seurat on the Channel coast. By focusing on these works, *Seurat and the Sea* offers the most detailed account of this major part of Seurat's production and reveals how vital they are in his oeuvre. It seeks to deepen our understanding of his seascapes as a key undertaking in his artistic practice.

1. Undated photograph of Georges Seurat, reproduced in Cousturier 1926

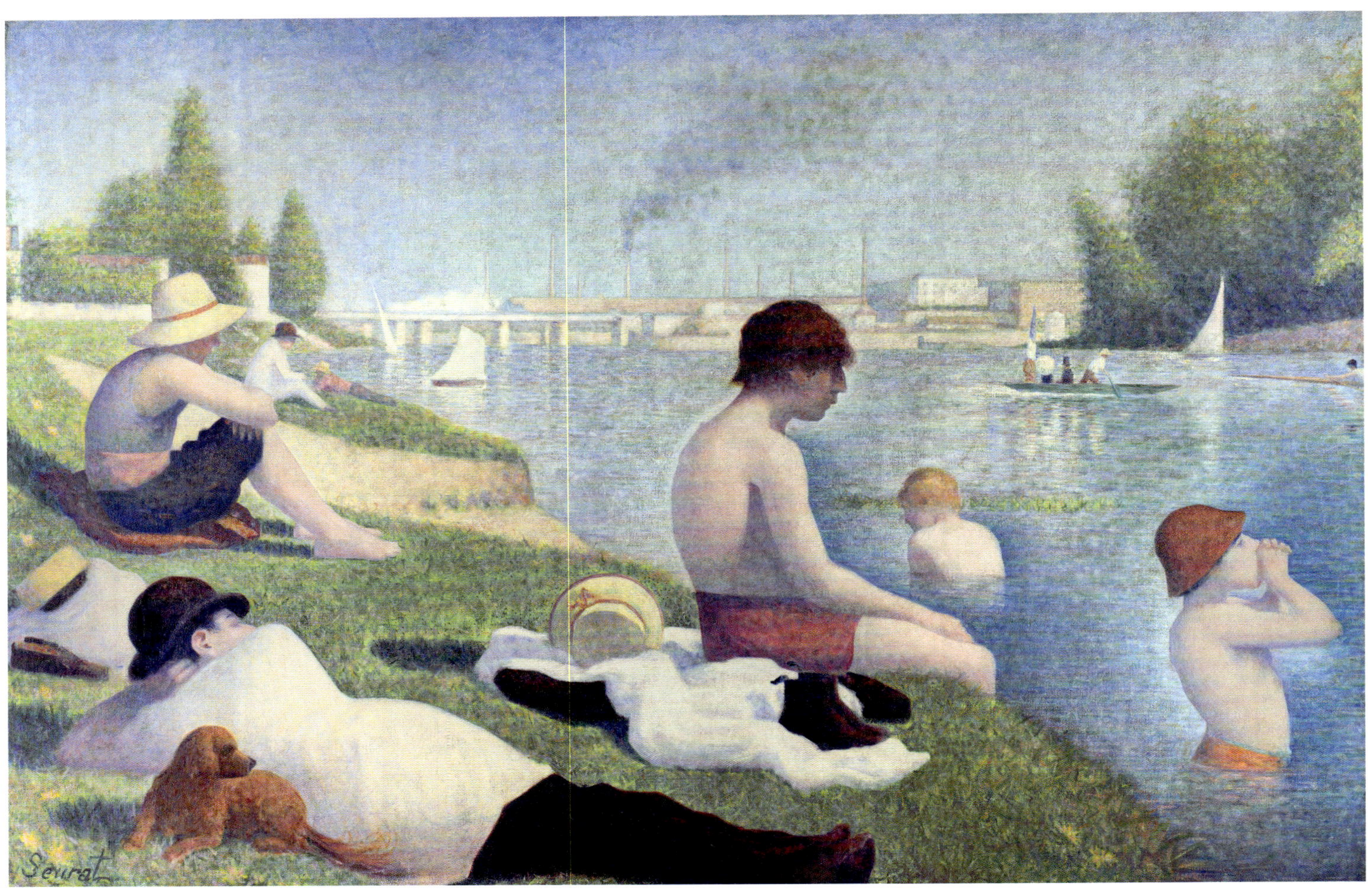

2. Georges Seurat, *Bathing, Asnières* (*Une baignade, Asnières*), 1884, oil on canvas, 201 × 300 cm, National Gallery, London

Seurat was born in Paris in 1859 into a bourgeois family that supported him financially throughout his career. His artistic training initially followed a traditional path. Drawing lessons at the École Municipale de Sculpture et de Dessin (1876–78) led to an admission to the École des Beaux-Arts in 1878. The following year, however, saw two important events for Seurat's career. The first was his visit to the Fourth Impressionist Exhibition in April or May 1879. The other was the start, in November, of his year-long voluntary military service. The Parisian Seurat was posted in Brest, on the western tip of Brittany, and an early biographer dated his interest in seascapes from that period (albeit without a clear source):

All of his leave permits in hand, this one-year conditional conscript, who has never been reprimanded, roams all along the English Channel; he travels from Brest to Saint-Brieuc, to Saint-Malo, to Cherbourg, to Le Havre and as far as Dunkerque, stopping at Perros Guirec, the islands of Guernsey and Jersey,

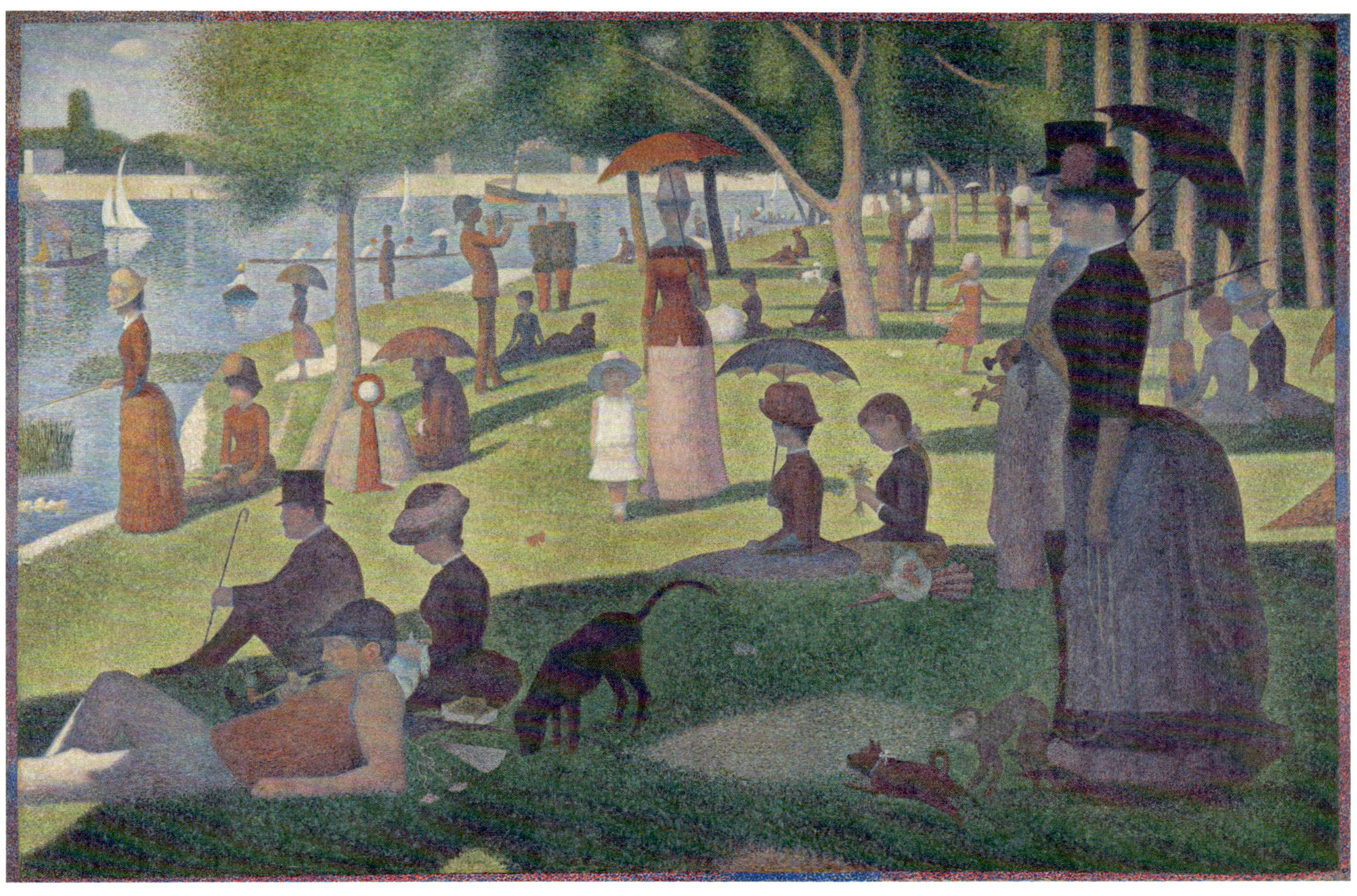

3. Georges Seurat, *A Sunday on La Grande Jatte* (*Un dimanche à la Grande-Jatte*), 1884–86, painted border c. 1888–89, oil on canvas, 207.5 × 308.1 cm, The Art Institute of Chicago

lingering even longer in this estuary of the Seine, where he falls in love with Grandcamp, Port-en-Bessin and Cabourg.[7]

Upon his return to Paris, Seurat left the École des Beaux-Arts and set up on his own. A drawn portrait of his friend and fellow artist Edmond Aman-Jean (The Metropolitan Museum of Art, New York) was accepted at the official Salon in 1883. At that same moment, however, Seurat was moving away from his conventional training and the artistic establishment to seek a radical new way of painting. The large canvas *Bathing, Asnières* (fig. 2) was its first manifestation. When the painting was rejected by the Salon in 1884, Seurat joined the new Groupe (later Société) des Artistes Indépendants, which championed exhibitions of contemporary art open to all, with no selection committees nor juries. These became the Salon des Indépendants, where Seurat exhibited every year until his death seven years later, in 1891.

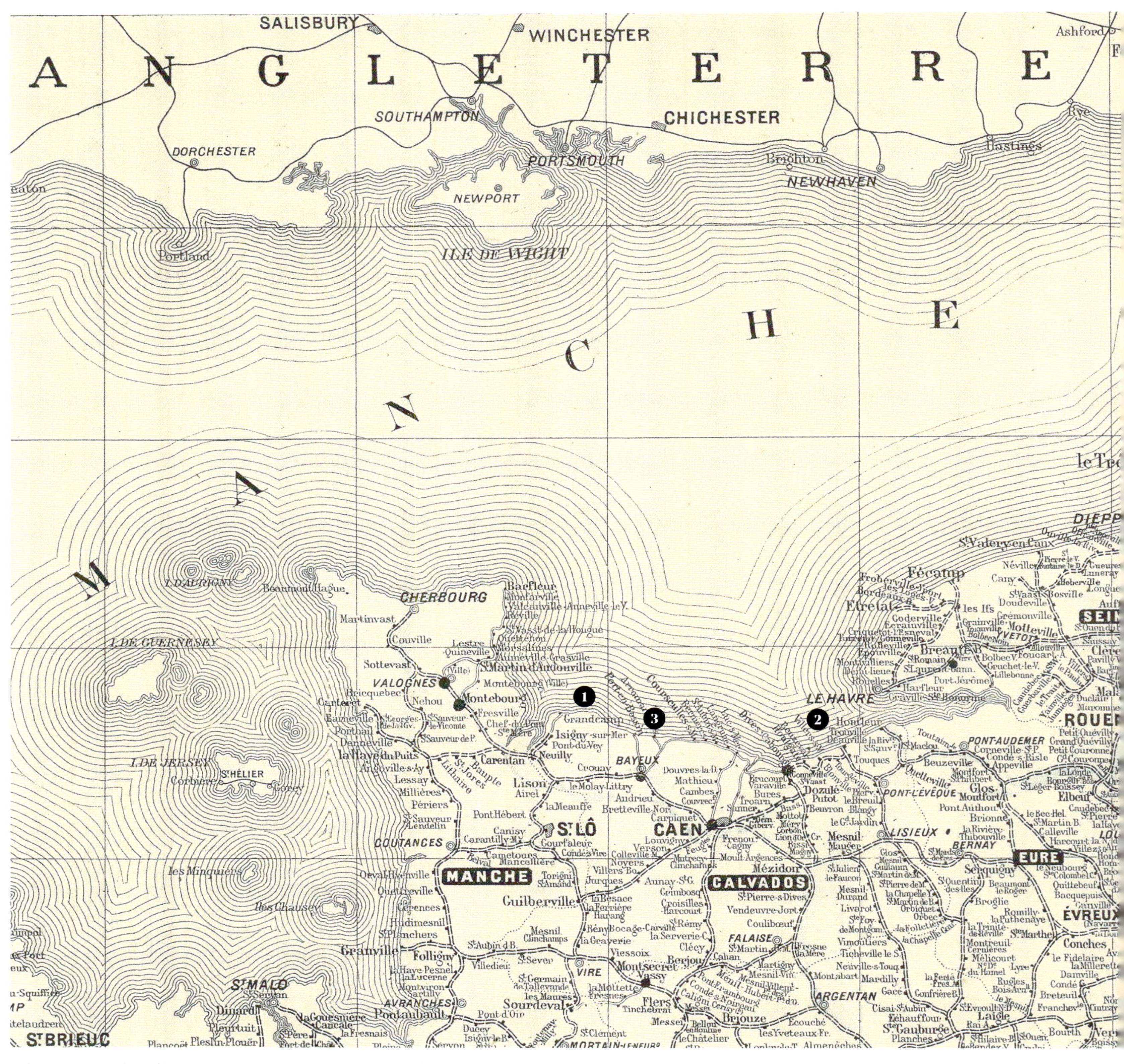

4. *General map of the rail lines of France …* (detail
showing the places visited by Seurat), Paris: Chaix, 1895,
Bibliothèque nationale de France, Paris: the double and
black lines map out the rail network but are differentiated
because they were run by separate companies.

1 Grandcamp, 1885
2 Honfleur, 1886
3 Port-en-Bessin, 1888
4 Le Crotoy, 1889
5 Gravelines, 1890

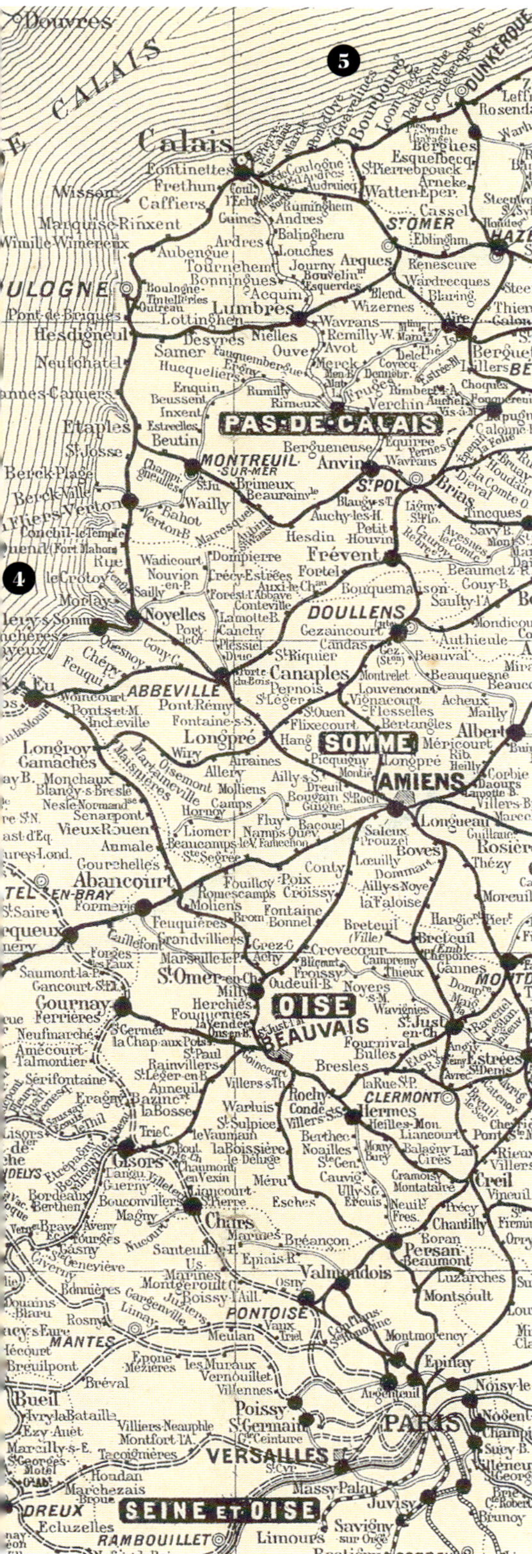

In leaving the city during the summer months, Seurat was following the well-trodden path of the middle classes who fled the sweltering capital for the coast or countryside, thanks in large part to the rapid expansion of the French railway network. When Seurat was forced to stay in Paris during the summer of 1887 (perhaps to finish work on his large *Models* and *Circus Sideshow*), he complained that the city was deserted.[8] Despite this lament, Seurat was by all accounts a highly reserved, introspective person who rarely let anyone into his studio. Similarly, he always went to the coast on his own, not for a holiday but as a change of pace from the city, to capture a different kind of light and to experiment with a different approach to his technique.

Seurat's reserve and short life mean that sources on his work, life and ideas are rare. We must rely on a handful of letters; testimonies from friends and fellow artists; reviews at the time; and the works themselves to elucidate his career. Seurat's contemporaries were certainly aware of his yearly routine. Recounting a conversation with Seurat in 1887, the Belgian poet Émile Verhaeren contrasted Seurat's seascapes – 'his summer's work' – with the 'large canvas' he pursued every winter in Paris. He described seeing in Seurat's studio

A few landscapes, including one on an easel. It was his summer's work, the one he undertook every year at the seaside or around Paris … He concluded: 'a large canvas in winter, a canvas of experimentation and ideally of conquest…'
 - A thesis canvas ('*Une toile à thèse*'), I interrupted.
But he did not agree and continued … 'then, in the summer, cleansing one's eyes of the days spent in the studio and translating as accurately as possible the bright light, in all its nuances.' A life divided in two, by art itself.[9]

The French poet and art critic Gustave Kahn, another of the few privileged visitors to Seurat's studio, also commented on his divided year:

In this small, narrow studio [on boulevard de Clichy], inconvenient, freezing in the winter and sweltering in the summer, Seurat sat daily in front of his three-month canvas; he emerged emaciated and, to rest, went to paint seascapes, returning with six canvases of a variety of motifs and intentions.[10]

One must, however, be careful not to place Seurat's 'winter' canvas and 'summer' work in opposition, as one strongly informed the other. Seurat's seascapes played a crucial role in the development of his technique and he often reworked his large figural paintings after his summer campaigns. As Thomson has noted, 'At times they [the seascapes] served as the laboratory for experiment, with the dotted touch, directional brushwork, the painted border.'[11]

As this essay describes, Seurat's choice of subject matter during his stays on the coast and its development are equally illuminating, as he progressed from a clear debt to Impressionist landscapes – and Claude Monet's Normandy works in particular – in his early work to more geometrical and abstracted compositions in the later ones. Nevertheless, he always remained remarkably faithful and accurate in the representation of his chosen sites, as the contemporary postcards and modern photographs reproduced in this publication make clear. This is perhaps surprising given the highly constructed nature of his figural works. The painter Charles Angrand reminisced that Seurat 'was not a slave to nature, oh! no; but he was respectful of it, not being imaginative.'[12] Seurat was equally attentive to weather and its effect on light. As he wrote from Honfleur to his friend and fellow artist Paul Signac in 1886, 'The wind and therefore the clouds have bothered me these past few days. The stability of the first days should come back … What else can I say? Well, that's it for today, let us get drunk on light once again, it's a consolation.'[13] Seurat's seascapes carefully depict the fall of light and shadow, and render the unmistakable pearly glow and overcast skies of the northern coast.

Grandcamp

Seurat's first summer campaign took place in 1885 in Normandy, in the small fishing village of Grandcamp. This would be followed by four further stays, in Honfleur in 1886, Port-en-Bessin in 1888, Le Crotoy in 1889 and Gravelines in 1890. By going to Normandy to paint, Seurat was following in the footsteps of a long line of artists, most famously Eugène Boudin and Monet. Signac, a great admirer of Monet, had worked in Port-en-Bessin over three summers from 1882 to 1884, and might have encouraged his friend to go to the coast. Thomson's essay in this publication charts the tradition of artists painting in the towns frequented by Seurat.

The opening of the railway line between Paris and Normandy around 1850 had made the coast easily accessible from the capital, for painters and holidaymakers alike. Indeed, it is notable that all the spots chosen by Seurat could be reached by train (fig. 4). Over the previous decades, towns like Honfleur had progressively been transformed from fishing villages into resorts, ready to welcome French and foreign tourists. At the same time, ports on the Channel were expanding their infrastructure to cater to increased commercial traffic, most especially with Great Britain and Scandinavia, an industrialisation captured in Seurat's works, most notably his views of Honfleur and Port-en-Bessin.

This was yet to come, however, as Grandcamp in 1885 had no commercial infrastructure and few tourists. The small fishing village, located at the westernmost point of the Norman coast before it juts out into the Cotentin peninsula, had a sheltered harbour (cat. 3) but no port, forcing the fishing boats to moor on the beach (fig. 5). Five paintings from that summer are known, alongside twelve small oil sketches. Four sketches are preparatory for larger works (see, for example, cat. 2), while the others are either independent studies or perhaps made in preparation for paintings never realised (cat. 4). Seurat explored the area and painted from both the beach and the cliffs. His most dramatic view is certainly of the rock formation Le Bec du Hoc (also known as La Pointe du Hoc) slightly east of Grandcamp (cat. 1). While the depiction of open water from an elevated vantage point inevitably calls to mind Monet's views of Normandy, Seurat boldly undermines the expected panorama by having the rock cut the horizon line and almost touch the top of the canvas. He used a similar device in *The Roadstead of Grandcamp* (cat. 3),

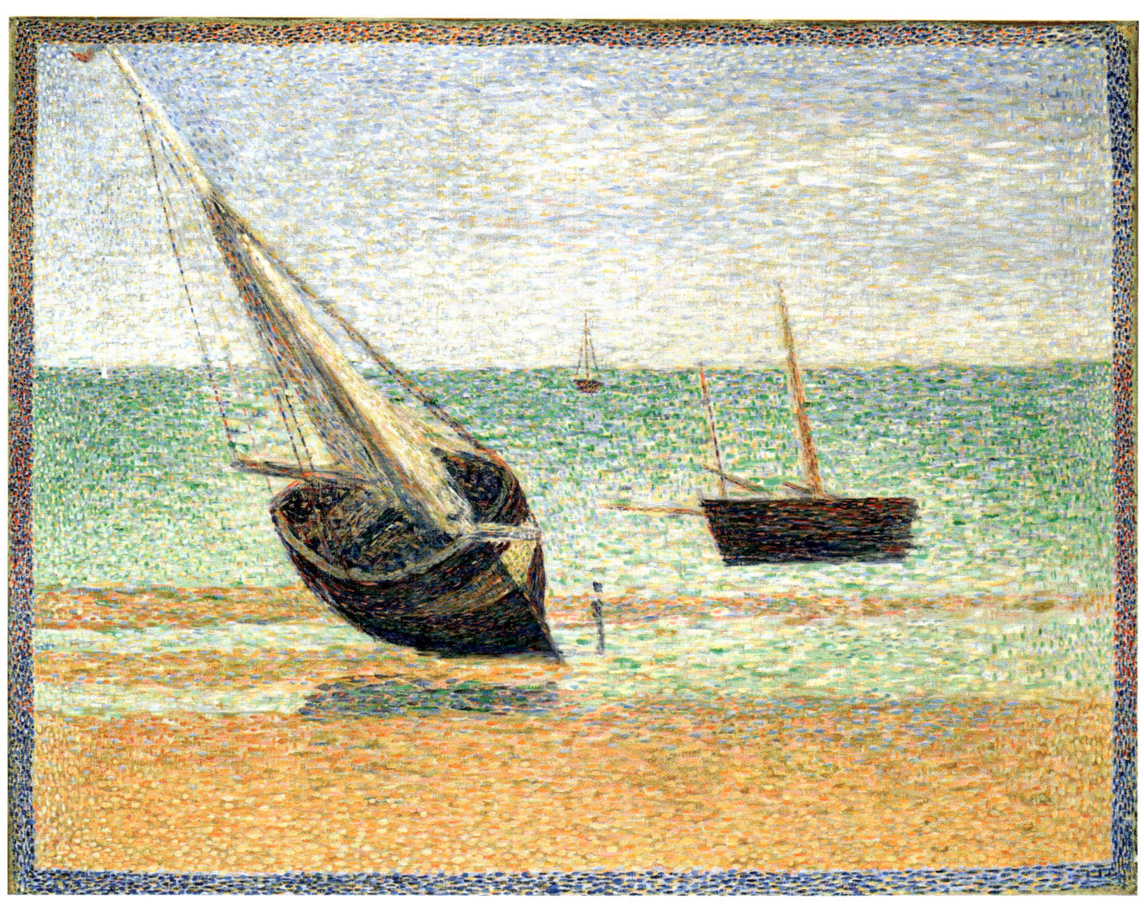

5. Georges Seurat, *Boats (Bateaux)*, 1885, oil on canvas, 66 × 82 cm, Pola Museum of Art (Japan)

whose foreground vegetation blocks the view of a passing regatta – another echo of Monet. Another favoured composition, which recurred throughout Seurat's seascapes, can be seen with the view of the seventeenth-century fortification Fort Samson, this time west of Grandcamp (fig. 6). The main purpose of the structure is to serve as a transition in the middle distance between the large expanse in the foreground and the sea beyond. The combination of sand and creeping vegetation that takes up more than half of the canvas is particularly suited to Seurat's emerging pointillist technique of using short brushstrokes of pure colours. The fifth Grandcamp painting (fig. 7) looks back towards the town as the sun is setting, allowing Seurat to deploy a different tonal range, using soft pinks and purples to capture the fading light. In all these canvases, Seurat broke up the vast expanse of sea with a passing sailboat or a buoy, signs of human presence in compositions otherwise devoid of figures. Those elements are always painted over existing paint and were added at the end, no doubt to balance the composition.

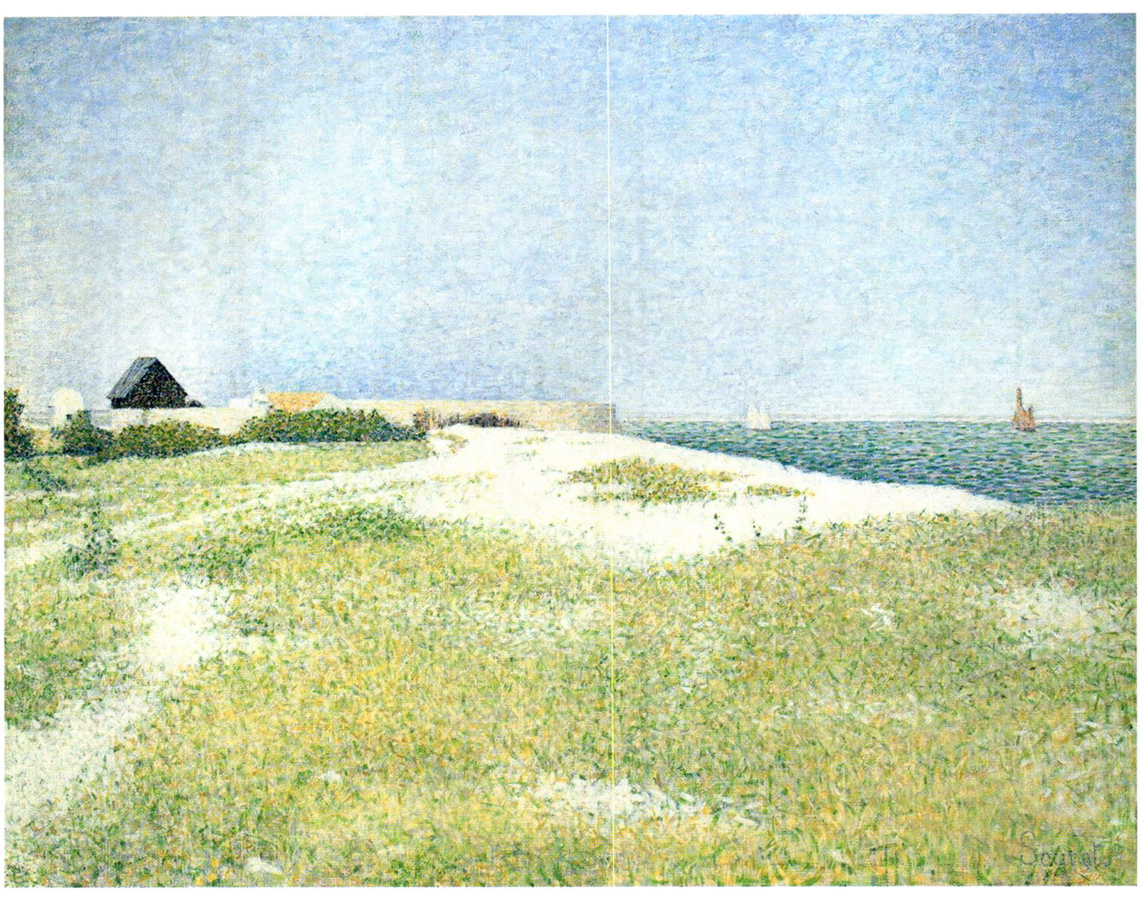

6. Georges Seurat, *Fort Samson (Grandcamp)*
(Le fort Samson [Grandcamp]), 1885, oil on
canvas, 65 × 81 cm, Hermitage Museum,
Saint Petersburg (Russia)

The Grandcamp paintings give only a partial insight into Seurat's early
style as several were reworked years later as his technique evolved. Painted
borders were added to *Le Bec du Hoc (Grandcamp)*, *Grandcamp (Evening)* and
Boats around 1889, along with a skin of small, tight dots to enhance certain
areas (see the entry for cat. 1).[14] The unreworked areas, however, show that
Seurat initially adopted two types of short brushstrokes: broken horizontal
lines, which indicate, for example, the waves on the water or clouds in the
sky, and overlapping strokes in a criss-cross pattern, principally to render
vegetation and sand. The latter technique was dubbed '*balayé*' ('swept' or
'sweeping'), a term adopted early on in Seurat literature.[15]

This loose application echoes the one found in the small oil sketches Seurat
made at that period. These spirited works – called '*croquetons*' at the time,
a derivative of '*croquis*', or sketch[16] – fascinate for the insight they offer into
the freer side of a painter now associated with control and precision in his
application of paint. From the start, they were central to Seurat's practice,
both as tools in the creative process and as independent studies. Angrand
remembered seeing in Seurat's studio 'On the wall, in closely spaced frames,

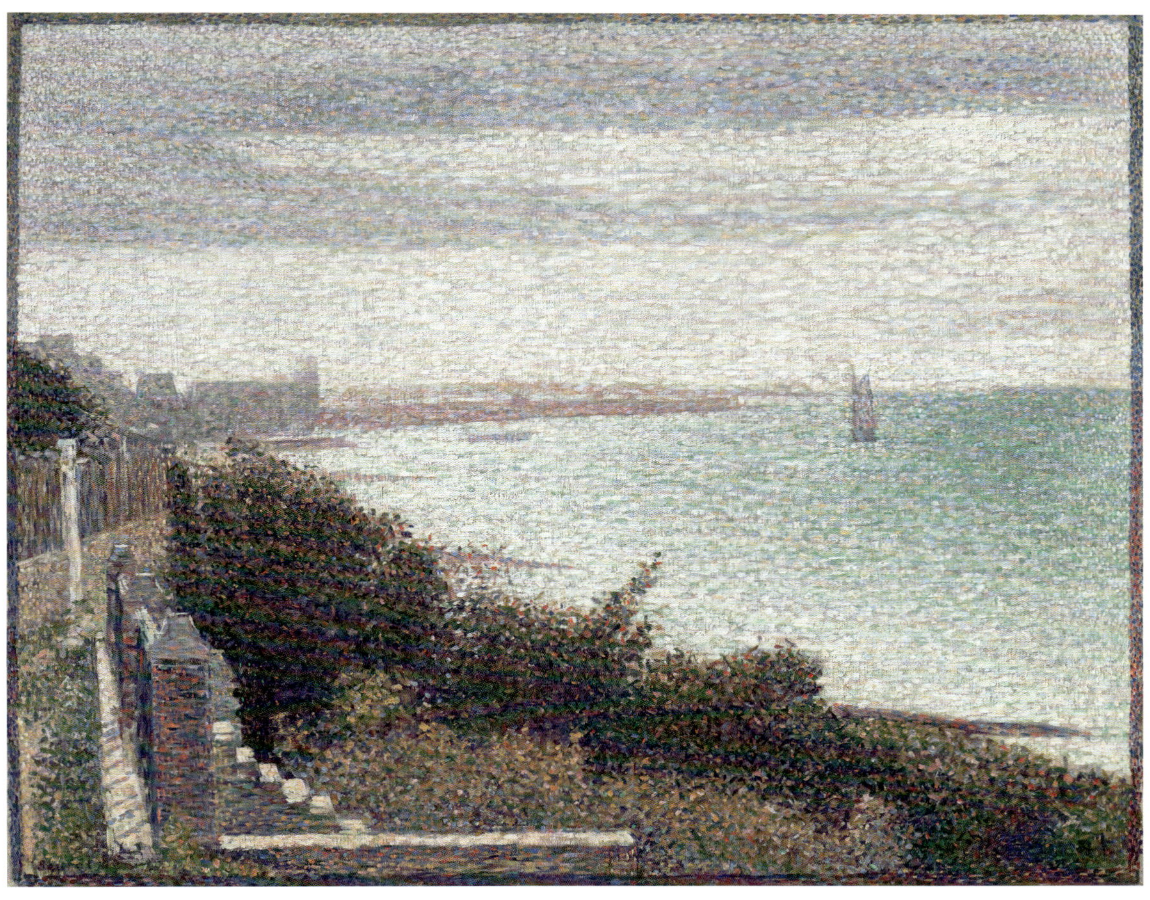

7. Georges Seurat, *Grandcamp (Evening) (Grandcamp [soir])*, 1885, painted border c. 1888–89, oil on canvas, 66.2 × 82.4 cm, The Museum of Modern Art, New York

many of those small studies from a travel paint box, which he said were his greatest joy.'[17]

Seurat made frequent use of sketches in preparation for his large figural canvases as well and 163 were inventoried in his studio after his death.[18] He also included them in public exhibitions, on their own or framed together. Indeed, the first seascapes he ever exhibited were two *croquetons* from Grandcamp, framed alongside 10 other studies and included in the exhibition *Works in Oil and Pastel of the Impressionists of Paris*, which opened in New York in April 1886 (see cat. 2).

Seurat seems to have made (or, more probably, kept) the greatest number of *croquetons* in Grandcamp. Of the nineteen known from his overall time in northern France, twelve date from that summer. Was this high number a mark of his hesitancy in finding motifs? As Seurat wrote to Signac the following year, shortly after arriving in Honfleur, 'It's been nice here for the past five days. I hope to get started on my canvases in earnest soon. So far, I have only done sketches to acclimatise myself.'[19] *Croquetons* were thus a way of settling into painting.

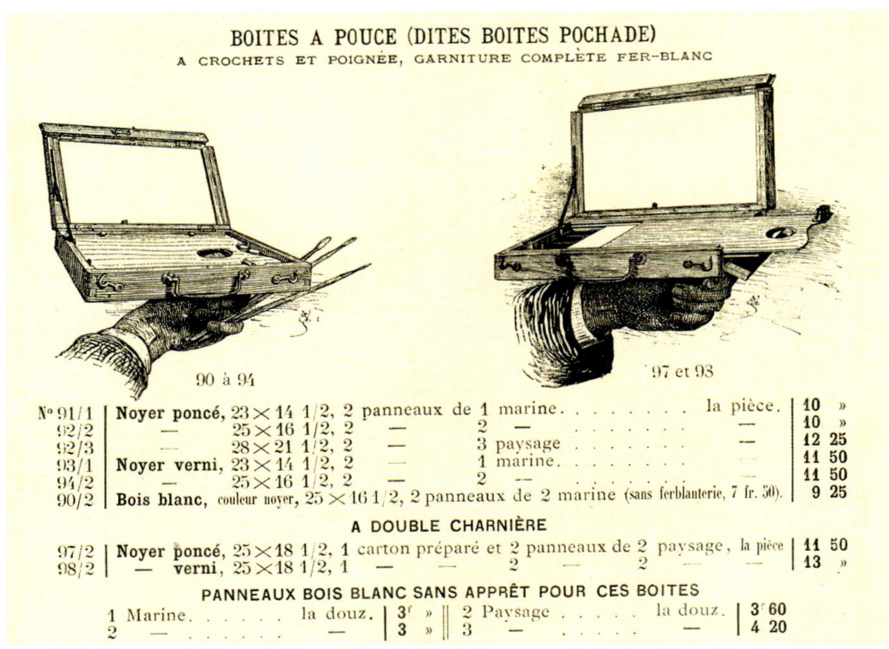

For his sketches, Seurat found early on a format that suited him and never deviated from it. They all measure 16 × 25 cm, a slightly unusual size that is more elongated than the traditional 'landscape' format. It was fittingly called a 'marine' and considered particularly suited to panoramas. The panels were available primed or unprimed in several types of wood, including 'white wood' and mahogany. An important aspect of Seurat's technique is that he never covered the whole panel with paint but instead used the colour of the white priming or bare dark wood as part of his colour scheme (cat. 7 and 21).

The wood panels were meant to be slotted into the small travel paint box mentioned by Angrand, a '*boîte à pouce*'. Its name derives from the fact that there was an opening for the thumb to stabilise the box and allow it to rest on the back of the artist's hand. The bottom held a small palette, paint tubes and turpentine, while panels were fitted on the inside of the lid; several of Seurat's *croquetons* bear grooves indicating where they were held in place (cat. 21). Artists' supply catalogues advertised several types of boxes and it is most likely that Seurat procured his from the firm Bourgeois Aîné, whose trade brochure offered two at the right size (fig. 8: Seurat's was no. 92/2 or 94/2).[20] An ideal set-up for a reserved artist who disliked having anyone watch him paint, it allowed Seurat to work discreetly on site. Grains of sand found embedded in the paint of several *croquetons* confirm they were made outdoors (for example, cat. 21 and 26). No sand was found in the larger canvases and it is more likely that they were painted in his lodgings and finished in Paris.

Seurat's seascape canvases made their debut at the *Eighth Impressionist Exhibition*, which opened on 15 May 1886. Seurat and Signac had been invited to exhibit by Camille Pissarro, who supported the young painters and was trying his hand at their new technique. The last of its kind, the Exhibition showcased how fragmented the movement had become. The reviews set the tone for those garnered by Seurat for the rest of his career. While his large figural composition attracted most of the attention and negative criticism, his seascapes were well received. This may be due to their clearer lineage with Impressionist landscapes, by then a known quantity, as well as with the longer tradition of seascape painting. They fit more easily within an established genre than Seurat's unclassifiable and stagey Parisian works. It may also be that Seurat's technique, sometimes perceived as strange and austere, was felt to be better suited to the rendering of landscapes, imbuing them with a feeling of calm and contemplation. The emerging pointillist technique seemed particularly apt in representing sand, ripples on the water, cloudy skies and wild vegetation, all composed of a myriad of colours.

As one reviewer reported in 1886, 'Mr Seurat's marines', displayed alongside his controversial *A Sunday on La Grande Jatte* (fig. 3), 'were not even contested by the journalists. Their calm immensity shines through from the start, with their burrowed, jagged, aligned cliffs, their waves in the distance reborn, and the huge amount of air circulating between the sky and the water. Mr Seurat manages, as does Mr Pissarro, the feeling of visual void in the atmospheric expanses.'[21] Critics took pains to highlight the contrast between Seurat's strange figural compositions and his seascapes: as one noted,

> In fact, when Mr Seurat uses his method in a more subdued manner, he achieves charming effects. Thus, in his landscapes of *the Bec du Hoc*, *the fort Samson* [sic], *the Roadstead of Grandcamp, the Seine at Courbevoie*, although the pointillist technique still seems too apparent to me, there is a vibration of light, a richness of colour in the shadows imbued with light, a soft and poetic harmony, something milky and flowery that voluptuously strokes the eye.[22]

Another commented, 'If we judge the overall effect of his canvases, we find an extreme delicacy of colours in his suite, particularly of the seascapes of Grandcamp... However, we cannot abide his *Sunday at La Grande Jatte*, which is *crude* in tone and in which the figures are cut out like poorly made mannequins.'[23]

Most importantly, critics all perceived a strong vein of melancholy in Seurat's seascapes. Unlike Monet's, his seas are never agitated but are refined and wistful – feelings enhanced by his pearly-grey touches. In 1886, at least three critics used the same expression – 'a penetrating melancholy' – to describe the sentiment conveyed by Seurat's Grandcamp seascapes.[24] As Thomson notes in his essay in this publication, the sea had long been associated, in the mind of poets and painters, with a cleansing of the soul – or of the eye, in Seurat's case. These feelings of regeneration, however, coexist with a sense of sadness and longing. As another reviewer of the 1886 Impressionist Exhibition noted, 'Some paint in a tranquil manner, with clarity in their solid tones, such as Seurat, whose seascapes are skilfully executed and vibrating with fresh air, with an impression of sadness that is charming.'[25]

Seurat was well aware of these reviews as he subscribed to a press clipping service and diligently pasted the articles onto loose pages.[26]

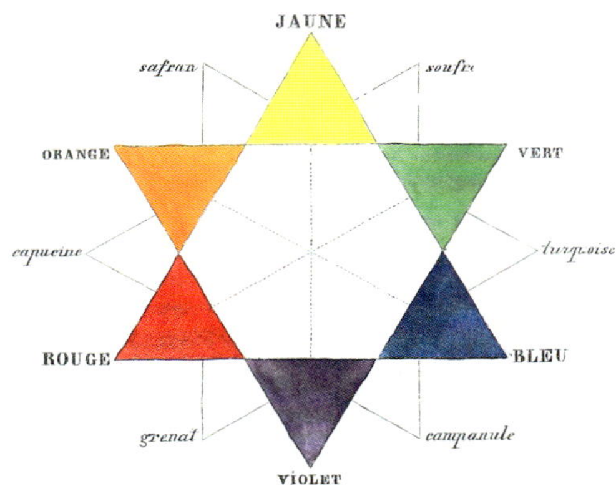

9. Chromatic circle published in Charles Blanc, *Grammaire des arts du dessin: architecture, sculpture, peinture*, Paris: J. Renouard, 1867, p. 599

Angrand remembered him rejecting these interpretations of his work: 'He added: "They – meaning the literary hacks and critics – they see poetry in what I do. No, I apply my method and that is it." Wasn't his point of view sensible? Isn't poetry the very definition of imponderable?'[27] The review by Octave Maus, a Belgian art critic and head of the avant-garde artists' collective Les XX ('Les Vingt', or The Twenty, after the number of artists in the group), would have been more to Seurat's liking, focusing as it did on how the artist rendered light. Seurat's seascapes, he noted, 'reveal an artistic nature singularly adept at breaking down the phenomena of light, penetrating its prism and expressing, through simple but skilfully combined means, its most complicated and most intense effects. We consider Mr Georges Seurat to be a sincere, thoughtful, observant painter, whom the future will rank.'[28]

As we saw, Seurat's 'method' had not yet fully coalesced in the Grandcamp seascapes but their display, alongside *A Sunday on La Grande Jatte*, in May 1886 marked an important milestone in the development of Neo-Impressionism. It spurred the young writer and critic Félix Fénéon (1861–1944) to begin formulating, in his review of the Impressionist Exhibition, the characteristics of the works shown there by the new group of young painters led by Seurat.[29] In consultation with some of them (albeit seemingly not Seurat himself)[30], he expanded on the 'Neo-Impressionist method' in an article a few months later, coining the term.[31] Although the designation might be seen as an homage to these artists' predecessors, Fénéon very much presented the new style in opposition to Impressionism. In the latter, 'nothing was precise: the works of these painters looked like an improvisation; their landscapes were corners of nature glimpsed as though through a porthole quickly opened and closed: it was basic and approximate. This rigorous technique, Impressionism has now possessed it since 1885 thanks to a painter of some 25 years of age, Mr Georges Seurat.'[32] While the Impressionists, he stated, sought to render an instant in a landscape, capturing the sky, sea and vegetation as they would never be seen again, 'To synthesise the landscape into a definitive form that perpetuates its sensation, such is the aim of the Neo-Impressionists.'[33] Signac put the contrast more pithily in his account of the movement, written in 1899: the Impressionist technique is one of 'instinct and inspiration' while the Neo-Impressionists' is 'methodical and scientific'.[34]

To the term 'Neo-Impressionism', Seurat much preferred 'chromo-luminarism' or 'divisionism'. Seeking to render light through colour in a systematic way, he turned to optical theories developed in the previous decades to devise a 'method'. This supposedly scientific approach to art-making was heavily mediated through the work of the historian and art critic Charles Blanc and his *Grammaire des arts du dessin* (1867).[35] Instead of blending colours on the palette or on the canvas itself – thus moving away, according to Fénéon, from the haphazard nature of the Impressionist technique, created 'by means of mysterious sauces put together on the palette'[36] – Seurat applied paint in short strokes (later dots) of pure colour placed side by side. The aim was to 'divide the tone', to separate the colours that make up an image. When viewed from a certain distance, these dots were meant to merge in the beholder's eye. This phenomenon, called 'optical mixture' or 'optical fusion', was believed to confer a greater vibrancy to the surface of the works. Contributing to this vibrancy was the interweaving of cool and warm tones, and the juxtaposition of complementary colours – colours on opposite sides of the colour wheel – whose contrast enhanced the properties of each hue (fig. 9).

Painters had instinctively gravitated towards such colour harmonies long before their scientific formulation and Seurat particularly admired the use of tones in the work of Eugène Delacroix (1798–1863). What he sought, however, was a truly objective approach, to create a modern kind of painting. Crucially, the technique was perceived as inherently modern in that it activated the role of the viewer in new ways, making them part of the process of the picture coming into being. As Signac wrote to Pissarro in February 1887, 'The *pointillé* intrigues people and forces them to think; they sense there is something behind it.'[37]

In practice, however, and as his seascapes make clear, Seurat's method was iterative and experimental, and took many forms. In his early works, he first applied broad planes of colour and used the *balayé* technique to block out the elements in the composition before overlaying then with a loose 'skin' of large overlapping dots. Despite his exactness and commitment to this painstaking pointillist method in his later works, his dots are never uniform but often elongated and directional; they adapt in scale and shape to the forms they model.

In contrast, Seurat's palette shows a steadfast commitment to applying pure colours (fig. 10).[38] Neatly aligned on one side of the board, his hues include several types of greens and blues to render the vegetation, sky and sea. Although he occasionally combined two types of pigments, he most often used unblended tones, mixing them only with white to produce a lighter tint.

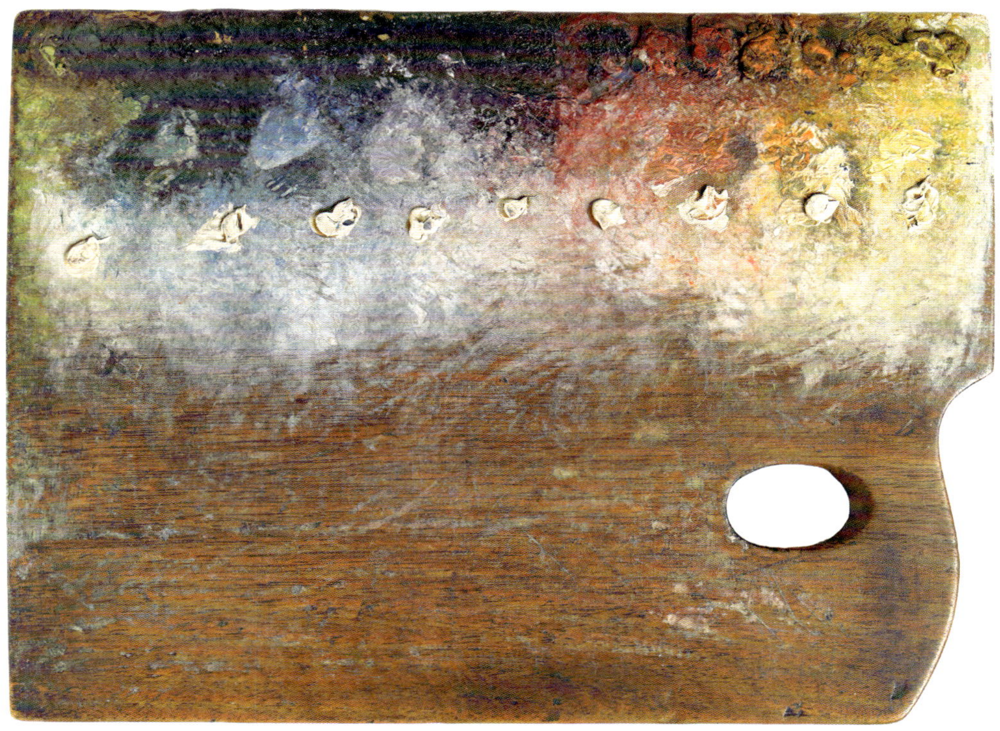

Honfleur

Seurat arrived in Honfleur on 21 June 1886, less than a week after the closure of the *Eighth Impressionist Exhibition*. He lodged west of town, at 15 rue de Grâce, in the home of 'Mr Hélouin', the local tax collector.[39] The eight weeks Seurat spent there were the most productive of all his summer campaigns. He began work on seven large canvases, as well four oil sketches and two drawings.

In contrast to Grandcamp, Honfleur had a long tradition of tourism, thanks to its picturesque medieval cobbled streets, as well as its busy port, located on the mouth of the river Seine, opposite Le Havre.[40] Seurat chose a variety of sites near the port and along the coast. Three views of the shore follow a similar composition, with a strong diagonal in the foreground that contrasts with the horizon beyond (cat. 5 and 6, and fig. 26). In Honfleur, Seurat returned to the overcast skies and pearly water he had painted the previous summer. However, as he wrote to Signac, instead of the open expanse of the Channel, he now saw 'the Seine – an almost indefinable grey sea, even in the brightest sunshine under a blue sky, at least during the last few days.'[41] Two other paintings focused on the port, with an emphasis on horizontal lines (cat. 8 and fig. 20). For all these works, Seurat created preparatory oil sketches (cat. 7 and fig. 55) or Conté crayon drawings outlining their compositions (cat. 9 and fig. 19). The final two paintings moved away from the river and widened Seurat's range of motifs, with views of harboured ships – *The 'Maria' (Honfleur)* (cat. 10) and *Corner of a Harbour (Honfleur)* (fig. 18).[42]

Contemporary postcards and works by previous artists depicting the same sites testify to their popularity. However, it was undoubtedly their striking geometric arrangement that most attracted Seurat. He sought to balance the strong horizon of the waterline and piers with the verticals of the lighthouses and ships' masts, and the diagonals of the cliffs and beaches. It is interesting that critics read emotion into those lines. In his review for the *Third Salon des Indépendants* in April 1887, Kahn described how, in Seurat's Honfleur works, 'Straight lines, schematic angles accentuate the sadness. The earth and open sea end who knows where!'[43] Fénéon echoed his sentiment, writing at that same moment of Seurat's 'seascapes of Honfleur, and the wonder of those infinite skies. The predominance of horizontal lines helps fix their serene character.'[44] Both were reading Seurat's work through the lens of recent theories published by the mathematician Charles Henry, who sought to associate the direction of lines with specific emotions, linking science and aesthetics.[45] Several years later, outlining aspects of his painterly approach to a journalist, Seurat would note that 'Calmness of tone is the balance between dark and light; of colour, between warm and cool; and the Horizontal for the line.'[46] While such theories might have influenced the composition of Seurat's highly constructed figural paintings, one must be wary of applying such theory to his seascapes, whose horizons and calmness stem from their very subject matter – calm seas and empty spaces.

A letter written to Signac six weeks after Seurat's arrival on the coast takes stock of his summer production. In early August, as he was getting ready to leave Honfleur, he described having

6 canvases only ...
1 considered finished, the motif having long ago broken up (boats in a corner of a harbour) [fig. 18]
2 others worked up but not yet satisfactory (shores) [cat. 6 and fig. 26]
1 canvas of [size] 10 overcast weather, still needing to be worked on (end of a jetty) [fig. 20]
That leaves one canvas of 25 [cat. 5] and 1 of 15 [cat. 8] sketched out.
That's all I was able to do.[47]

The telegraphic letter nevertheless provides two important insights: Seurat worked on all the canvases at the same time and none were finished by the time he left Honfleur.

In his article describing the new Neo-Impressionist movement, Fénéon stressed that, in contrast to the Impressionists' *plein-air* working method (by then an oft repeated cliché), the younger artists' paintings 'cannot tolerate haste and involve work in the studio'.[48] The lengthy genesis of Seurat's seascapes is corroborated by visual and technical examination. In the Honfleur paintings, the initial layers, created with a flurry of vigorous brushstrokes in a *balayé* effect, had had time to dry fully before a coat of dots of varying sizes was applied. Indeed, this is particularly visible in *The Hospice and the Lighthouse of Honfleur* (cat. 5), which Seurat stated having worked on for two and a half months.[49] The paintings made in Honfleur are particularly revealing because, by March 1887, five of the seven started the previous summer had been given away or sold by Seurat, preventing him from reworking them years later as he did with the Grandcamp paintings.[50]

Unlike Seurat's earlier seascapes, the Honfleur works did not make their debut altogether but were unveiled in a piecemeal fashion. Seurat had not planned on showing his summer works, still unfinished, at the *Second Salon des Indépendants*, which opened only a week after his return from the coast. In his letter to Signac, however, he toyed with the idea of presenting the '1 considered finished, the motif having long ago broken up', *Corner of a Harbour (Honfleur)* (fig. 18), depending on 'what it looks like in a frame'.[51] As he told Verhaeren, he had worked on 'the large sketch' for a week and stopped when the ship left port.[52] The painting was included in the end, alongside paintings of Grandcamp and *A Sunday on La Grande Jatte*.

By October 1886, *The Hospice and the Lighthouse at Honfleur* (cat. 5) and *The Shore at Bas-Butin* (cat. 6) were ready for exhibition and unveiled at the *Exposition des Beaux-Arts* in Nantes, where Pissarro had once again intervened to ensure Neo-Impressionism was included.[53] This was followed by the display of four of the seven Honfleur paintings in March 1887 in Brussels, at the annual exhibition of Les XX, who had invited the promising young artist.[54]

Reception of Seurat's work in Belgium mirrored that bestowed by the Parisian public, with the large figural canvas *A Sunday on La Grande Jatte* scorned and the seascapes much admired. As Verhaeren recounted, 'visitors, all the while rejecting the painter's major submission, allow themselves to be drawn to his small landscapes: Marines and Ports. Two canvases found buyers .... Never has anyone been able to render with such precision details within grandeur. The *Bec du Hoc* and the *Lighthouse of Honfleur* are at once meticulous and vast.'[55] Verhaeren does not disclose that he was one of the two buyers, having acquired *The Hospice and the Lighthouse at Honfleur* praised in his review. The other purchase, of *The Shore at Bas-Butin (Honfleur)* by the Belgian painter and patron of the arts Henri Van Cutsem, is notable as a very rare acquisition by someone outside Seurat's orbit. It bears witness to the importance of Belgian collectors and Symbolist circles for the recognition of Neo-Impressionism.[56] While Seurat might have been pleased with these sales, he was mostly preoccupied by the fact that they depleted his stock of new canvases to show at the *Third Salon des Indépendants* opening in Paris the following month, on 26 March 1887. He therefore only ceded the paintings on the condition that their new owners would agree to lend them for a few months.[57]

To understand Seurat's career, it is essential to consider the changing landscape of contemporary art exhibitions in Paris in the 1880s. Seurat's regimented annual routine – an ambitious 'winter' canvas and his 'summer' haul – was geared towards producing new work every year for public display. The short period of his activity witnessed a revolution in how artists were able to show their work. As the official Salon, with its conservative jury, became less powerful – upending two centuries of tradition – commercial dealers on the one hand and the artists themselves on the other took over the display of contemporary art. The former organised exhibitions in their premises, seeking to shape the market, while the latter formed societies to give voice and power to the creators.[58] Of these, the Société des Artistes Indépendants, founded in 1884, was one of the most active. It organised the annual Salon des Indépendants, a public exhibition of avant-garde art where artists themselves were free to choose what to display. Seurat was a founding member and dedicated participant of the installation committee. Although it initially lacked a fixed schedule and permanent home, the Salon des Indépendants became a driving force in the promotion of new artists, most especially the Neo-Impressionists. Seurat focused on having a large figural painting to unveil at the Salon des Indépendants every year, alongside a group of landscapes.[59] Freed from any commercial considerations thanks to his family's financial support, he was less concerned with sales than making his mark. He never worked with a dealer and there are recorded purchases of only three canvases in his lifetime, all of which are included in the present exhibition (cat. 5, 6 and 13).[60]

Drawings

Seurat's Honfleur campaign seems to have been the first time he turned his hand to drawing the coastal sites. Two works on paper from that summer are known, both related to larger paintings: *The Port of Honfleur* (cat. 9) is taken from the same vantage point as the painting *Entrance of the Port of Honfleur* (cat. 8), while *The Lighthouse at Honfleur* (fig. 19) depicts the same jetty and lighthouse seen in *End of the Jetty of Honfleur* (fig. 20) but from the water level rather than higher up on the hill.

Both drawings are remarkable in their scale and ambition. As he had for his *croquetons*, Seurat settled on a medium and support early on in his career and remained faithful thereafter.[61] He always used a type of handmade paper called Michallet, whose watermark often shows through. This paper was very textured, with chain and laid lines so prominent as to cause the crayon to skip over them. Seurat used those skips and the resulting reserves to create specks of light with the white of the paper and animate his surfaces, as he had done in letting the wood or priming show through in his *croquetons*. What is more, technical studies have shown that Seurat used a toothing plane to rough up the smooth surface of his small wood panels, emulating the textured paper of his drawings.[62] At around 24 × 31 cm, the drawings are larger than his oil sketches. Michallet paper came in standard sheet sizes of 48 × 63.5 cm, which Seurat cut into quarters. He used the same format for all his later drawings, including *Gravelines, An Evening* (cat. 24) and *Sailboats* (fig. 16).

Instead of the ubiquitous charcoal, Seurat favoured a greasy stick called 'Conté crayon', which did not smudge and allowed forms to be built up easily by layering strokes. It had been patented by Nicolas-Jacques Conté in 1795 and consisted of compressed powdered graphite and carbon black in a clay base. Conté crayon had the advantage of being harder than pastel and producing deeper blacks than any other medium simply by adding pressure to the round or square stick. Seurat often took advantage of this feature to create darker areas in his compositions – the black bollard in the foreground and the ship on the other side of the quay in *The Port of Honfleur*; the tall mast of the boat, the jetty and the lighthouse in *The Lighthouse at Honfleur*. In both drawings, he added touches of white gouache for contrast, to striking effect. Although closely related to his painted seascapes, Seurat's drawings serve a different function. They allowed him to explore the tonal contrasts between the different elements of his compositions and enhance his understanding of light and shadow in his motifs.

Port-en-Bessin

After staying in Paris in the summer of 1887, Seurat returned to the coast in 1888. He settled in Port-en-Bessin, located twenty or so kilometres from Grandcamp. In a postcard to Signac, who had stayed in the town a few years earlier and was working that summer further west, in Brittany, Seurat wrote that he could be reached 'at Mr Marion's' but his exact address and the dates of his stay are unknown.[63] It seems, however, that he was renting rooms with a local, as he had done in Honfleur, instead of staying in a hotel.

Seurat brought back six canvases from his trip, no oil sketches and only one possible drawing.[64] Scholars have noted that the Port-en-Bessin paintings, as a group, could be seen as forming a composite image of its harbour, with certain features recurring in different works.[65] Despite some accommodation for tourism (and the production of postcards for holidaymakers to send home; fig. 59–61), the town, nestled between two tall cliffs, was principally sustained by its port and fishing activity. Seurat painted three views on the quays themselves: the sequence seems to start with *Port-en-Bessin – A Sunday* (cat. 11), which is listed first in the exhibition catalogues in Seurat's lifetime. The painter positioned himself inside the inner basin, looking out towards the moored ships bedecked with flags and to the harbour beyond. One recognises, in the middle distance, the swivelling steel bridge that is the subject of *Port-en-Bessin – The Bridge and the Quays* (cat. 12). The third work, *Port-en-Bessin – The Outer Harbour (Low Tide)* (cat. 13), is painted from the outermost point of the harbour, looking back towards the inner port. The three other views were taken from higher up in the surrounding cliffs west of town, with the painter rotating his viewpoint: one painting looks eastwards back towards the port (cat. 14), one faces north (cat. 15) and the final work turns west, away from the town and towards the cliffs and the open sea (cat. 16). While it is perhaps speculative to consider these works as a series per se – for one, they are not all the same size, with four canvases of a standard 'size 25 portrait' (which Seurat rotated to use in landscape mode) and two of a 'size 15 portrait' – the Port-en-Bessin paintings show Seurat adopting a more methodical approach in his choice of views than the more organic one suggested by his letter to Signac at the end of his Honfleur stay.

Seurat continued to work on the six paintings in Paris that winter and unveiled them in February 1889 at the *Sixth Exhibition of Les XX* in Brussels. Reviewing the works, Maus relished the exploration of Port-en-Bessin they offered, as Seurat had undoubtedly planned:

And the eye rejoices in following, alongside the artist, the straight quays, the jetties, the bridges, the piers, dominated by the grassy mass of the cliffs; in probing the depth of the green water marbled by the fleeting shadows of the clouds; in measuring the height of the lighthouses; in searching the distant horizon of the sea.[66]

The Brussels showing would be the only time the six paintings were displayed together, until now. The exhibition *Seurat and the Sea* brings them back together 137 years later.

As Maus sensed and as we have seen in the Honfleur works, the most striking feature of the canvases are the geometrical lines of their compositions. Seurat focused on the strong horizontals and diagonals created by the infrastructure of Port-en-Bessin's harbour, which had undergone an extensive expansion only a few years earlier.[67] This grid-like aspect makes the works appear relatively flat, their different planes simply superimposed rather than interwoven, like theatre décor.[68] A few attempts at creating a sense of depth can be seen with the swing bridge in *The Bridge and the Quays* or the sharp angle of the balustrade in the foreground of *A Sunday*. This, and many other aspects of Seurat's style, are examined in Paul Smith's essay in this publication.

Contrasting with the grid-like constructions of Seurat's Port-en-Bessin paintings are the sinuous lines he introduced in his skies, most especially the elongated, wave-like clouds found in *The Semaphores and the Cliff* and *The Outer Harbour (High Tide)*. While earlier canvases demonstrate Seurat's attentiveness to weather pattern and cloud formation, the skies in his Port-en-Bessin paintings seem much more fanciful, drawing less on nature than on the highly constructed backgrounds of his contemporary figural paintings, such as *Circus Sideshow* (fig. 11). Other artificial elements include the wisps of tall grass on the edge of the cliff, individually silhouetted against the sea, in *The Outer Harbour (High Tide)* (fig. 27); the ellipsoidal shadows cast by the clouds on to the sea in *Entrance to the Outer Harbour*; and the flags fluttering in the wind in *A Sunday*, mimicking the scalloping of the clouds. Even as staunch a

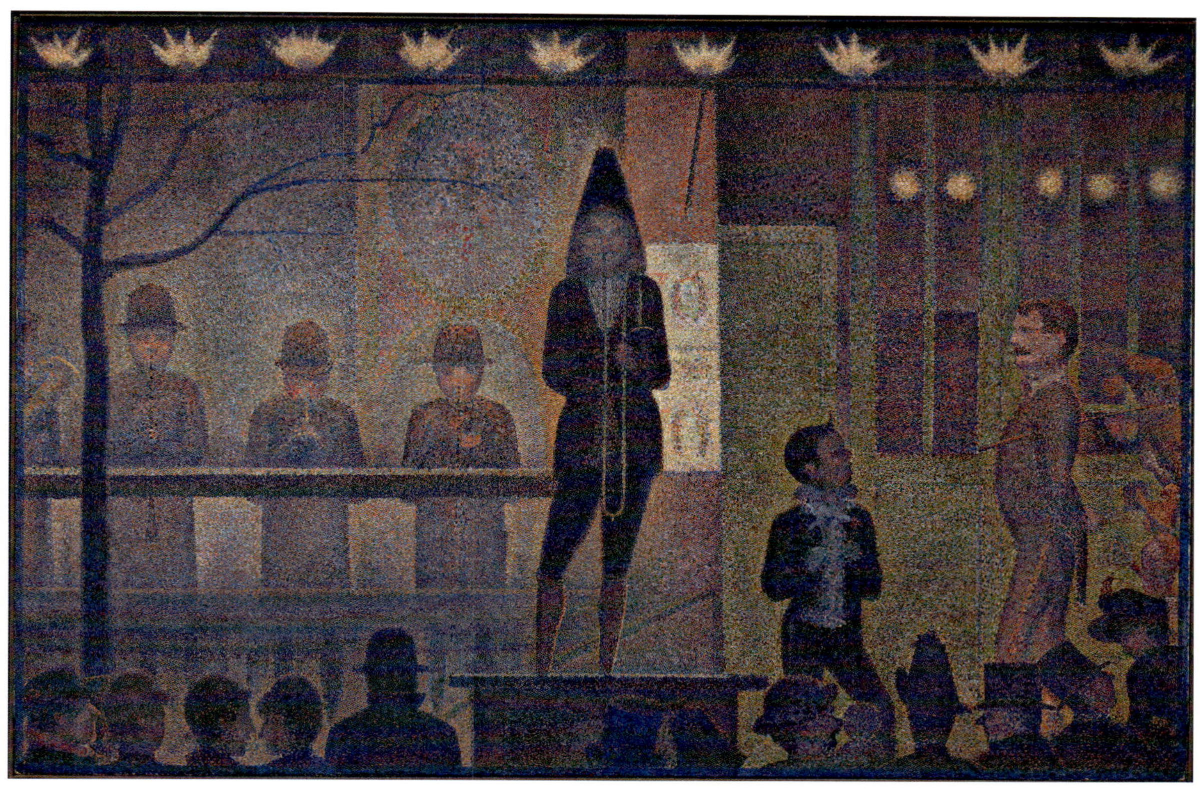

11. Georges Seurat, *Circus Sideshow (Parade de cirque)*, 1887–88, oil on canvas, 99.7 × 149.9 cm, The Metropolitan Museum of Art, New York

supporter as Fénéon cast a wary eye on such developments. He objected to the crossover with Seurat's Parisian production and, most especially, his interest in the posters of Jules Chéret (1836–1932), which advertised the capital's many entertainments.[69]

Similarly, Fénéon lamented the introduction of figures into Seurat's coastal paintings, which had been previously devoid of human presence. Commenting on *The Bridge and the Quays*, he noted that

> one would want the figures walking along the quay of *Port-en-Bessin* to be less stiff: while the appearance of the wandering baby [in English in the original] is charming and authentic, the nebulous customs officer and the woman carrying firewood or seaweed remain implausible; that customs officer, we have known him for the past two years: he was the ringmaster in the *Parade* by the same Mr Seurat.[70]

The 'baby' in the foreground is equally reminiscent of the frontal child in the centre of *A Sunday on La Grande Jatte* (fig. 3). In addition to these three staged characters, Seurat introduced more indistinct figures in the backgrounds of both *The Bridge and the Quays* and *A Sunday,* where they can be seen crossing the swing bridge so prominently represented in the former painting. This would prove a short-lived experiment.

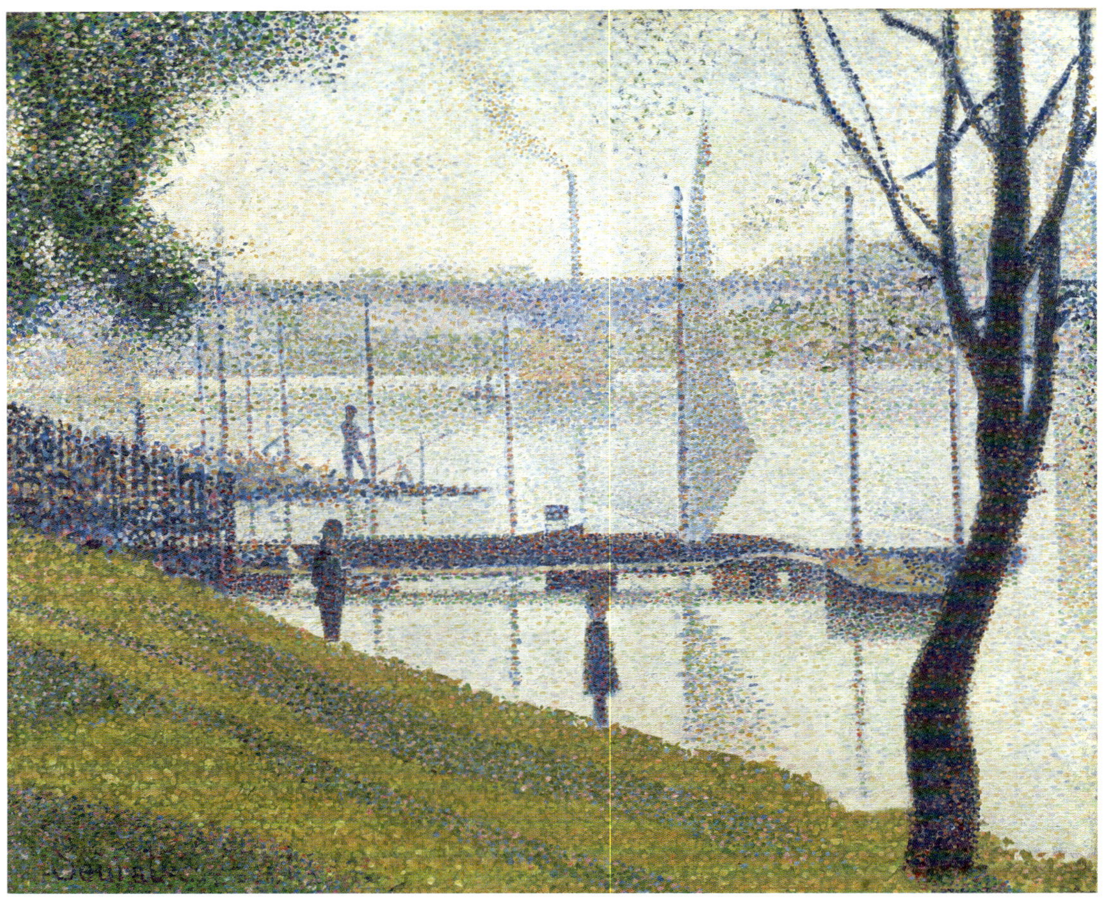

12. Georges Seurat, *The Bridge of Courbevoie (Le Pont de Courbevoie)*, c. 1886–87, oil on canvas, 46.4 × 55.3 cm, Courtauld Gallery, London (Samuel Courtauld Trust)

A comparison between the Honfleur port views and seascapes of 1886 and the paintings from Port-en-Bessin reveals the strides Seurat made in the intervening years in developing his 'method'. The vegetation on the cliff of *The Semaphores and the Cliff*, for example, is still rendered with a layer of directional strokes but a skin of tight dots has been meticulously applied over the surface. Whereas the dots in the Honfleur works were larger and used in discrete areas to indicate shadows and light, they are here much smaller, more widely used and in a greater range of colours. In an interesting development, when a wider paint mark has been applied, Seurat broke it up by placing a smaller dot of its complementary colour in the centre.

The period between the Honfleur and Port-en-Bessin seascapes had also been marked with a renewed interest on Seurat's part for depicting the banks of the Seine north-west of Paris. It coincided with the summer he stayed in Paris and landscapes such as *Gray Weather (Grande Jatte)* (The Metropolitan Museum of Art, New York) and *The Bridge of Courbevoie* (fig. 12) allowed Seurat to explore a different kind of light. As Verhaeren noted, 'Asnières! nowhere in the world did he find places with a wetter and more charming bright light.'[71]

Seurat had first represented suburban landscapes in 1884–85, before his time
on the Channel coast. He depicted fields and houses just outside the capital,
as well as the river and its activity – paintings that informed *A Sunday on La
Grande Jatte*. In late 1886 and 1887, Seurat returned to the island of La Grande
Jatte to depict once again the banks of the river. Albeit much less numerous
than the seascapes, these landscapes should be considered alongside them as
they showcase the development of Seurat's technique at a critical moment of its
evolution. In particular, *The Bridge of Courbevoie* embodies a transition of sorts
from the prominent use of criss-cross brushstrokes to the more insistent use of
dots to animate the surface of the work.

Le Crotoy

Little is known about Seurat's stay in Le Crotoy in the summer of 1889.
He seems to have made only two paintings during his time there, and no
croquetons or drawings. As a destination, Le Crotoy was a dramatic departure
from previous summers in Normandy. Located further north along the coast,
the town is on the estuary of the Somme river, a flat region of low dunes ideally
suited to Seurat's love of representing large expanses of sand. The geography
of the area is a far cry from the tall cliffs and busy ports of the Norman coast.
This deliberate choice marked a move away from representing congested port
scenes in favour of more expansive vistas and greater amplitude, an aspect
that would be taken further the following year in Gravelines.

Seurat's two Crotoy paintings continued his systematic approach of
capturing a specific site, an approach echoed in the paintings' symmetrical
titles: *Le Crotoy (Upstream)* and *Le Crotoy (Downstream)*. The former
represents a view of the southern end of the town, with the artist looking
out towards the Channel across a tidal bay (fig. 13). The latter captures the
houses along the beach and the estuary from the other direction, looking
back towards the mouth of the river (cat. 17). They both demonstrate a certain
level of abstraction as forms are smoothed and somewhat subjugated to the
decorative patterns created by the tight application of dots of paint. Their
execution is incredibly intricate and may explain the smaller haul. However,
the paintings were, unusually, ready to be presented that September in the
Fifth Salon des Indépendants. The more restrained campaign was particularly
well timed as Seurat would not have been able to show more paintings
(nor did he show a large figural composition) because the *Indépendants*'
move to smaller premises that year meant that artists were limited to three
submissions. In addition to the two Le Crotoy paintings, Seurat included *Port-
en-Bessin – The Bridge and the Quays* (cat. 12), the first of the Port-en-Bessin
canvases to be shown in Paris.

Painted borders and frames

It was around this period that Seurat began considering how his paintings'
presentation affected the way they were perceived. This led to two
developments in their framing: the addition of a coloured border painted
directly on the canvas and the creation of bespoke external frames.

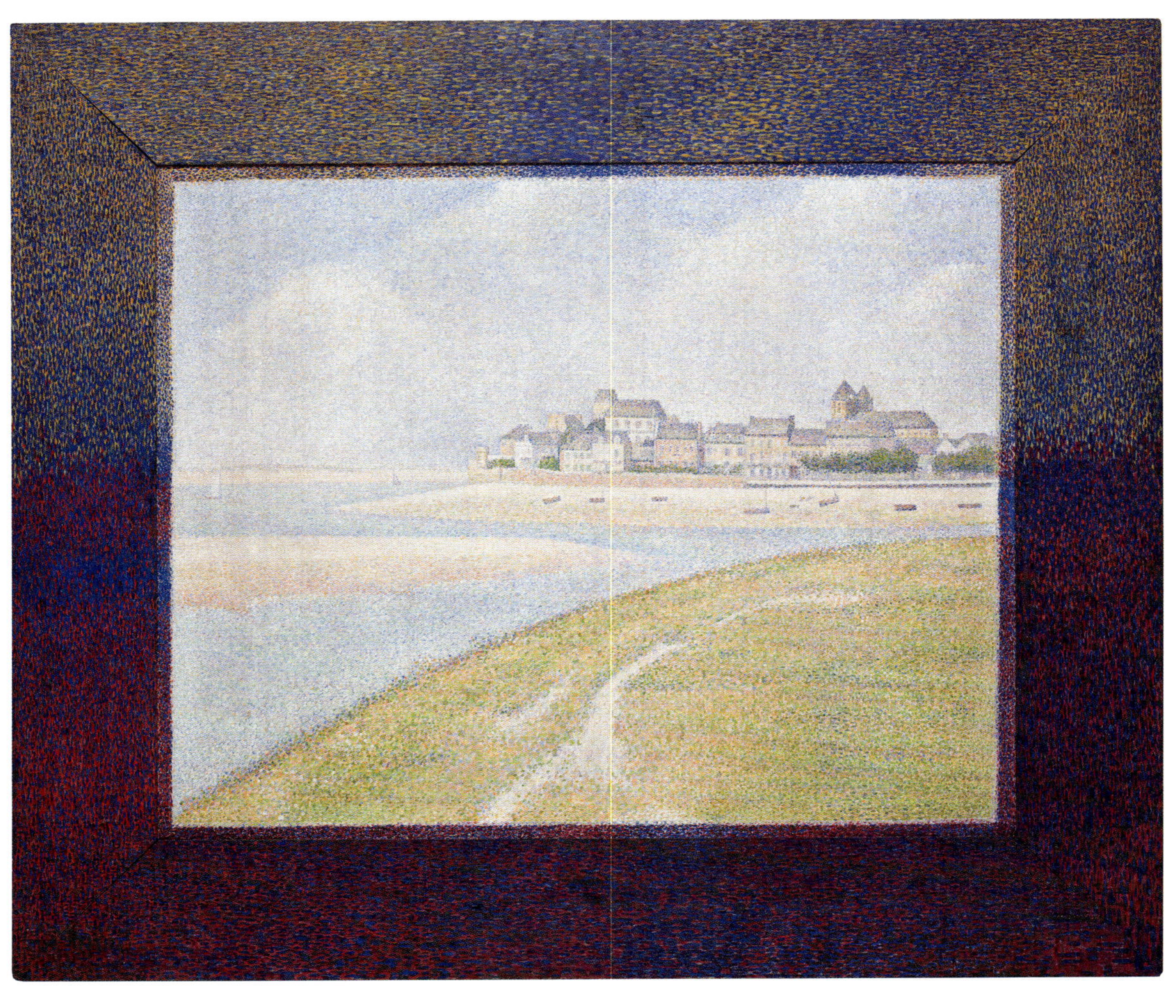

13. Georges Seurat, *Le Crotoy (Upstream)*
(Le Crotoy [amont]), 1889, oil on canvas,
70.5 × 86.7 cm (98.7 × 114.6 cm with painted
frame), Detroit Institute of Arts

Five of the six Port-en-Bessin paintings have a painted border. Technical examination has shown that these were added retroactively, over the existing composition and after the underlying paint had had time to dry.[72] Seurat favoured a dark blue border, animated by red and orange dots, to set off the composition. His colour scheme was relatively simple and, in some cases, such as *Port-en-Bessin – The Bridge and the Quays*, the lower border is simply a series of long, Morse code-like brushstrokes, which echo the pattern on the side of the steel bridge. Crucially, when adding the borders, Seurat also took the opportunity to rework the paintings themselves. For example, the same red pigment found in the later border of *The Semaphores and the Cliff* (cat. 16) was also used to add scattered dots throughout the composition. Seurat must have felt it important to revisit the image and balance his colour scheme, inevitably affected by the addition of a dark border. Similarly, the small orange dots animating the blue border around *The 'Maria' (Honfleur)* (cat. 10) seem to

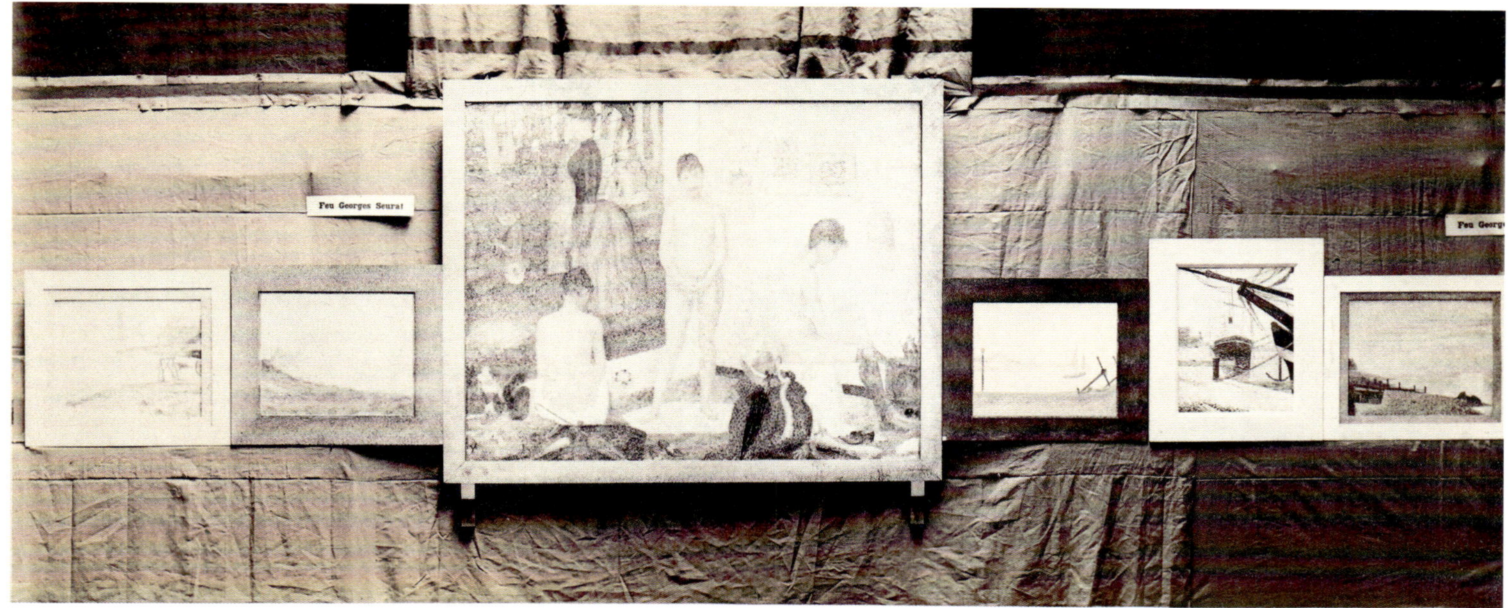

14. Installation view of Georges Seurat's works in the first annual exhibition of the *Association pour l'art*, Antwerp, May–June 1892, photograph, on long-term loan from the Bibliothèque royale (FS XII 157/1) to the Archives et Musée de la Littérature, Brussels

spill out of their lane and wander on to the image itself like fireflies, creating a visual transition between the two. Indeed, Seurat not only revisited the Port-en-Bessin works but also returned to the earlier Grandcamp and Honfleur seascapes still in his studio (see cat. 1 and fig. 26), as well as larger canvases, most notably *A Sunday on La Grande Jatte* (fig. 3).[73]

In contrast, the borders around the paintings made in Le Crotoy and, later, Gravelines were conceived at the same time as the compositions themselves and relate closely to the colours immediately adjacent to each section, offering nuanced complementary tones and values. For these works, Seurat went further and added a separate painted frame that prolonged the colour scheme of the border. Most of these frames have been lost but, in a rare survival, the original frame around *Le Crotoy, Upstream* (fig. 13), with its wide, flat profile, gives a sense of the effect sought by Seurat. A photograph taken in 1892 (fig. 14) shows the other Le Crotoy work (cat. 17; second from left) and *Gravelines, An Evening* (cat. 22; third from right) in their original painted frames. Displayed alongside them, in broad white frames, are the two seascapes (fig. 18 and cat. 5) acquired in 1886 and 1887 by Verhaeren, who retained the simpler frames favoured by Seurat in those years.

This development divided artistic circles; it was lauded and emulated by some but decried by others, including Fénéon and Pissarro.[74] In a letter to his son, Pissarro reported that all of Seurat's Gravelines paintings 'are framed in chromatic colours, which together create an intense blue or purple stain that I find very unpleasant and disharmonious.'[75] Writing a day after Seurat's death on 29 March 1891, Pissarro was describing the *Seventh Salon des Indépendants*, which had opened ten days earlier and presented the four paintings made by Seurat the previous summer in the port of Gravelines: 'Poor Seurat has a beautiful exhibition; his seascapes are very refined as always, a little white and weak in colour, but very artistic.'[76] That campaign had been his last.

Gravelines

The 'refined' seascapes described by Pissarro were painted in the summer of 1890 in the town of Gravelines, located in northernmost France, between the ports of Calais and Dunkerque. Seurat focused almost exclusively on the canalised river Aa, which provided the seventeenth-century fortified town, situated slightly inland, with access to the sea. On either side of the canal as it reached the Channel were the hamlets of Grand-Fort-Philippe (to the west) and Petit-Fort-Philippe (to the east), whose designations derived from fortifications named in honour of King Philip IV of Spain. Grand-Fort-Philippe had become independent from Gravelines in 1884 but Petit-Fort-Philippe, where Seurat was staying, remained part of the town.

In a letter to Fénéon on 24 June 1890, Seurat indicated that he was 'going to the Nord department, around Calais'.[77] He was still there on 19 August, when he sent his condolences for the death of the Neo-Impressionist painter Albert Dubois-Pillet and noted his return address as 'rue de l'Esturgeon au Petit Fort Philippe'.[78] According to the 1891 census, the adults in the 25 households living on that street were all sailors, fishermen and -women, save for one '*cabarétier*', who may have run a hotel or guest house.[79] Despite Baedecker's 1894 description of Gravelines as 'an uninteresting town with 5952 inhab.',[80] it was easily accessible by train from Paris and obviously inspired Seurat, who made four major paintings, four *croquetons* and at least eight Conté crayon drawings that summer, the largest number for a coastal sojourn.

The four Gravelines paintings mark a decisive shift from the works Seurat had made in Normandy. In addition to a more restricted colour palette, the paintings are also much sparer. They inevitably respond to the specificities of the site – no longer a busy port amidst tall cliffs but a canal in a low region – but equally demonstrate a new interest on Seurat's part in capturing sweeping vistas and open skies. This move had begun the previous year in Le Crotoy but finds its fullest expression in the works made in summer 1890. In paring down his compositions, Seurat created a feeling of expansiveness that is particular to this summer campaign. In the Gravelines paintings, Seurat conjured up a sense of infinity that belies the constricted and highly constructed space in which he worked. In many ways, the canalised river corresponds perfectly to his preference for controlled and contained seas and for calm waters – a far cry from the agitation sought by other artists working on the coast.

What the Gravelines paintings do share with their predecessors is that the viewpoints seem deliberate and planned. Key motifs recur in several works and attest to the small perimeter in which Seurat was working: the white lighthouse in *Petit-Fort-Philippe* (cat. 20) is also found in *Direction of the Sea* (cat. 19) while the tall pole of the tide signal station at the far left of the latter composition can also be seen in both *Grand-Fort-Philippe* (cat. 18) and *An Evening* (cat. 22; see also fig. 32 and 33). The art historian Michelle Foa has argued that Seurat's seascapes are sustained explorations of the nature of visual experience itself and related them to contemporary theories of perception. She posited that port towns, with their combination of solid structures and infinite horizons, offered Seurat subjects that tested the range and limits of visual perception.[81]

For her part, Ellen Lee has suggested that the four Gravelines paintings were meant to represent different times of day, based on the way Seurat positioned the shadows in each work.[82] She noted that *Grand-Fort-Philippe* must have been painted in the morning; *Direction of the Sea* at noon; *Petit-Fort-Philippe* in the late afternoon, the long shadow of the bollard in the foreground being a prominent tell; and *An Evening* at dusk, giving it a pink glow. This sequence corresponds to the way the paintings were listed in both catalogues of the exhibitions in which Seurat included them, at Les XX in February 1891 and the Salon des Indépendants in March. As before, however, the paintings are not the same size, with two of a standard '25 portrait' size (81 × 65 cm) and two of '30' size (92 × 73 cm), all turned on their sides. Seurat's preference for these squarer canvases over the traditional elongated 'landscape' and 'marine' formats signals the singularity of his approach.[83] He was less interested in panoramic views of the open sea than in more evenly proportioned canvases to depict open skies, which now occupy half of the compositon, and vast foregrounds. The presence of a bollard close to the picture plane in *Petit-Fort-Philippe* serves only to accentuate the empty space behind it, as do the large anchors and lamp post in *An Evening.* They echo similar compositions in *Entrance of the Port of Honfleur* (cat. 8) and *The 'Maria' (Honfleur)* (cat. 10), where a large single element is placed in the foreground.

Prolonging the developments of Le Crotoy, the Gravelines paintings demonstrate an incredibly controlled technique. The dots of colour covering the surface of the canvases are tighter than in earlier works. Nevertheless, they are never applied mechanically but always with purpose. Each mark is conferred thickness and texture by the bristles of the paintbrush, which give them individuality in a sea of similar tones. In addition, conservators have noted how the dots in the foreground of the Gravelines paintings, for example, are more akin to dashes – thicker and looser than those used in the middle ground and in the distance, in order to convey a sense of spatial recession.[84]

When Seurat's first seascapes were unveiled in May 1886, critics already noted that the artist 'breaks down the prism with relentless logic'.[85] With the Gravelines paintings, Seurat's 'method' reached its full development, atomising the light. For Signac, Seurat's late seascapes managed to create their own internal glow. Seeing them again in the apartment of Seurat's mother three years after her son's death, Signac noted, 'The last seascapes from Crotoy and [missing word], in their colourful frames, look wonderful there. It is soft and harmonious light that is hanging on those walls. You don't feel the technique at all. All the awkward aspects of the craft disappear – and only the benefit of light and harmony remains. I believe that the soft light of an apartment is very favourable to this type of painting, which does not need bright light since it creates its own.'[86]

Not everyone agreed however and, while Seurat's seascapes had always managed to evade the criticism directed at his large figural paintings, some reviewers echoed Pissarro's description of the Gravelines paintings as 'a little white and weak in colour'.[87] One of them denounced Seurat's seascapes as 'white

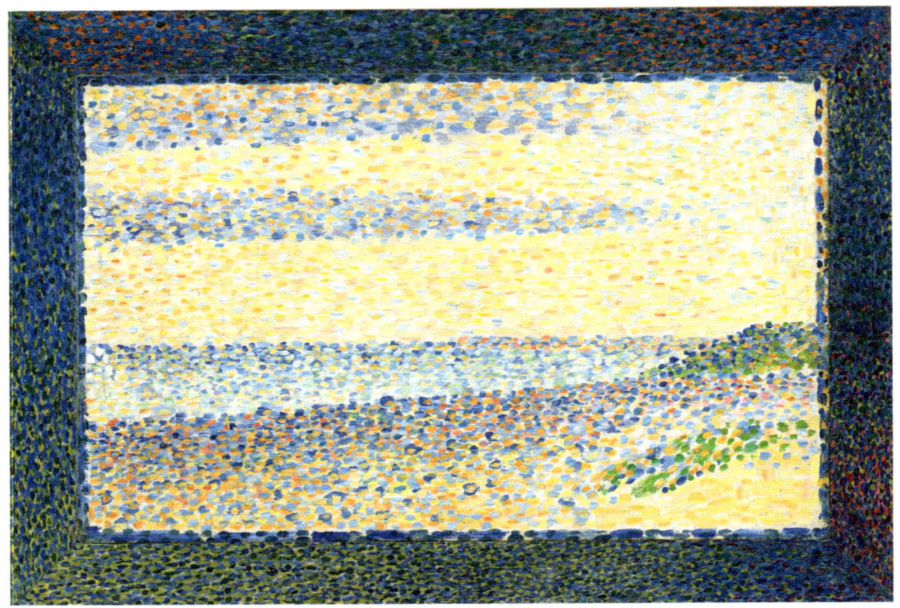

and monotonous due to his excessive pursuit of luminosity'.[88] It seems that even the (now lost) coloured frames mentioned by Signac were not enough to counter the paintings' subdued countenance. They do retain, however, the thick painted border on the canvases themselves. To the dark blue are added dots of colour complementary to the adjacent tones in the composition. The transition between image and border is treated with great care and subtlety, and varies widely around the whole perimeter to enhance the image.

The handling of paint in the four *croquetons* made by Seurat that summer is similarly tight and controlled, a far cry from the loose brushstrokes of the Grandcamp and Honfleur panels. Two of the four known oil sketches (cat. 26 and fig. 15) are likely to have been created as standalone works and both have a summary blue border, emulating the larger canvases. The two other sketches (cat. 21 and 23) are preparatory for *Petit-Fort-Philippe* and *An Evening*. In both, the composition is already fully worked out and close to the final canvas. In an unprecedented development, Seurat also used drawings to complement the sketches. *An Evening* has a full compositional drawing (cat. 24), as well as studies of individual elements for the composition, such as the large anchors in the foreground (cat. 25) and different types of boats that could be added to the scene (fig. 16). All are on quarter-page Michallet paper and demonstrate Seurat's continued subtle handling of the Conté crayon, from a light application of grey lines to evoke the hazy background to the use of the crayon's edge to create strong black outlines.

By the time of Seurat's sudden death on 29 March 1891, probably of diphteria, his seascapes had been the most admired and exhibited part of his oeuvre. Writing to Henri-Edmond Cross, Angrand noted that 'Last week, while in Dieppe where I spent ten days or so, I thought of him (Seurat) as I

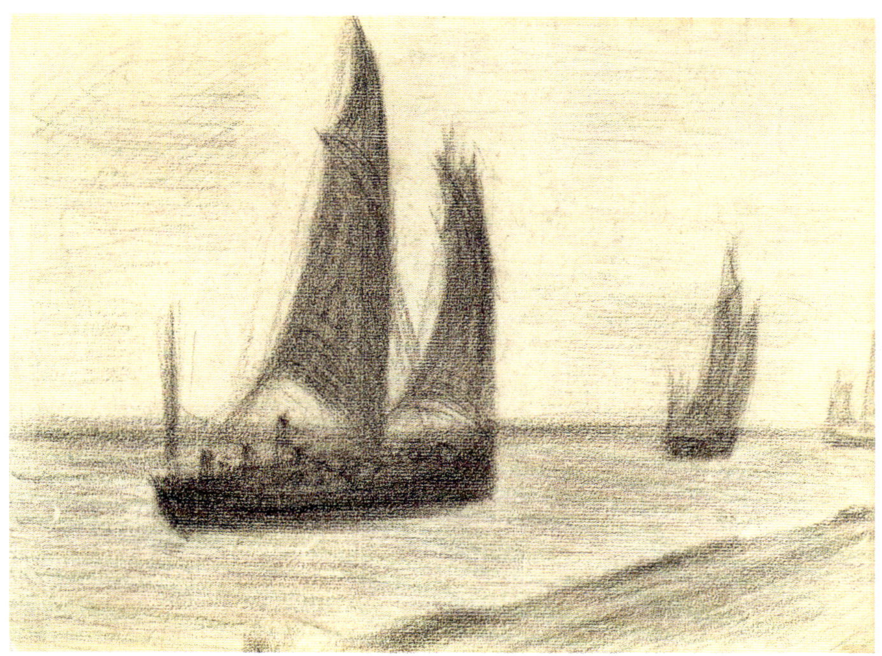

16. Georges Seurat, *Sailboats*, 1890, Conté crayon on laid paper, 23 × 31 cm, private collection

always do when I am looking out to the sea. He was the first to capture the feeling it inspires on quiet days …. The truth was that the tone of his palette, a unique tone, captured the essence of things – the iridescent and unlimited fluidity of the element. He produced some admirable seascapes ….'[89]

Seurat's seascapes remained hugely influential in Neo-Impressionist circles in the following decades.[90] As Angrand's reminiscences show, they also transformed the way that viewers saw the sea: calm waters and a passing boat were now experienced through the prism of Seurat's paintings. Thirty years after Seurat's death, Fénéon recounted a (probably apocryphal) anecdote: 'The late Octave Maus was travelling with his wife in Normandy, in a small train making its way along the coast. Suddenly, the landscape appeared to him so delicately sparkling and nuanced that he exclaimed: Oh! A Seurat!'[91]

Although not as shocking to his contemporaries as his large Parisian paintings, Seurat's seascapes nonetheless enacted a quiet revolution in their approach to the genre, reinventing it for modern eyes. In doing so, they combined a search for objective truth through an innovative technique with a very personal feeling for the subject, imbued with emotion. Seurat's seascapes represented an ongoing vital campaign that allowed him to test and develop his radical way of painting in front of the complexities of his port subjects. The result are works that absorbed viewers – then and now – in their sense of place and evocation of mood and deep contemplation.

Note to the reader: Throughout this publication, Seurat's works are referenced using the titles chosen by the artist himself, who was especially attentive to the issue, when they were first exhibited. The titles are given in their direct English translation. In the figure captions or upon first mention, the original French is included.

1 The remaining three are *Chahut* (1889-90, Kröller-Müller Museum, Otterlo), *Young Woman Powdering Herself* (*Jeune femme se poudrant*, 1889–90, Courtauld Gallery, London, Samuel Courtauld Trust) and *Circus* (*Cirque*, 1891, Musée d'Orsay, Paris).

2 Thomson 1985, pp. 157–81; Zimmermann 1991, pp. 205–12 and 393–439; Smith 1997; and Foa 2015, pp. 7–61 (this chapter is a revised and expanded version of her earlier essay 'On the Spaces of Painting and Perception: Seurat and Helmholtz', in Becker and Burckhardt Bild 2009, pp. 113–23).

3 Darragon 1984 and 1991.

4 Herbert 1991, pp. 233–55; 318–27 and 349–59.

5 Veldink 2014.

6 Lee 1990.

7 Coquiot 1924, p. 33. Seurat's sketchbooks from that period contain only figure studies, most likely of Seurat's fellow soldiers.

8 Dorra and Rewald 1959, pp. LX–LXI.

9 Verhaeren 1891 pp. 432–33.

10 Kahn 1891, p. 108.

11 Thomson 1985, p. 173

12 Quoted in Coquiot 1924, p. 40.

13 Letter written after 5 July 1886, first published in Rewald 1948, p. 111.

14 Kirby et al. 2003, p. 28.

15 On its use, see Coquiot 1924, pp. 215–19.

16 See, most recently, Callen 2015, pp. 250–51.

17 Quoted in Coquiot 1924, p. 39.

18 Hauke 1961, vol. 1, p. xxx; Dorra and Rewald 1959 counted 145 and Herbert 1991, p. 4 says 170.

19 Letter from Georges Seurat to Paul Signac, Honfleur, 25 June 1886, first published in Rewald 1948, p. 111. It is likely that some are lost as only four are known from his time in Honfleur.

20 See Stonor 2001, pp. 13–16, Kirby et al. 2003, p. 18 and Callen 2015, p. 252.

21 Paul Adam, 'Peintres impressionnistes', *La Revue contemporaine*, vol. 4, April 1886, pp. 541–51, at p. 550.

22 Maurice Hermel, 'L'Exposition de peinture de la rue Laffitte', *La France libre*, 28 May 1886, pp. 1–2, at p. 2.

23 Émile Hennequin, 'Notes d'art: Les Impressionnistes', *La Vie moderne*, 19 June 1886, pp. 389–90, at p. 390.

24 George Auriol, 'Huitième exposition', *Le Chat noir*, 22 May 1886, p. 708; 'Labruyère', 'Les Impressionnistes. II', *Le Cri du peuple*, 3rd year, no. 942, 28 May 1886, pp. 1–2, at p. 2, and Octave Mirbeau, 'Exposition de peinture (1, rue Laffitte)', *La France*, 21 May 1886, pp. 1–2, at p. 2.

25 Jules Vidal, 'Les Impressionnistes', *Lutèce*, 29 May 1886, p. 1.

26 Some are preserved in the Hauke Archives, 36/4/1.

27 Quoted in Coquiot 1924, p. 40. Reminiscing in 1891 about Seurat, with whom he had discussed his 'method', one critic noted that the refinement and lightness of Seurat's landscapes, 'and the delicate melancholy that accompanies them, are, I believe, largely the result of Seurat's soul more than of his methods and of his theories': T. de Wyzewa, 'Georges Seurat', *L'Art dans les deux mondes*, no. 22, 18 April 1891, pp. 163–64.

28 Octave Maus, "Les Vingtistes parisiens', *L'Art moderne* (Brussels), 6th year, no. 26, 27 June 1886, pp. 201–04, at p. 204.

29 Fénéon 1886 (June), later expanded and published as the pamphlet *Les Impressionnistes en 1886*.

30 Smith 1997, pp. 23–27.

31 Fénéon 1886 (Sept.).

32 Félix Fénéon, 'L'Impressionnisme', *L'Émancipation sociale*, 3 April 1887, reprinted in Fénéon 1970, pp. 65–68, at p. 66.

33 Fénéon 1887, p. 139.

34 Signac 2014, pp. 127–28.

35 The literature on Seurat's relationship with contemporary theory and science is vast. For a review, see Herbert 1991, pp. 5–6.

36 Fénéon 1886 (June), p. 270.

37 Quoted in Dorra and Rewald 1959, p. LVIII.

38 See William I. Homer, 'Notes on Seurat's Palette', *The Burlington Magazine*, vol. 101, no. 674, May 1959, pp. 192–93 and, more recently, Stonor 2001 and Kirby et al. 2003.

39 Letter from Georges Seurat to Paul Signac, 25 June 1886, Honfleur, first published in Rewald 1948, p. 111.

40 Darragon 1984, p. 270, gives a thorough account of the extensive infrastructure investments made in Honfleur, starting in the 1830s and ramping up in the 1870s, with jetties, canals, docks and locks.

41 Letter from Georges Seurat to Paul Signac, 25 June 1886, Honfleur, first published in Rewald 1948, p. 111.

42 According to Seurat, this painting was left unfinished because the ship left port after a week. He nevertheless exhibited it that year and described it as 'a large sketch'. For an exploration of the different sites depicted by Seurat in Honfleur, see Smith 1984.

43 Kahn 1887, p. 229.

44 Fénéon 1887, p. 140.

45 Henry's *Introduction à une esthétique scientifique* (*Introduction to a Scientific Aesthetics*, published in book form in 1885 after appearing as articles in *La Revue contemporaine*) was highly influential and followed by several other important publications on the subject. Seurat met Henry in spring 1886.

46 He was opposing 'calmness' to 'joyfulness' and 'sadness': draft of a letter from Georges Seurat to the writer and journalist Maurice Beaubourg, 28 August 1890, published, for example, in Rey 1921, p. 132. In it, Seurat corrects some of the misunderstandings he felt had occurred in the recent publication on him by Jules Christophe, *Georges Seurat*, Collection 'Les Hommes d'aujourd'hui', no. 368, April 1890.

47 Letter from Georges Seurat to Paul Signac, Honfleur, early August 1886, first published in Rewald 1948, pp. 111–12. *The 'Maria' (Honfleur)* is not mentioned.

48 Fénéon 1887, p. 139.

49 Letter from Georges Seurat to Émile Verhaeren, late February or early March 1887, Paris, published in Herbert 1959, p. 322.

50 See the list of owners of Seurat's works in the Hauke Archives, 36/1/2/2. Two paintings were gifts: *Entrance of the Port of Honfleur* to Fénéon (who likely returned the work in 1890; see cat. 8) and *End of the Jetty of Honfleur* (fig. 20) to the writer Paul Adam. Two were purchases, most likely made at the *Fourth Exhibition of Les XX*: *The Shore at Bas-Butin (Honfleur)* (cat. 6) was bought by Henri Van Cutsem and *The Hospice and the Lighthouse of Honfleur* (cat. 5) by Verhaeren. It is unclear if Verhaeren's earlier acquisition of *Corner of a Harbour (Honfleur)* (fig. 18), most likely during a visit to Seurat's studio in autumn 1886, was a gift or purchase. The two remaining canvases, *The 'Maria' (Honfleur)* (cat. 10) and *Mouth of the Seine. Evening* (fig. 26), were given a painted border and a surface of tight dots around 1889.

51 Letter from Georges Seurat to Paul Signac, early August 1886, Honfleur, first published in Rewald 1948, pp. 111–12.

52 Letter from Georges Seurat to Émile Verhaeren, late February or early March 1887, Paris, published in Herbert 1959, p. 322.

53 See Lévy and Sciama 2018.

54 These included the three exhibited previously and *Mouth of the Seine. Evening* (fig. 26). Two earlier seascapes were also included: *Le Bec du Hoc (Grandcamp)* (cat. 1) and *The Roadstead of Grandcamp* (cat. 3).

55 Verhaeren 1887, p. 138.

56 For the relationship between Seurat's work and Symbolism, see Thomson 1985, pp. 177–81, and Paul Smith, 'The Neo-Impressionist Painter.

Color, Facture, and Fiction', in Homburg 2014, pp. 47–71.

57 Letter from Georges Seurat to Émile Verhaeren, late February or early March 1887, Paris, published in Herbert 1959, p. 322.

58 See, for example, Martha Ward, 'Impressionist Installations and Private Exhibitions', *The Art Bulletin*, vol. 73, no. 4, December 1991, pp. 599–622, especially pp. 619–21.

59 Exceptions were the *Third Exhibition* in 1887, when no large figural painting was ready to be exhibited. The following year, two figural paintings, *Models* and *Circus Sideshow*, were presented but without accompanying seascapes, as Seurat had not gone to the coast the previous year. In 1889, smaller premises for the *Exhibition* meant that Seurat was unable to display a large figural work and showed only three seascapes.

60 As noted above, it is unclear whether *Corner of a Harbour (Honfleur)* was given or sold to Verhaeren in October 1886: see Herbert 1959, p. 321 ('There is no mention of a sale and probably Seurat had given the canvas to him') and Robert L. Herbert, 'Seurat and *La Grande Jatte*, 1886–91', in Herbert 2004, pp. 132–51, at p. 135 ('Seurat's first sale, as far as we know'). Seurat also sold a few drawings in his lifetime. Other paintings, sketches and drawings were gifted to friends, supporters and members of his family.

61 For a recent overview of Seurat's materials and technical examination of his drawings, see Jodi Hauptman, 'Introduction', pp. 9–15, and Karl Buchberg, 'Seurat: Materials and Techniques', pp. 30–42, with previous literature, both in Hauptman 2007.

62 Richard Shiff, 'Seurat Distracted', in Hauptman 2007, pp. 16–29, at p. 27.

63 Postcard from Georges Seurat to Paul Signac, 1888, Port-en-Bessin, Fondation Custodia, Paris, Collection Frits Lugt, inv. 1977-A.1730. The postcard is tentatively dated 7 June 1888 based on the postmark but the legibility of the postmark is compromised. It is unclear whether a letter to Signac dated 26 August (Dorra and Rewald 1959, p. LXV) was written from Port-en-Bessin. Census records indicate that all of the 'Mr Marions' living in Port-en-Bessin at that time were fishermen or sailors.

64 *L'Estacade de Port-en-Bessin* (H 692), 27.5 × 29 cm, sold at Sotheby's, London, 9 December 1997, lot 362.

65 See Darragon 1991; Herbert 1991, p. 318, and Foa 2015, pp. 45–51.

66 Octave Maus, 'Le Salon des XX, à Bruxelles (VIᵉ Exposition annuelle)', *La Cravache parisienne*, 9th year, no. 417, 16 February 1889, p. 1.

67 See Darragon 1991 and Richard Thomson's essay in this publication.

68 The question of the influence of Japanese prints on Seurat's works has been raised. While there was wide interest in this art form within his circle, there is no evidence that Seurat himself collected prints or attended the exhibitions organised in Paris at that time. On the subject, see Henri Dorra and Sheila C. Askin, 'Seurat's Japonisme', *Gazette des beaux-arts*, vol. LXXIII, no. 1201, February 1969, pp. 81–94.

69 Fénéon 1889, p. 339.

70 Ibid.

71 Verhaeren 1891, p. 433.

72 *Port-en-Bessin – The Outer Harbour (Low Tide)* (cat. 14) is the only work with no painted border. As it was possibly purchased in February 1889 (at the *Sixth Exhibition of Les XX*) and was thus out of Seurat's hands thereafter, that date could provide the earliest date for when the borders on the other paintings were added.

73 See Herbert 2004.

74 See Dorra and Rewald 1959, pp. CII–CIII, and Herbert 1991, Appendix A.

75 Letter from Camille to Lucien Pissarro, 30 March 1891, in Pissarro 1950, p. 222.

76 Ibid. They were shown alongside his last large figural work – still unfinished – *Circus*.

77 Hauke Archives, 36/1/2/13.

78 Draft of a letter from Georges Seurat to Mr Valton, 19 August 1890, Hauke Archives, 36/1/2.

79 A local historian quoted in Ellen W. Lee, 'Seurat at Gravelines: The Last Landscapes', in Lee 1990, pp. 24–59, at p. 57, note 9, suggested that Seurat might have stayed at the Hôtel du Phare, although it seems to have been located on another street.

80 Quoted by Ellen W. Lee, 'Seurat at Gravelines: The Last Landscapes', in Lee 1990, pp. 24–59, at p. 25.

81 Foa 2015, pp. 7–61.

82 Ellen W. Lee, 'Seurat at Gravelines: The Last Landscapes', in Lee 1990, pp. 24–59, at p. 27.

83 However, as we have seen, he favoured 'marine' formats for his *croquetons*.

84 Kirby et al. 2003, p. 29.

85 Maurice Hermel, 'L'Exposition de peinture de la rue Laffitte', *La France libre*, 28 May 1886, pp. 1–2, at p. 2.

86 Rewald 1949, p. 114 (diary entry for 29 December 1894).

87 Letter from Camille to Lucien Pissarro, 30 March 1891, in Pissarro 1950, p. 222.

88 J. Krexpel, 'Les XX', *La Revue blanche (série belge)*, 3rd series, vol. II, no. 12, March 1891, reprinted by Geneva: Slatkine Reprints, 1972, pp. 379–81, at p. 381.

89 Quoted in Rey 1921, p. 95. Ellen W. Lee, 'Seurat at Gravelines: The Last Landscapes', in Lee 1990, pp. 24–59, at p. 57, note 2, dates the letter to summer 1908, seventeen years after Seurat's death, based on information provided by Angrand's family.

90 See, for example, Marina Ferretti Bocquillon, ed., *Radiance. The Neo-Impressionists*, exh. cat. National Gallery of Victoria, Melbourne, 2012, especially the section 'The Lure of the Sea'.

91 Félix Fénéon, 'Paroles', *Bulletin de la vie artistique*, n.d. (between 1919 and 1926), reprinted in Fénéon 1970, vol. 1, p. 497. The end of the anecdote has a passenger seated in Maus's carriage thinking his companion had just spotted a rare seagull and saying he was happy to learn the name of this particular species.

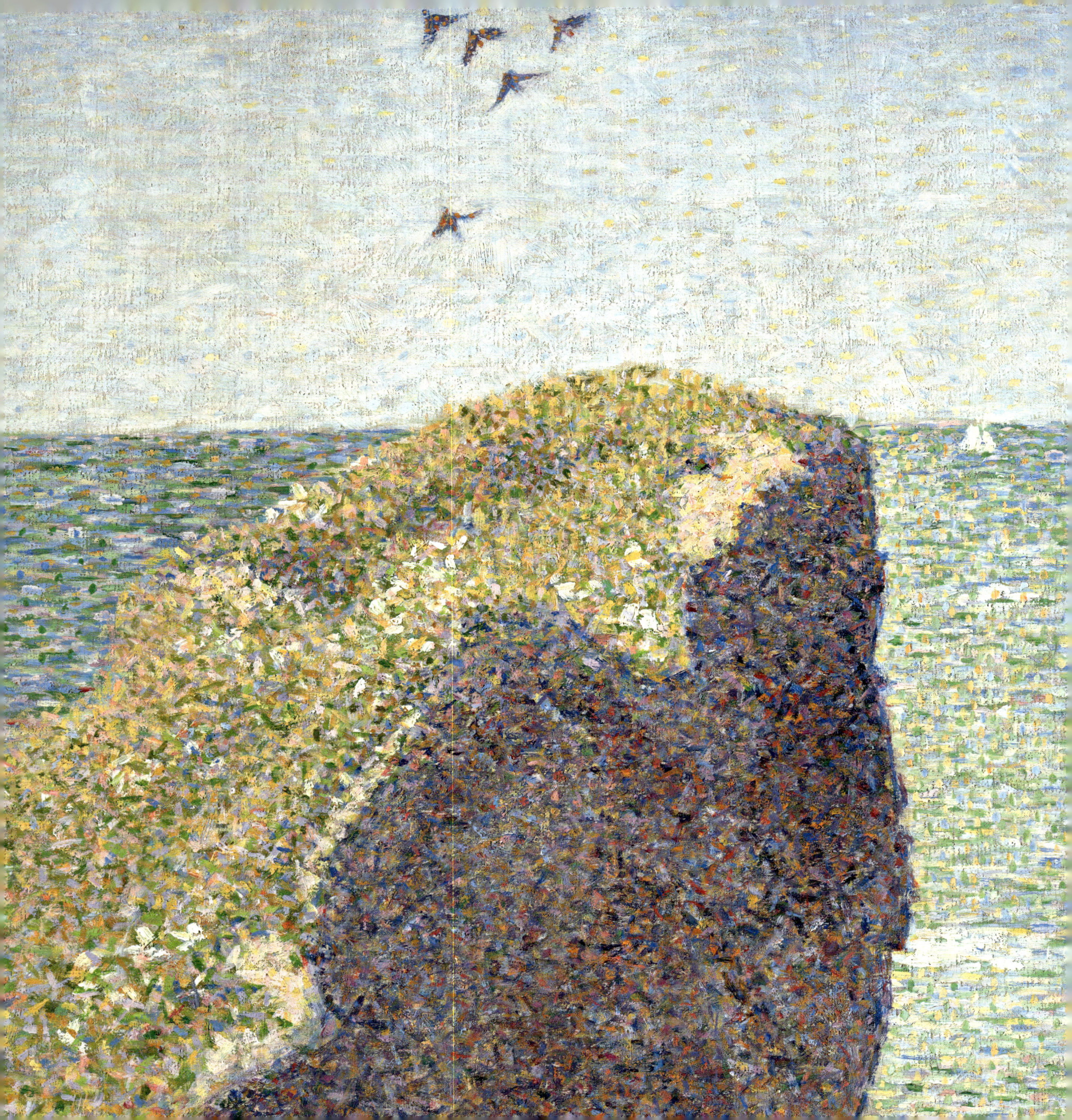

‘Nothing resembles M. Seurat more than M. Signac’
—Albert Michel[1]

‘A Signac … no more resembles a Seurat than a
Hokusai resembles a Hiroshige’
—Paul Signac[2]

Both of these statements concern style, at least implicitly. They nevertheless appear to contradict one another. The first states that Georges Seurat's and Paul Signac's styles are closely similar, whereas the second maintains they are quite different. In fact, however, they are not at odds at all, since they each refer to a different kind of style. Albert Michel's concerns what the philosopher Richard Wollheim calls 'general style', in this case the style Seurat's contemporaries dubbed Neo-Impressionism.[3] Signac's, in contrast, is about 'individual style', or his own style and Seurat's (and those of Hokusai and Hiroshige). What is more, because the two kinds of style are in many respects diametrical opposites, both statements are perfectly correct. As will become clear, paintings such as Seurat's *The Hospice and the Lighthouse of Honfleur* (cat. 5) and Signac's *Les Andelys, Côte d'Aval* (fig. 17), both of 1886, not only exhibit strong generic similarities, but also significant individual differences.

That Seurat did have an individual style is manifest in the large difference between the Normandy that appears in his paintings and its counterpart in reality, insofar as this can be gauged from first-hand experience and from photographs. Seurat nevertheless insisted on giving his seascapes matter-of-fact titles that simply specify the sites he painted. In a letter of early 1887, he even wrote to the Belgian poet Émile Verhaeren, who was closely involved with the art group Les XX, to tell him that *Corner of a Harbour (Honfleur)* (fig. 18), which 'featured at the Indépendants under this title', could appear in the catalogue of their forthcoming exhibition under the title 'Corner of a harbour (Honfleur)' ('*Coin d'un bassin [Honfleur]*') or 'The Corner of a harbour' ('*Le Coin d'un bassin*'), but it could not be described as a painting of 'just any corner or any harbour'.[4] Taken on their own, at face value, such titles imply that there is no more to Seurat's paintings than the topographical facts. But when read alongside the paintings, the situation is not so clear-cut.

To appreciate why, it is useful to consult some of the philosophical accounts that draw a distinction between what can be seen in a stylistic painting and what can be seen in the real world. Notably, Lambert Wiesing has argued that because the 'image object', or the thing represented in a picture, 'always appears in a particular style', it is not the same as the 'image subject', or the actual thing it refers to.[5] Wiesing none the less accepts that the two can be connected by appeal to the artist's intention, which is most often indicated by a title. By this account, Seurat's titles are incongruous, since they merely name real places rather than indicate the artist's transformation of them (as, for instance, Monet's *Impression, Sunrise* did in alluding to the role played by the artist's subjectivity in forming the corresponding painting of 1872). Or at least this is the case until they are read in front of the paintings, when it becomes

‘A Higher, Exalted Reality’ Seurat, Sea, Style

PAUL SMITH

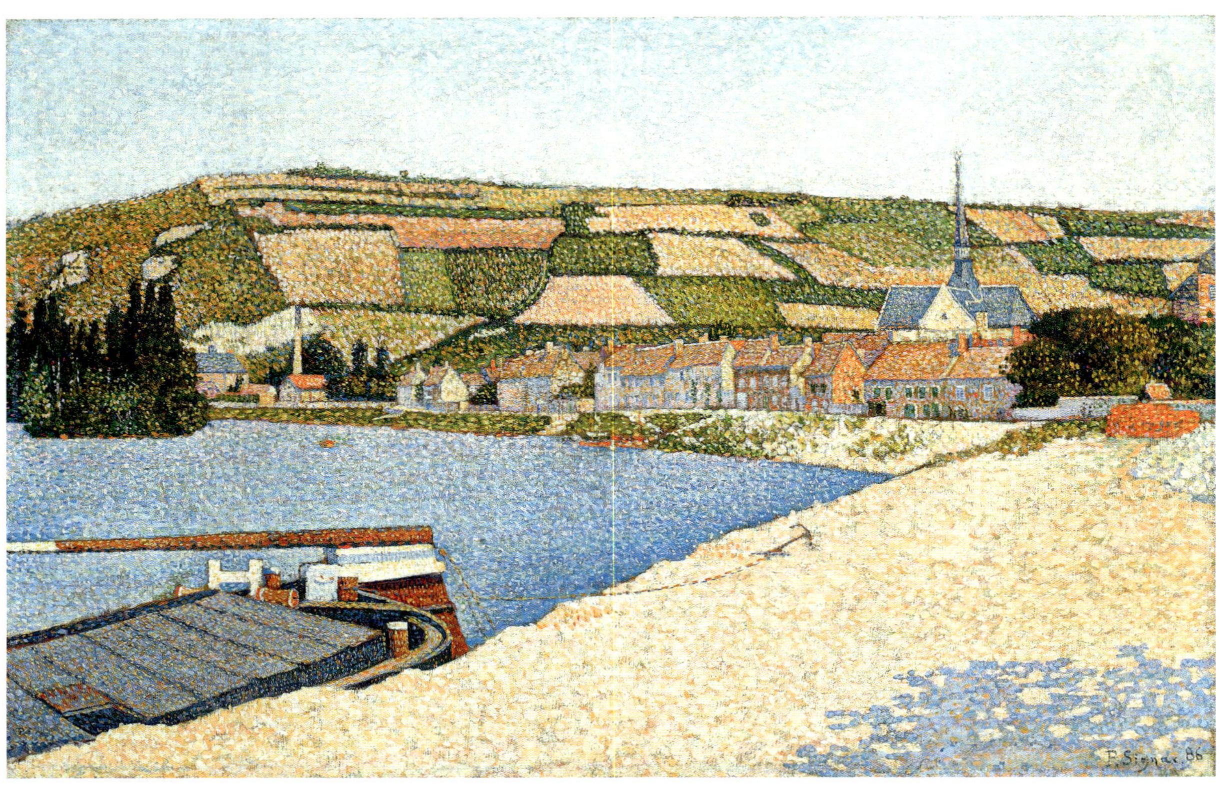

17. Paul Signac (1863–1935), *Les Andelys, Côte d'Aval*, 1886, oil on canvas, 60 × 92 cm, The Art Institute of Chicago

clear that they are ironic, or intended to create bathos.[6] Their very banality, in other words, is designed to point up how Seurat's 'style' creates a 'world' of its own, to use the langue of Nelson Goodman.[7] And arguably, this world is identical in all his seascapes, irrespective of the fact that their titles indicate different geographical locations – much as Shakespeare's 'style' and 'language' create 'their own world' across the 'whole *corpus* of his plays' wherever they are set, according to Ludwig Wittgenstein.[8]

To appreciate what Seurat's individual style is, and how it is different from the general style of Neo-Impressionism he shared with Signac, it is necessary to look further into Wollheim's theory of the two kinds of style. The most important aspect of this for present purposes is its contention that a competent artist like Seurat does not manufacture the painting piecemeal, but adjusts his marks as he goes along to ensure that they produce the right look when they are seen all together.[9] This means that style is a holistic phenomenon, which cannot be identified with specific features of the painting's surface, nor of the image in it. Rather, it flows through and inflects both, and hence can only be recognised in larger, less determinate visual structures. In this respect, it is not unlike the gestalt (or overall impression) produced by a face, which subsumes the appearances that its component features exhibit in isolation, and gives that face its characteristic look.[10]

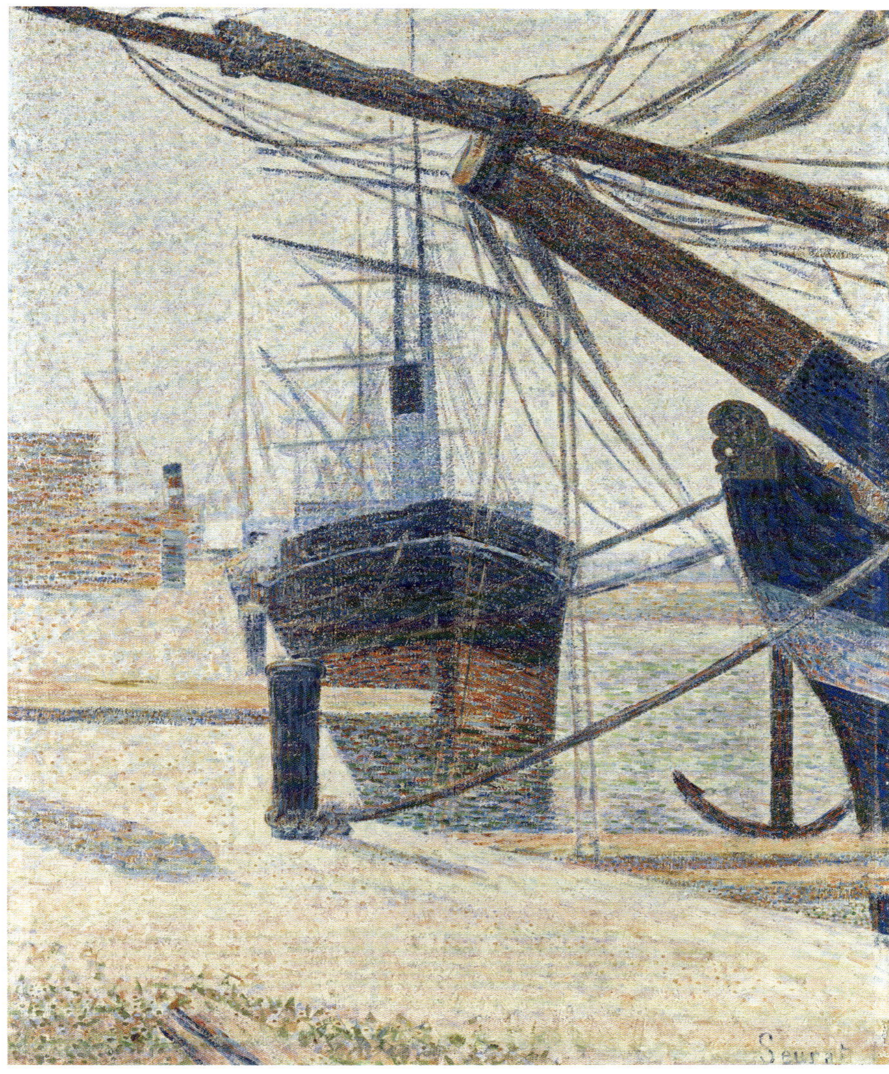

18. Georges Seurat, *Corner of a Harbour (Honfleur)* (*Coin d'un bassin [Honfleur]*), 1886, oil on canvas, 79.5 × 63 cm, Kröller-Müller Museum, Otterlo

Similarly, individual style may be hard to pin down, but it is what makes a Seurat a Seurat, as opposed to a Signac.

General style is quite different, since it is relatively easy to specify in terms of features of the painting's surface, or the image it contains. The Neo-Impressionist style shared by Seurat and Signac involves the use, for instance, of the dot, spectral colours and simplified silhouettes. What is more, these techniques can be learned by following rules, unlike individual style, which cannot. This explains why Signac and others could make perfectly good Neo-Impressionist paintings, but not Seurats.

Despite Wollheim's understandable reticence to specify what individual style consists in, he did suggest that it might be identified with how discrete components of the painting are 'concatenated', or drawn together into larger complexes with their own distinct identity.[11] Although he did not pursue this insight, John Willats did by developing a psychological method which could demonstrate how the various 'systems' employed in a picture to create depth work together to form its 'style' as well.[12] In what follows, therefore, I will apply Willats's ideas to Seurat's seascapes. And I will draw on other ideas from psychology to show how concatenation operates in his treatment of light and movement.

Another key aspect of Seurat's style is its dependence on the medium. Willats's ideas help explain how Seurat used his medium when depicting depth. But Seurat's engagement with his medium is also crucial to his depiction of light and movement. A useful route into these issues is provided by Michael Podro's argument that the artist can only be said to work with a medium when he makes the inert materials he begins with responsive in his hands.[13] In Seurat's case, this process manifested itself in the fact that his paintings did not become fully stylistic until some time after his drawings. Scale is also an important factor here. That is, although Seurat used paint with aplomb in his seascapes, it is questionable whether he did so in his much larger figure paintings, notably *A Sunday on La Grande Jatte* of 1884–86 (fig. 3), which several contemporary commentators found stiff, or too large for the comparatively minute dot it employed.[14] It would seem, then, that Seurat set himself a technical challenge he could not rise to in these paintings, with the result that they were 'extra stylistic' in Wollheim's terms.[15] By corollary, making seascapes must have been decisive to his formation of a painterly style.

As will become clear, the systems an artist like Seurat employs, and his media, impose a number of constraints on his capacity to render depth, light and movement. It could seem, then, that individual style is simply a function of these limitations. But rather than characterise Seurat's style as impoverished, I will try to show that it exemplifies an extraordinary ability to make a virtue of necessity.

Shallowness

> 'a flat imitation of Miss Kate Greenaway'
> —Firmin Javel[16]

Firmin Javel's sardonic comparison between the monumental *Grande Jatte* and the diminutive book illustrations of the British artist and writer Kate Greenaway leaves no doubt that he found the painting devoid of depth. Shallowness is nonetheless inherent in pictorial space, which Willats describes as a 'third domain' intermediate between the depth of the three-dimensional world and the flatness of the physical picture surface.[17] It has this character, he explains, because pictures cannot deploy the same range of depth clues as reality, notably 'motion parallax', or how objects move relative to one another when we move around them. Nor can they exploit stereo disparity, or the difference between the two views an object presents to our eyes.[18] Seurat clearly worked against these limitations, however, by engaging with them creatively.

The principal tool at the artist's disposal for creating depth in a picture is what Willats calls its 'drawing system'. This is effectively the perspectival

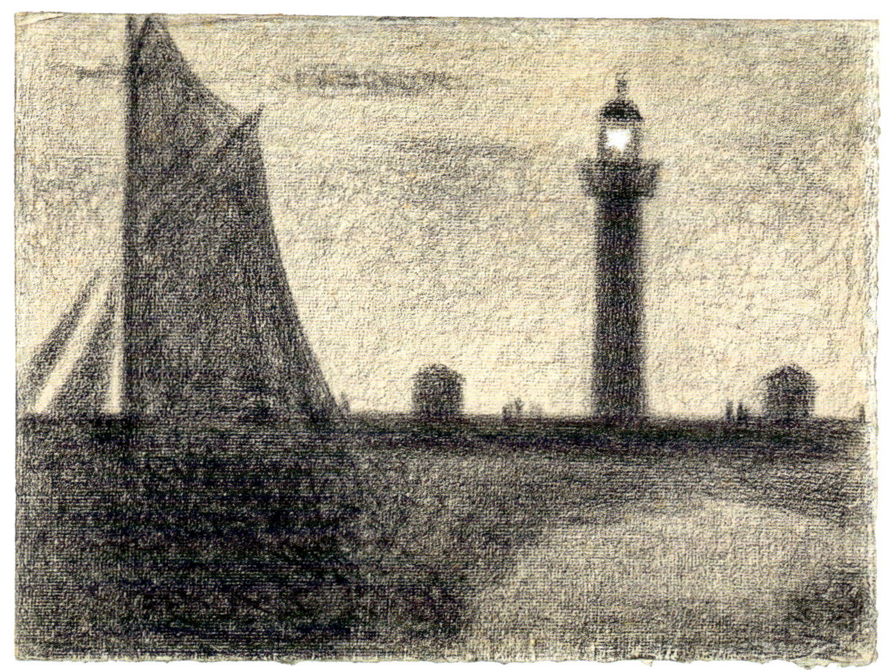

algorithm that projects three-dimensional shapes onto a two-dimensional surface. Any particular drawing system also acts as an overarching structure which organises its component elements in its own way, by governing how they can be combined.

In the drawing *The Lighthouse at Honfleur* (fig. 19), Seurat used an informal version of the system known as 'orthographic projection'.[19] This treats objects as though they are viewed head-on or in profile, with little or no foreshortening, so that they appear in their 'true' shapes, undistorted by convergence towards a vanishing point. In effect, orthographic projection represents objects as if they were viewed from a long way away, and hence yields the kind of space produced by a powerful telephoto lens, in which the distances between them appear compressed. The lighthouse and the sailing boat in *The Lighthouse at Honfleur* consequently appear closer together than they would in a normal viewing situation. Seurat's drawing system is quite distinctive in these respects, and quite unlike the one Signac employed in *Les Andelys, Côte d'Aval*. This uses a relatively traditional perspective to generate a more familiar recessional space along the foreground shoreline, and in the row of houses leading back into the picture from the right.

In Willats's scheme, a drawing system articulates basic structures such as lines or shading known as 'picture primitives', which correspond to elements of the visual array like edges or tonal variations.[20] These primitives, it must be emphasised, are virtual structures, and are not the same as the physical marks in which we see them.[21] What is more, a particular drawing system can only employ picture primitives belonging to an appropriate 'denotation system'.[22]

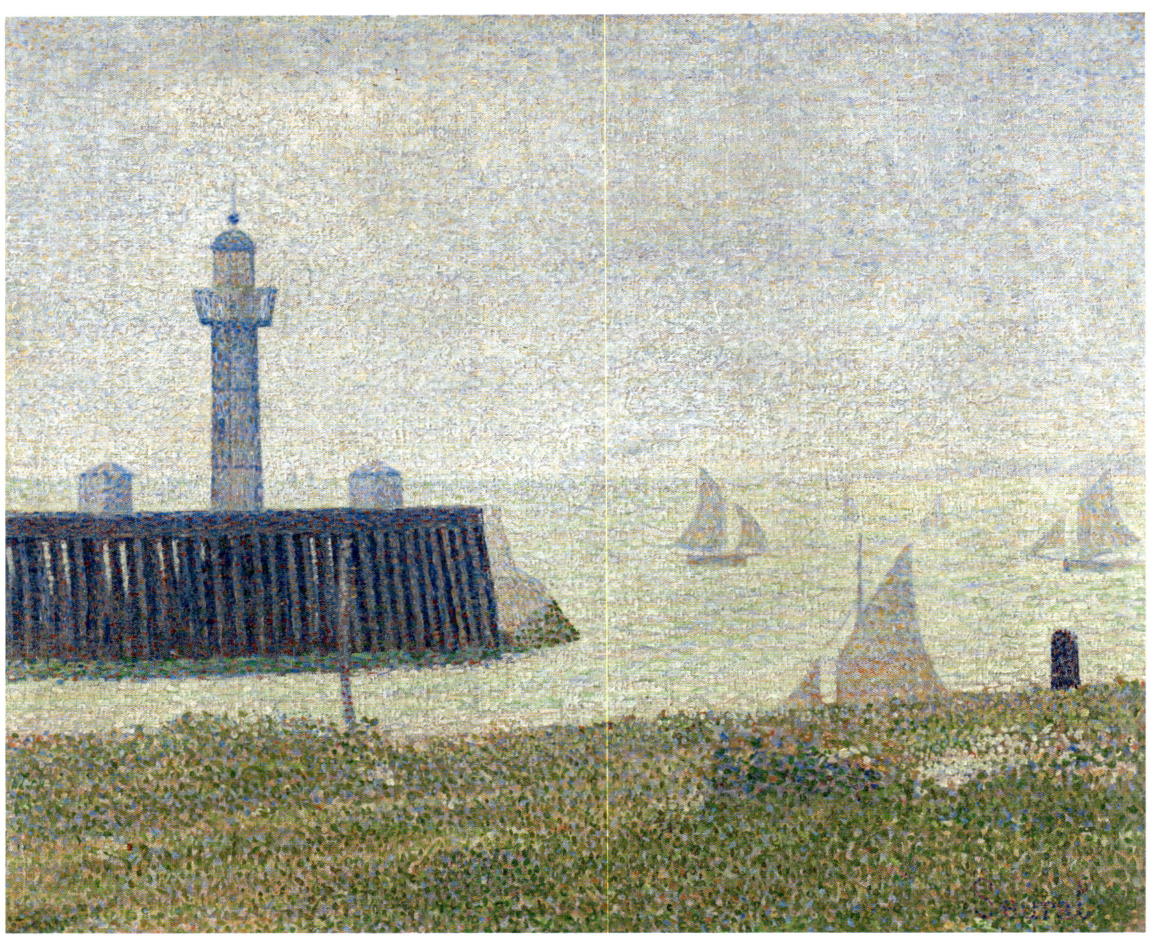

20. Georges Seurat, *End of the Jetty of Honfleur (Bout de la jetée d'Honfleur)*, 1886, oil on canvas, 46 × 55 cm, Kröller-Müller Museum, Otterlo

This is because not all primitives work in every drawing system. Orthographic projection, more particularly, cannot readily accommodate primitives that create tonal variation.[23] Accordingly, in *The Lighthouse at Honfleur*, Seurat employed silhouettes instead, which create depth largely through occlusion or overlap.[24] In principle, however, these are incapable of mapping shadows, and are devoid of modelling.[25] Seurat's choice of drawing system thus inevitably bestowed a particular character on the space that its primitives could create.

The material dimension of his medium imposed its own constraints as well. Seurat nevertheless bent the rules and used Conté crayon to introduce a measure of tonal variation into his drawing. In *The Lighthouse at Honfleur*, he rubbed it gently over the textured surface of the Michallet paper to generate marks that have the 'attributes' of softness and semi-transparency.[26] These create shading and modelling in several places, but particularly in the whitish object in the bottom right of the drawing.

Other marks in front of the sail in the left foreground exhibit 'wiggliness', and appear to sit on the surface of the paper – an effect amplified by the

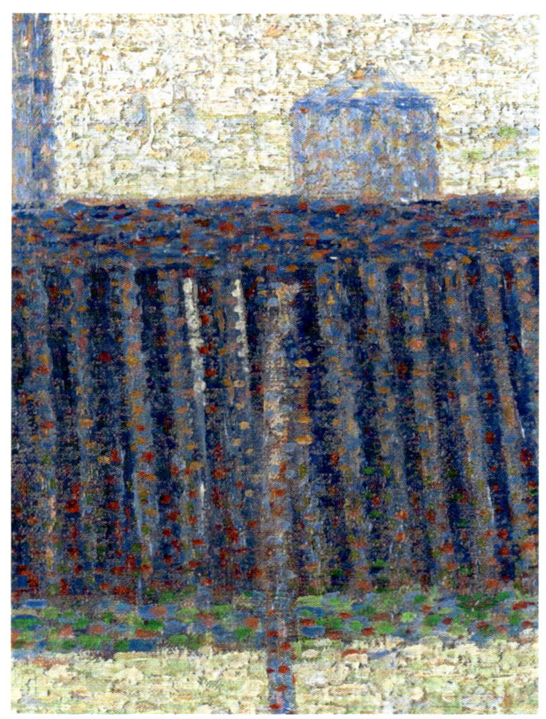
21. Detail of fig. 20

difficulty of resolving them into an identifiable object.[27] Flattening is not the whole story, however. Rather, *The Lighthouse at Honfleur* creates depth because its drawing system does not simply project a particular 'view' of the scene, but also maps what David Marr called 'object centred' descriptions, or the mental representations we make of objects in the round.[28] This is apparent in the fact that *The Lighthouse at Honfleur* preserves the true (or objective) relationships in size between the front edges of objects. More significantly, the slender cylindrical silhouette of the lighthouse is that of a 'generalised cone', or a three-dimensional shape produced by rotating an edge around an axis.[29] Depth thus reasserts itself here, even in the notionally flat silhouette.

Seurat's use of the medium enhances this shallow depth. Notably, the soft, repeated marks around the lighthouse create a 'contour', which gives a sense of the curvature of the building where it glances across our line of sight.[30] Seurat's fluent use of Conté crayon also exploits 'chance', by making his marks vague and hence suggestive enough for depth to be projected into them.[31] What is more, space is established by the device the art theorist David Sutter called 'irradiation' in articles he published in the journal *L'Art* in 1880, which Seurat knew.[32] Thus, faint halos of light around the edges of the lighthouse and the sail help them to 'stand out' in relief.

Depth and flatness vie with one another as well in the related painting *End of the Jetty of Honfleur* (fig. 20), which depicts a slightly different view under an overcast sky. Here, Seurat compressed space by employing a loose version of orthographic projection, and by dispersing a diffuse greyness over the sea and sky, which elides the boundary between them. Elsewhere, Seurat applied touches of lighter-coloured paint to the upper section of the mast in the foreground to make it sit in the same plane as the whites immediately to its left, which stand for streaks of light glimpsed through the pillars of the jetty (fig. 21). Similarly, the deliberate alignment of the lower edges of the roofs of the two small structures on either side of the lighthouse with the horizon creates a 'false attachment' that collapses the distance between them.[33] Moreover, touches of paint that culminate in skins of 'dots' remain visibly distinct at a normal viewing distance, and hence draw attention to the physical surface of the painting.

Again, though, flatness does not have it all its own way. The orthographic drawing system in this work is loose enough for the jetty to enjoy some recessional depth. In concert with this, picture primitives which create shading give the lighthouse and the structures flanking it a measure of volume. Subtle tonal variations distinguish the illuminated sides of the jetty's pillars from those in shadow, while stronger contrasts make the structure stand proud against the sea. Since the use of picture primitives which map tonal variations is quite unusual within orthographic projection, Seurat was clearly prepared to contravene the rules here once again by employing creatively what Willats calls 'ungrammatical' combinations of drawing and denotation systems.[34]

Broadly summarised, the resulting pictorial world is distinguished by a 'tension' between the flatness of the physical surface and the virtual depth it contains.[35] Several examples of this are in play in *Entrance of the Port of Honfleur* (cat. 8). Its orthographic drawing system creates a series

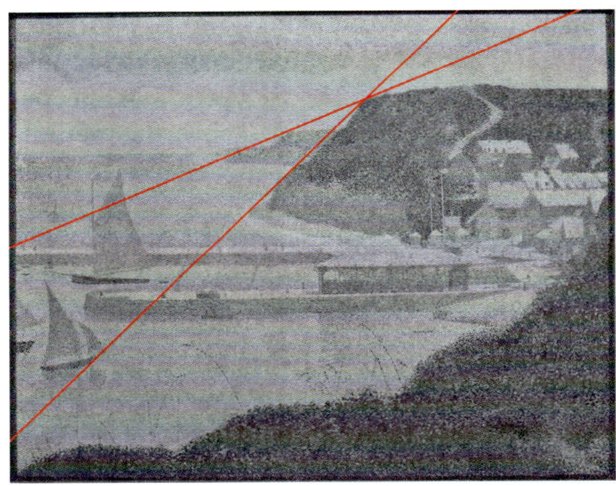

22. Diagram of 'aesthetic lines' in *Port-en-Bessin – The Outer Harbour (High Tide)* (cat. 14)

23. Detail of *Port-en-Bessin – The Outer Harbour (High Tide)* (cat. 14)

of overlapping *coulisses* (stage flats) that lie behind one another in shallow depth. In principle, the bollard at the front should deepen space by acting as a *repoussoir* that stands proud of the scene behind it. And arguably, it serves this purpose in the related drawing, where it only casts a weak shadow (cat. 9). In the painting, by contrast, the green bollard projects a deep reddish shadow, which abuts the painted border later added to the work. It thereby creates a false attachment that draws the bollard into the wall behind it, even as its position implies it lies in front.

Seurat employed a more sophisticated form of false attachment in *Port-en-Bessin – The Outer Harbour (High Tide)* (cat. 14), where he aligned certain terminal points in the scene with one another along what Sutter called 'aesthetic lines'.[36] These are illustrated in a diagram (fig. 22). In perceptual terms, their effect is to create 'eye directions' that draw elements of the scene located at different distances closer together.[37] What is more, Seurat manipulated tonal relationships to produce the same effect. Notably, he camouflaged the smaller house below the brightly lit roof of the large house immediately to the right of the circular artillery tower to make it melt into its neighbour (fig. 23).

The ambition of making space tense also explains why Seurat introduced two anchors into *The Channel of Gravelines: An Evening* (cat. 22), which are absent from the painted study (cat. 23). He first drew these in a separate Conté drawing (cat. 25), where he carefully aligned the top ('head') of the anchor with the lower edge of the sandbank behind it, and contrived to abut the tip ('bill') of its arrow-shaped head ('fluke') with its shank. These false attachments not only flatten the picture space here but in the painting as well, where it is clearer that the termination of the first anchor's stock is aligned with the bill of the second anchor's fluke.

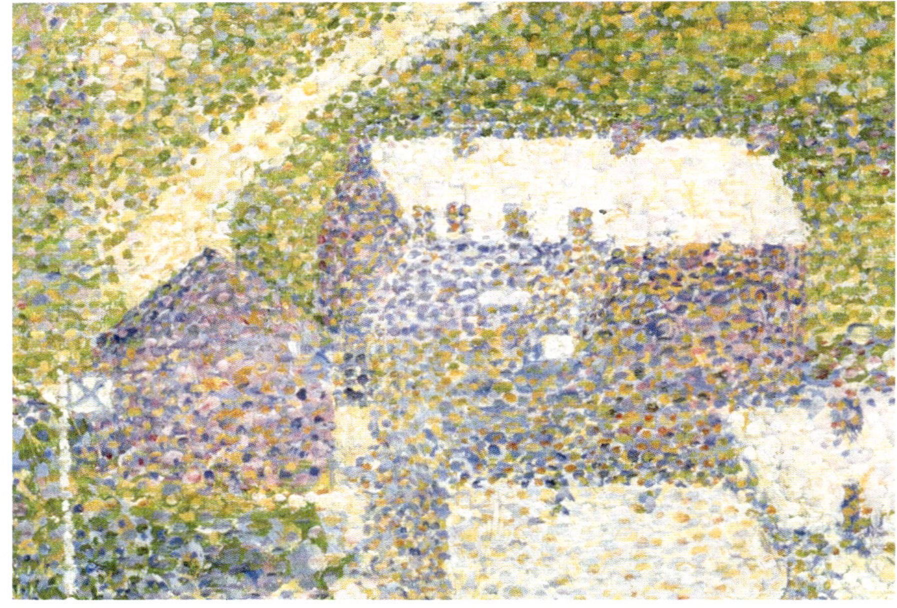

Detail of cat. 14

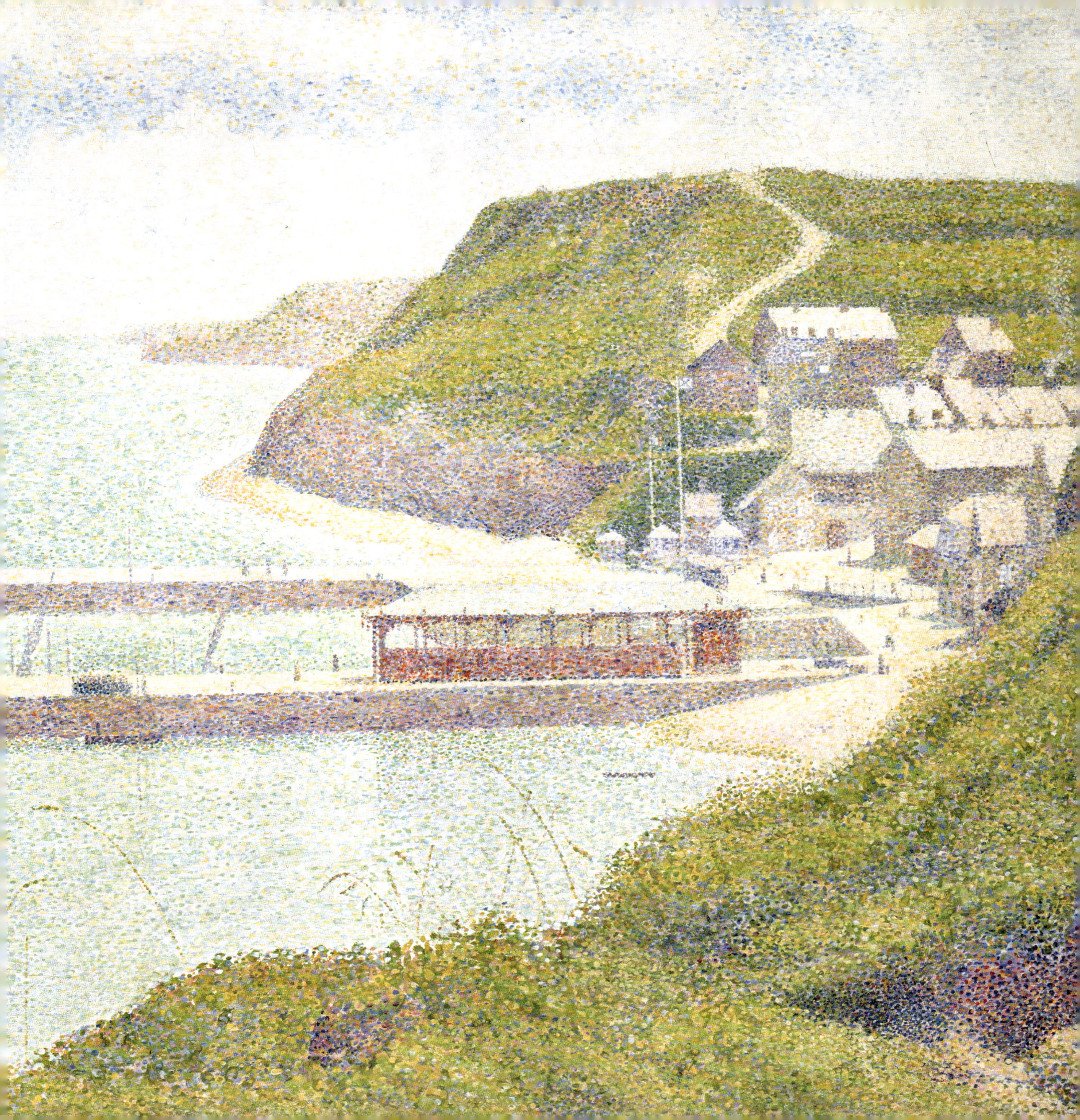

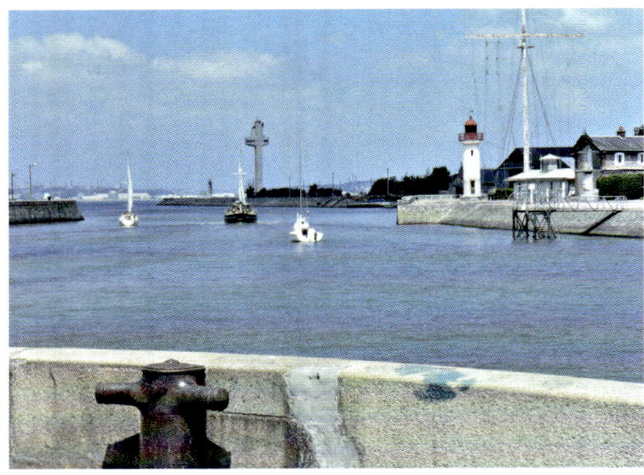

24. Photograph by the author of the motif of
Entrance of the Port of Honfleur (cat. 8), July 1982

In 1891, Seurat famously told his Symbolist colleague the poet Gustave Kahn that painting was 'The art of hollowing out a surface'.[38] But the foregoing analysis makes it apparent that – as with his titles – it would do him an injustice to take this statement literally.

Scaling

> 'If you find Les Andelys colourful, for my part, I see the Seine – an almost indefinable grey sea, even in the brightest sunshine under a blue sky'
> —Georges Seurat[39]

The letter which Seurat wrote to Signac on 25 June 1886 from Honfleur attests to his appreciation of the subtleties and paradoxes of natural light. The appearance of the light in a scene depends on a number of factors including the weather, the elevation of the sun and its azimuth position in the sky, and the artist's viewpoint.[40] It is quite possible, then, that Seurat contrived some of the views he rendered at Honfleur to suit his taste for even, subdued illumination, including those in broad daylight. And indeed, it is easy to appreciate just how comparatively subdued a work like *Entrance of the Port of Honfleur* (cat. 8) is by comparing it with Signac's *Les Andelys, Côte d'Aval* (fig. 17), which exemplifies his preference for 'brilliance'.[41]

It seems likely, too, that Seurat's liking for grey was not simply a matter of taste but was motivated by the fact that painting cannot capture the brightness of intense sunlight. Seurat could have arrived at this conclusion from his own experience of painting. An argument leading to it is also set out in the essay 'Optics and Painting' by the German scientist Hermann von Helmholtz, which was published in French in 1878 and which Seurat almost certainly knew.[42] In it, Helmholtz contended that the artist cannot create 'a simple copy of the object' but must instead supply 'a translation of his impression into another scale of sensation belonging to the different level of excitability of the viewer's eye'.[43] One reason for this, he argued, is that a painting hung under dull indoor light cannot replicate the much greater objective luminosity of the scene it represents. It must therefore lower (and compress) the range of value differences that we perceive in the real world.[44] Helmholtz also recognised that these objective differences are reduced in our subjective experience by the limited sensitivity of the observer's eye.[45] And he noted, in addition, that we assess such subjective or perceptual differences in relation to the 'total light intensity' of the scene.[46] Taken together, then, these facts mean that a painting can look convincing if only its light and dark values exhibit similar *ratios* between themselves to those we perceive in the corresponding scene.[47]

The advantages and limitations of Seurat's media were also important factors in his ability to capture natural light. In *End of the Jetty of Honfleur* (fig. 20), paint works perfectly well as a means of representing the modest illumination of a grey day, while Conté crayon is perfectly suited to the nocturnal conditions in *The Lighthouse at Honfleur* (fig. 19). Here, though, Seurat not only boosted the brightness of the lamp by adding a touch of white gouache to it but also increased the depth of his darks in so doing.

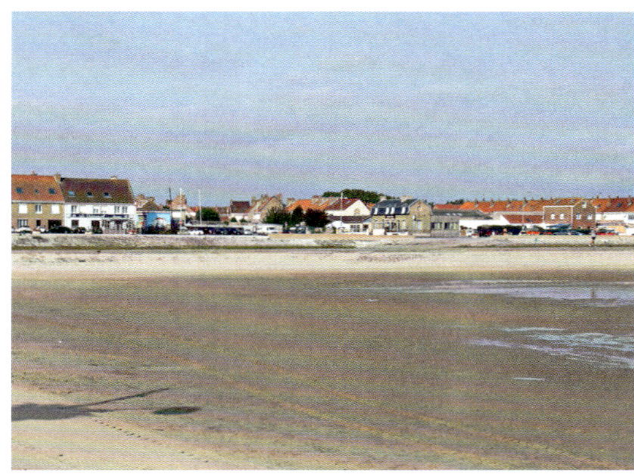

25. Photograph by the author of the motif of
The Channel of Gravelines: Grand-Fort-Philippe
(cat. 18), August 2025

The intrinsic strengths and weaknesses of Seurat's media are easier to discern by comparing *Entrance of the Port of Honfleur* with the corresponding drawing (cat. 9), since both represent the identical scene under the same light. Perhaps the most revealing fact about the drawing is that it sets the lighthouse against a section of sky which is darker than the section to its left. This suggests that the inherent darkness of Conté crayon obliged Seurat to employ contrast quite arbitrarily here to capture the brilliant white of the lighthouse. This conclusion is confirmed by the presence of the dark boat moored below the lighthouse to its left, which creates more contrast, as does its companion in the centre.

Things are very different in the painting, which – like the paint out of which it is made – is slightly more luminous overall. The lighthouse, for example, is much closer in brightness to the sky behind it. The painting could also afford to attenuate contrast by dispensing altogether with the larger of the two dark boats in the drawing, while shrinking the other one considerably. There is some contrast between the white sails of the boats and the sea behind them, but this is softer than in the drawing. The lighting in the painting is thus closer to the even illumination of a daylight scene – a conclusion that can be confirmed by comparing the painting with a photograph of the motif (fig. 24).

The idea that Seurat aspired towards greyness in his paintings runs counter to the familiar contention that he attempted to maximise the luminosity of his colour by exploiting 'optical mixture', or the process whereby the eye fuses the coloured light reflected by an array of separate touches. This is a misconception, however. The fact is that, to the limited extent that optical mixture does operate in Seurat's work, the eye only averages the luminosity of the colours involved.[48] The only advantage of optical mixture when it comes to luminosity, therefore, is that it avoids the muddying effect produced by mixing pigments, which combines their ability to absorb light.

Instead, Seurat's paintings have what luminosity they do largely as a result of the significant amount of white he routinely blended into their colours. This is particularly apparent in *The Hospice and the Lighthouse of Honfleur* (cat. 5) in the beach and the sunlit (right) side of the lighthouse. But close examination shows that Seurat also mixed white copiously into the sea and sky.[49] Seurat took the use of white to its limit in the paintings he made at Gravelines. Notably, in *The Channel of Gravelines: Grand-Fort-Philippe* (cat. 18), white is present over large areas of the beach and the sky, allowing it to capture the somewhat bleached colour that the extremely flat and exposed scene acquires under gentle morning sunlight (fig. 25). White, moreover, not only lightens colours but also desaturates them. Kahn was quite correct, therefore, when he stated that Seurat's 'marines blanch and leech out their colour' in the inscription he placed inside the copy of his book *Les Palais nomades*, which he gave to Seurat.[50]

The relative, as opposed to absolute, quality of the luminosity of Seurat's seascapes is betrayed in particular by the fact the nocturnal paintings use similar quantities of white to those in their diurnal relatives. In *Mouth of the Seine. Evening* (fig. 26), white is used to particularly dramatic effect to capture the shimmering light of the setting sun on the horizon seen through a dense atmosphere. This area of paint does not make the painting as a whole

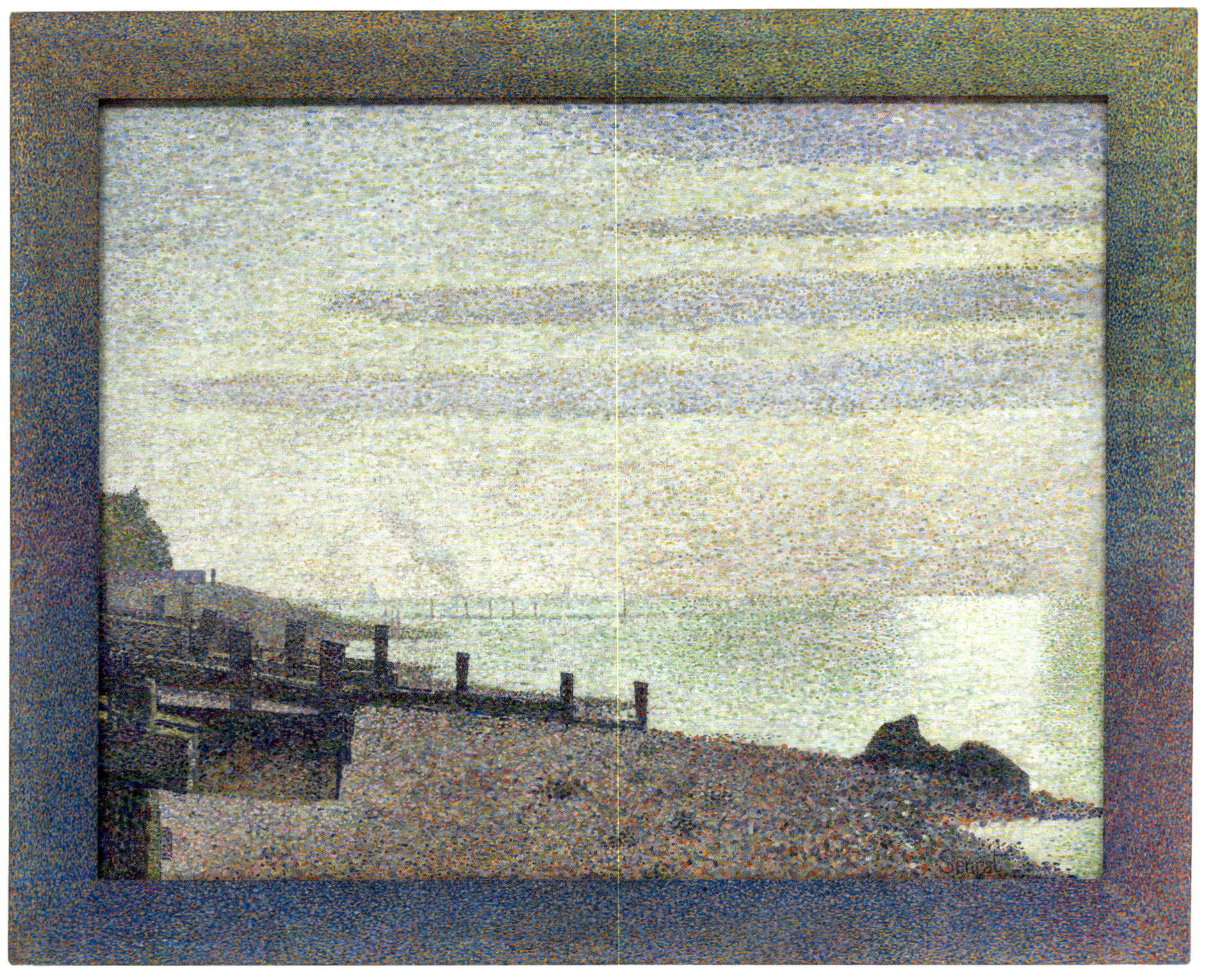

26. Georges Seurat, *Mouth of the Seine. Evening* (*Embouchure de la Seine. Soir)*, 1886, oil on canvas, 78.3 × 94 cm (including painted frame), The Museum of Modern Art, New York

particularly luminous, however, so much as it creates a bright spot (akin to the one in *The Lighthouse at Honfleur*) that expands the scale of value in the scene just enough for the darks to look convincing. White is used to a similar effect in the shimmering water of *The Channel of Gravelines: An Evening*, and more obviously so in the study. On several occasions, Seurat exhibited 'nocturnes' of this kind alongside seascapes painted under daylight.[51] It is tempting to believe that, in so doing, he intended to allude to the scenario devised by Helmholtz to introduce his argument about the relativity of painterly luminosity, in which a painting of a sunlit desert looks just as persuasive on a gallery wall as the moonlight scene hanging next to it.[52]

Crucial to Seurat's organisation of tonal relationships is the use of what he described, in a draft letter to the writer and journalist Maurice Beaubourg in 1890, as 'the analogy of similar and contrasting tones and hues'.[53] He calculated his use of colour, in other words, to create relationships of affinity and opposition for the purposes of 'harmony'.[54] Consequently, light and colour in his world – even while remaining plausible – are stylistic and *sui generis* in the last analysis, and more much harmonious than those in the actual Normandy.

Stasis

> 'Some may prefer less frigid or more lively impressions'
> —Joris-Karl Huysmans[55]

The writer and critic Joris-Karl Huysmans made these remarks about Seurat's Honfleur seascapes in 1887, when he also described them as depicting 'a nature at rest'.[56] Although he conceded that these paintings were not to everyone's taste, he nonetheless insisted that the stasis in them was less obtrusive than in the *Grande Jatte*, where 'the human frame becomes rigid and hard' and 'everything becomes immobile and frozen'.[57] Similarly, in 1889, Félix Fénéon criticised 'the figures walking along the quay of Port-en-Bessin' (in *Port-en-Bessin – The Bridge and the Quays* [cat. 12]) for being 'stiff'[58] (the accuracy of this remark can be gauged by comparing them with those in a postcard of the scene; fig. 60). As regards stasis more generally, Camille Pissarro stated in 1890 that both Seurat and Signac created 'a frozenness' that he found 'unpleasant'.[59] But in 1894 Octave Mirbeau argued that, whereas Signac 'made nature immobile and frozen', Seurat 'made the dust of light vibrate ... around his figures, in his skies, on his seas with their pure, melodious, washed-out colours'.[60] It would seem, then, that although critics did agree that Seurat's seascapes were affected by stasis, they could not pin down what made this different from the stiffness affecting his figures, nor what was particular about it to his individual style.

For all that the effects at issue are elusive, they were unquestionably deliberate. As Kahn stated in 1887, the Neo-Impressionists spurned 'all movement' in an attempt to give 'modern passers-by a little of the solemnity and timelessness of ancient statues'.[61] Similarly, he claimed that they 'wanted to capture not only the landscape at a particular moment, but also the silhouette it presented throughout the day'.[62] This is not strictly true since the seascapes Seurat made at Honfleur each captured light effects that lasted for only one or two hours. Among those he began in situ during the daytime, *Entrance of the Port of Honfleur* was painted around 1 pm, *The 'Maria' (Honfleur)* in mid-afternoon and *Corner of a Harbour (Honfleur)* in the early evening.[63] But it is fair to say that time appears to stand still in these paintings, so that a particular time of day is prolonged or arrested (and the tide along with it).

More generally, Seurat produced different kinds, and degrees, of stasis in his seascapes by employing techniques and devices that temper or suppress represented movement to a greater or lesser extent. Some of these operate directly through the medium, others involve the isolated parts of the painting, and yet others pertaining to the look of the whole painting involve concatenation. Seurat's stasis is so elusive, in other words, because its causes are multifarious.

Perhaps its most straightforward manifestation is the 'stiff' or 'rigid' look of Seurat's figures. This can be explained by his use of smooth, almost

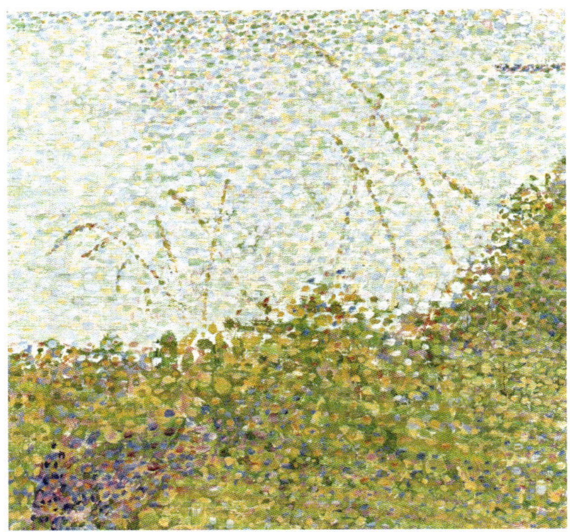

27. Detail of *Port-en-Bessin – The Outer Harbour (High Tide)* (cat. 14)

geometric, silhouettes, which play down the kind of inflections in posture that we have evolved to see as indicating movement.[64] Seurat's drawing also eliminates curved, convergent and diagonal lines from the draperies of his figures of the sort that imply movement (as can be seen in the postcard of Port-en-Bessin [fig. 60]).[65]

The appearance of the seascape in his work is more complex. In *Le Bec du Hoc (Grandcamp)* (cat. 1), for example, the shape of the rock itself is one we would normally experience as moving because it exhibits 'representational momentum'.[66] That is, our perception of a pointed shape like this will be inflected by our awareness of its potential to move in a particular direction, much as we tend to see a suspended shape as liable to sink under the pull of gravity ('representational gravity'). Any impression, however, that the rock is rising towards to the upper right of the scene is counteracted by a false attachment that pins its right tip to the horizon.

The movement of the seabirds at the top of the painting is also held in check. On an individual level, each bird has an arrowhead shape, which would normally look mobile. But because we are strongly disposed to interpret symmetry as indicating stability (rather as we tend to see imbalance as a prelude to collapse), their simplified, almost symmetrical silhouettes appear frozen.[67] Similarly, the look of the arrowhead that the birds form together (according to the gestalt principles of good continuation, proximity, similarity and common fate) is affected by its context in much the same way as the rock.[68] More specifically, although our perception of motion normally increases when a shape like this is directed towards a target, the flight of birds here is so close to the edge of the painting that it appears to hem them in.[69] The opposite is true, however, of the tiny sailing boat to the right of the rock, which moves into an expanse of open sea.[70] Comparison with the study for the painting (cat. 2) shows that Seurat added this boat at a late stage, perhaps to emphasise the becalmed appearance of the larger, dark sloop to its right.

The movement of the large sailing boat in *Entrance of the Port of Honfleur* is also mitigated. Seen in isolation, its pointed shape implies movement, as does the swelling of its sails, which we readily interpret as an effect caused by the wind pushing it.[71] But the fact that it is hemmed in by a flotilla of small boats, mostly viewed head-on, counteracts any sense of movement. Similarly, the distribution of shapes across the entire painting gives its composition a 'lucid order', in which they appear to hold one another in repose.[72] A related effect is at work in *Port-en-Bessin, Entrance to the Outer Harbour* (cat. 15), where the evenly spaced boats leaving the harbour at high tide form a procession that looks positively stately.[73]

Other paintings show how Seurat used the medium to create a sense of arrested movement. The crucial fact in this context is that we perceive movement as that of a continuous surface relative to a background.[74] This involves noticing 'kinetic texture', and particularly the effect of 'shearing' that an object produces as it moves.[75] Alongside this, as J.J. Gibson noted, the movement of an object involves 'wiping' the background ahead of it, and 'unwiping' the part in its wake.[76] Localised blurring effects of this kind are noticeably absent from Seurat's work, however. In *Port-en-Bessin – The Outer Harbour (High Tide)* (cat. 14), for example, where there is evidently enough

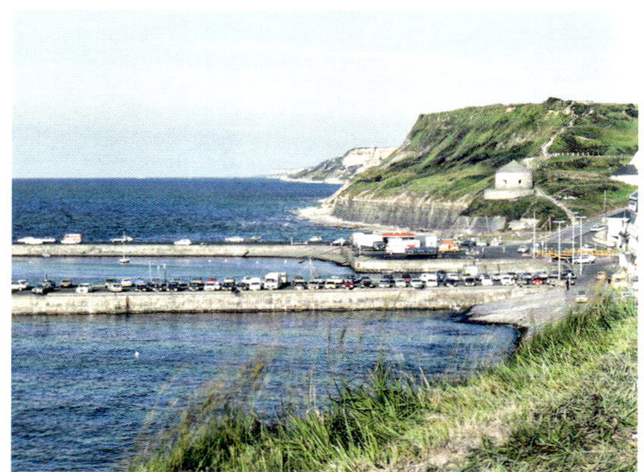

28. Photograph by the author of the motif of
Port-en-Bessin – The Outer Harbour (High Tide)
(cat. 14), July 1982

wind to fill the sails of the boats at the left, to keep the tricolour and the high water signal flag flying, and to inflect the smoke at the extreme right, this does not generate motion blur in any of them.[77] And, implausibly, the wind's effect is not registered at all in the grass on the edge of the cliff, which remains perfectly still. The dots out of which each stem is composed (fig. 27) may perhaps shimmer slightly at a distance, by creating an effect known as 'lustre'.[78] But since they do not sway about like their counterparts in a comparative photograph (fig. 28), they are devoid of kinetic texture.

Because localised motion blur is so important to the perception of movement, it stands to reason that Édouard Manet told Charles Toché, while watching the regatta at Mestre: 'Don't talk to me about precise, wiry lines in something that moves'.[79] Johan Jongkind nevertheless used sharp lines effectively to express the movement of ships, flags, clouds and smoke in the etchings he made in Honfleur in 1864, two of which represent motifs Seurat painted later. More particularly, the view in Jongkind's *Exit of the Port of Honfleur* (fig. 29) is recreated in *Entrance of the Port of Honfleur* (cat. 8), while that of *View from the Port to the Railway at Honfleur* (fig. 30) reappears in *The 'Maria' (Honfleur)* (cat. 10).

Admittedly, both of Jongkind's etchings represent quite gentle movement. In the former, the large ship at the left is becalmed, and only the flags and small vessels appear to be moving. But the scene is not frozen, as it is in the corresponding Seurat, because Jongkind's lines register the movement of his hand as it drew them. This gives them an 'impulse' which rubs off on the forms they represent.[80] Jongkind's *View from the Port to the Railway at Honfleur* looks a little more static – until it is noticed how the figures and the smoke in the left background are slightly agitated. The flags in Seurat's painting exhibit animation of a sort, too. But this effect is counteracted by the painting's insistent facture, which displaces localised effects of blur away from the edges of objects by spreading it across the whole scene indiscriminately.

Taken together, his various techniques and devices allowed Seurat to remake the mobile world created by his predecessor in his own way. Indeed, the fact that he not only painted the more obviously picturesque view of the harbour entrance etched by Jongkind, but also the drab view of the inner dock, suggests that he chose to measure how much he could make his Honfleur differ from Jongkind's more naturalistic version.

The tension between movement and stasis reaches a climax in *Port-en-Bessin – A Sunday* (cat. 11). Here, the tricolours and ships' pennants exhibit 'kinetic form', or the kind of abstract pattern we readily interpret as dynamic because of our innate sensitivity to movement.[81] They also seem to be agitated by the wind, or to flutter. Any impression of motion is nevertheless stemmed by their schematism, so that they appear frozen – rather as people do in photographs taken on a very short exposure. The same is true of the clouds to the right of the flags, which echo their shapes. And indeed, the clouds in *Le Crotoy (Downstream)* (cat. 17) are so schematic that Fénéon described them as 'conchoid', or shell-like.[82]

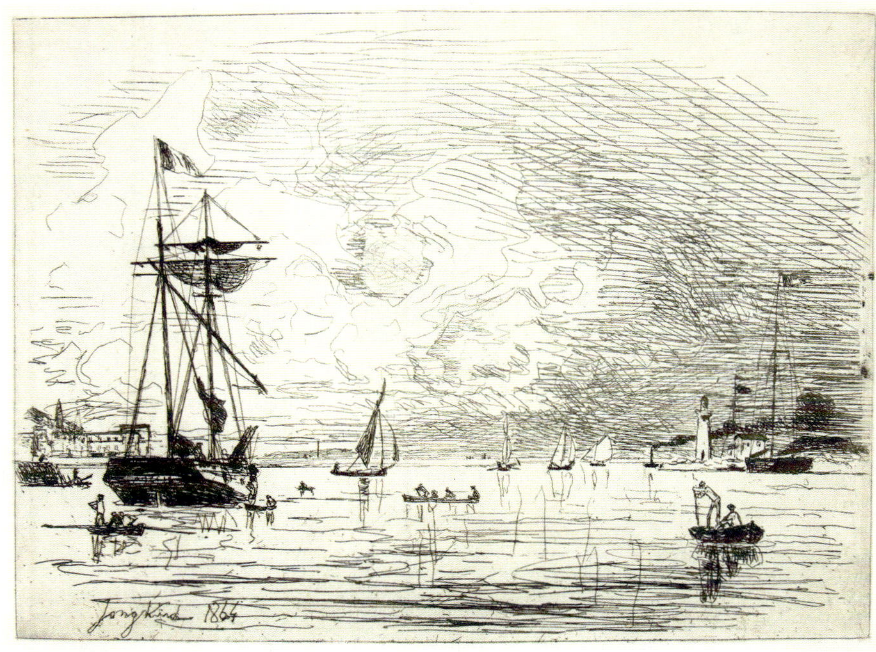

29. Johan Barthold Jongkind (1819–1891), *Exit of the Port of Honfleur* (*Sortie du Port de Honfleur*), 1864, etching, 24 × 31.8 cm (platemark), Yale University Art Gallery, New Haven

Conclusion

The world created by Seurat's style is not simply a function of the limitations inherent to drawing and painting, but it is also the result of his creative engagement with them. It is not just shallow, dull and frozen, therefore, so much as tightly integrated, harmonious and poised – so that the present moment dilates and persists in such a way that we, as spectators of this world, are placed outside of the flow of time. Fénéon came close to capturing this achievement in two remarks he made in an article of 1887. First, he correctly described how Seurat and his colleagues aimed 'to synthesise the landscape into a definitive form that perpetuates its sensation'.[83] And secondly, he hit on the importance of style to this process when he argued that for the Neo-Impressionists 'objective reality is simply a pretext for the creation of a higher, exalted reality into which their personalities are transfused'. It is none the less an indication of the persistent confusion between individual and general style that Fénéon did not distinguish Seurat's personal style from the one he shared with his colleagues.[84]

The artist himself said nothing about his individual style as such. He consequently said nothing to illuminate how it depended – as I have tried to show in this essay – on his unique engagement with his medium, and his particular way of concatenating pictorial elements into larger structures. But Seurat may have alluded to the role concatenation played in *how* he painted through *what* he painted. Notably, in *The Channel of Gravelines: Grand-Fort-Philippe* (cat. 18) and *The Channel of Gravelines: An Evening* (cat. 22) – which were exhibited together at the 1891 *Salon des Indépendants* –

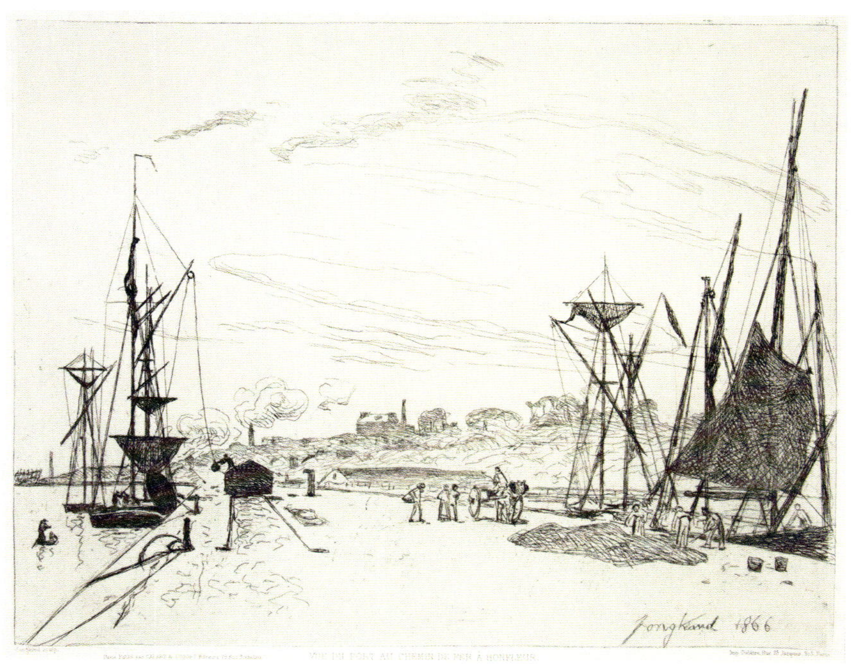

30. Johan Barthold Jongkind (1819–1891), *View from the Port to the Railway at Honfleur* (*Vue du port au chemin de fer à Honfleur*), 1864, etching, 25.5 × 32.5 cm (platemark), Yale University Art Gallery, New Haven

he depicted the combination of discrete components into larger structures in the arrangement of flags and balls displayed on the signal mast (behind the marine administration building) to announce the rising or falling of the tide and its height.[85] (This mast has since been demolished, but it can be seen in postcards and in a photograph by Georges Maroniez of 1904 [fig. 31], above the heads of the two fishermen left of centre.)

Seurat did not feature these signal systems in his paintings just because they were there. Rather, he evidently chose to do so because they held interest for him. Thus, he not only included a high tide signal flag in *Port-en-Bessin – The Outer Harbour (High Tide)*, but also represented the signal mast at Honfleur in *Entrance of the Port of Honfleur*, which displays three balls arranged symmetrically in a line immediately below the yardarm to indicate that the depth of the water is 3.75 metres.[86] In addition, Seurat depicted the semaphore on the cliffs above Port-en-Bessin in the top left corner of *The Semaphores and the Cliff* (*Les Grues et la percée*).[87]

In the daytime Gravelines painting, the larger rectangular flag with the cross lies beneath a smaller triangular pennant to signal that the tide is rising (fig. 32), while in the nocturne the flag sits above the pennant to indicate that the tide is ebbing (fig. 33).[88] Seurat may have seen these arrangements, but it is more than a little felicitous that movement of the tide in either painting coincides so perfectly with that of the light. What is more, in each work, these flags form groupings or gestalts that appear to be rising or falling in concert with both natural elements. Seurat, in other words, does not simply represent a conventionally meaningful combination of flags, but he also shows how

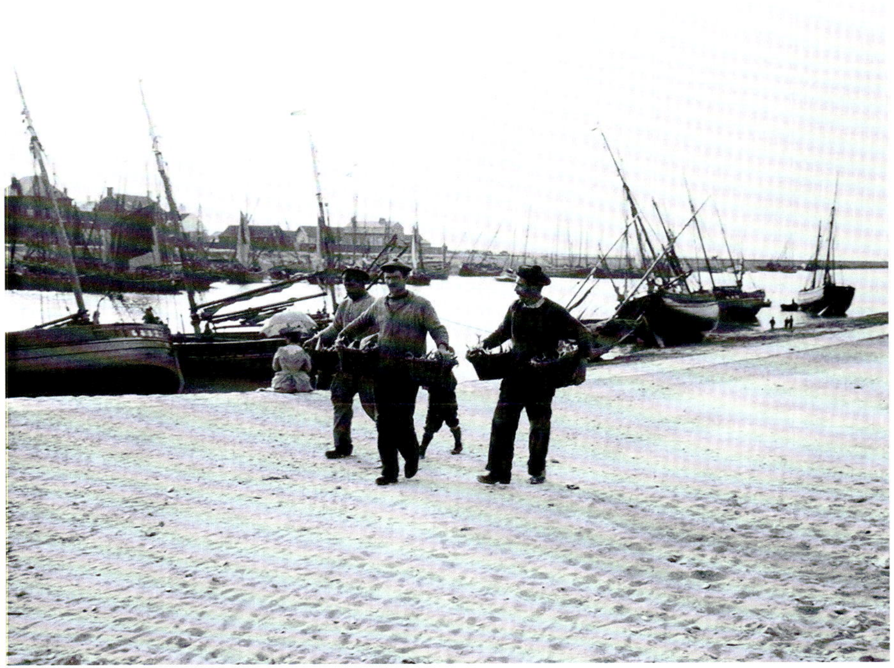

31. Georges Maroniez (1865–1933), Petit-Fort-Philippe, Fishermen carrying baskets full of fish at sunset, 1904, photograph, Bibliothèque nationale de France, Paris: Grand-Fort-Philippe is visible in the background.

these combine to create new, visually meaningful structures. Accordingly, they *exemplify* concatenation.[89]

The situation is rather different with the balls, since the combinations they form have no conventional meaning. In *The Channel of Gravelines: Grand-Fort-Philippe*, their irregular spacing means that they fail to form the same signal as their evenly spaced counterparts in *Entrance of the Port of Honfleur*.[90] Similarly, the two balls suspended to the side of the mast on brackets in *The Channel of Gravelines: An Evening* would need a flag with a blue border above them to create the signal prohibiting all movement in or out of the harbour.[91] The balls in both Gravelines paintings do nevertheless combine to form groupings that are *visually* expressive in that they, too, appear to float and to sink. What is more, being nearly round and almost identical, they signal the ability of the picture primitives we see in Seurat's medium – separate 'dots' of paint – to coalesce into a stylistic world.

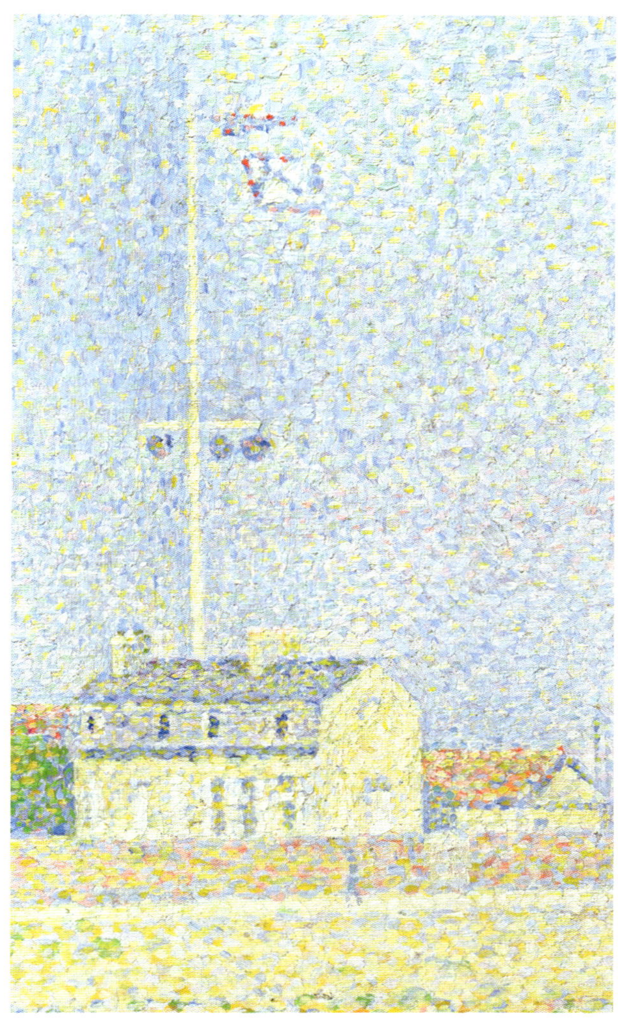

32. Detail of *The Channel of Gravelines:
Grand-Fort-Philippe* (cat. 18)

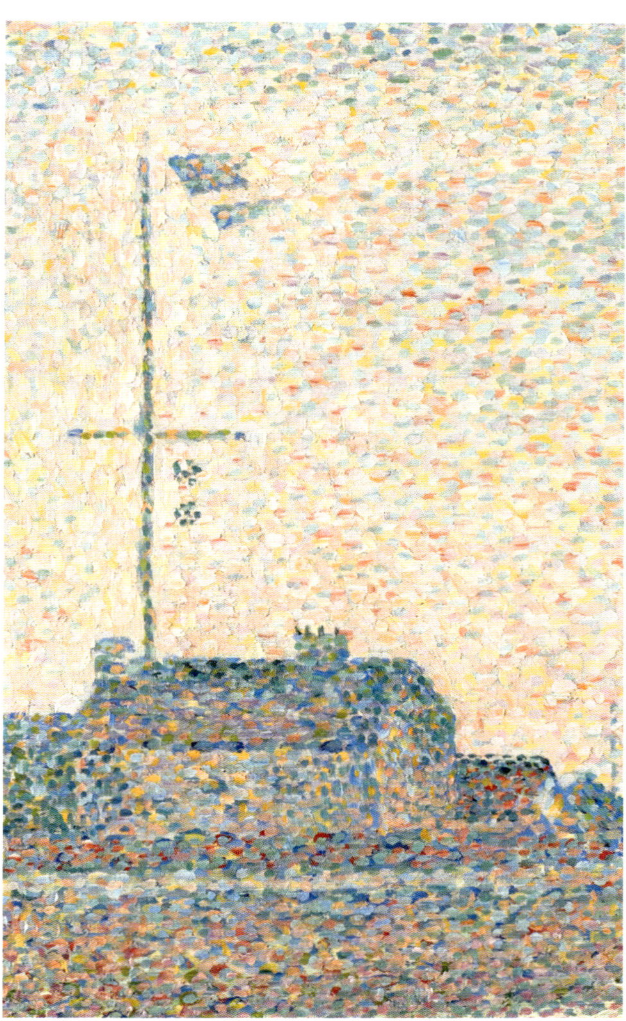

33. Detail of *The Channel of Gravelines:
An Evening* (cat. 22)

1 Albert Michel, 'Le Néo-impressionnisme', *L'Art moderne*, vol. VIII, no. 11, 10 March 1888, pp. 83–85, at p. 84.

2 Letter from Paul Signac to Camille Pissarro, 28 January 1894, cited in Pierre Michel and Christian Limousin, 'Octave Mirbeau et Paul Signac – Une lettre inédite de Signac à Mirbeau', *Cahiers Octave Mirbeau*, no. 16, March 2009, pp. 202–10, at p. 202.

3 See Wollheim 1987, pp. 26–27.

4 See Herbert 1959, p. 318.

5 Lambert Wiesing, 'When Images are Signs: The Image Object as Signifier', in *Artificial Presence: Philosophical Studies in Image Theory*, Nils. F. Schot trans., Stanford: Stanford University Press, 2020, pp. 24–57. See also John Hyman, 'Depiction', *Royal Institute of Philosophy Supplements*, vol. LXXI, October 2012, pp. 129–50.

6 See Joan U. Halperin, 'The Ironic Eye/I in Jules Laforgue and Georges Seurat', in Paul Smith ed., *Seurat Re-Viewed*, University Park, Pennsylvania: Penn State University Press, pp. 113–46.

7 Nelson Goodman, *Ways of Worldmaking*, Hassocks: Harvester Press, 1978, esp. pp. 7–17 and 27–40. See also Podro 1991, p. 173, for the argument that our awareness of the artist's procedure penetrates the appearance of the subject matter to create 'a new kind of world'.

8 Ludwig Wittgenstein, *Culture and Value*, H.G. von Wright and Heikki Nyman eds, Peter Winch trans., Oxford: Blackwell, 2nd ed., 1980, pp. 56 and 89.

9 See Wollheim 1973, pp. 196–98.

10 I am indebted to the late Andrew Harrison for this observation. On the holistic nature of face perception, see Graham Hole and Victoria Bourne, *Face Processing: Psychological, Neurophysical, and Applied Perspectives*, Oxford: Oxford University Press, 2010, pp. 246–51.

11 Wollheim 1973, pp. 200–01.

12 See Willats and Durand 2005, pp. 319–51.

13 Podro 1991, p. 185.

14 See the remarks on the painting by Huysmans cited below. In a letter to Pissarro of March–April 1887, Signac complained that the *Grande Jatte* employed a 'division … too mean for a large canvas of several metres'; cited in Dorra and Rewald 1959, pp. 161–62.

15 Wollheim 1987, pp. 31–36.

16 Firmin Javel, 'Les Impressionnistes', *L'Évènement*, no. 5166, 16 May 1886; cited in Dorra and Rewald 1959, p. 158.

17 John Willats, 'The Third Domain: The Role of Pictorial Images in Picture Perception and Production', *Axiomathes*, vol. XIII, no. 1, March 2002, pp. 1–15.

18 On Seurat's awareness of this argument in the writings of Hermann von Helmholtz, see Foa 2015, pp. 20–25. On Helmholtz's argument, see also Paul Smith, *Interpreting Cézanne*, London: Tate, 1996, p. 46.

19 See Willats 1997, pp. 43–46. This is the term used in the UK. The system's US name, 'orthogonal projection', is confusing because this system actually eliminates orthogonals, or lines that converge on the horizon at a vanishing point.

20 Willats 1997, pp. 4–8.

21 See Paul Smith, '"Between a Thing and a Thought": Syntax, Twofoldness, and the Wisdom of the Ancients', *Word & Image*, vol. XXIX, no. 3, July–September 2003, pp. 304–33, esp. pp. 305, 307, 309–10, 314 and 322.

22 Willats 1997, pp. 96–100.

23 Ibid., pp. 29, 154–58 and 251.

24 Ibid., pp. 109–11.

25 Ibid., pp. 236–37.

26 Willats and Durand 2005, pp. 343 and 348.

27 Ibid., p. 343.

28 Willats 1997, pp. 18–21 and 150–54. See also pp. 105–07 for an example of primitives that can be described either way. I am grateful to Sam Rose for drawing this passage to my attention.

29 Willats 1997, pp. 97 and 110.

30 Willats and Durand 2005, p. 325.

31 Ibid., p. 326.

32 Sutter 1880, p. 216. On Seurat and Sutter, see William Innes Homer, *Seurat and the Science of Painting*, Cambridge, Mass.: MIT Press, 1964, pp. 43–47.

33 False attachment is common with orthographic projection. See Willats 1997, pp. 24, 30, 113 and 231.

34 See Willats 1997, pp. 154–58 and 251.

35 Willats and Durand 2005, p. 325.

36 Sutter 1880, pp. 75, 124–25, 147–49, 196–97, 216 and 220.

37 Willats and Durand 2005, p. 333.

38 Kahn 1891, p. 109.

39 Letter from Georges Seurat to Paul Signac, 25 June 1886, Honfleur, first published in Rewald 1948, p. 111.

40 See Smith 1984.

41 See Signac 2014.

42 See Smith 1984, p. 172, note 66.

43 Brücke and Helmholtz 1878, p. 191. See also C.L. Hardin, *Color for Philosophers: Unweaving the Rainbow*, Indianapolis: Hackett, 1988, p. 25.

44 Brücke and Helmholtz 1878, pp. 189–90.

45 Ibid., p. 191.

46 Ibid., p. 192.

47 Ibid., p. 195.

48 See J. Carson Webster, 'The Technique of Impressionism: a Reappraisal', *College Art Journal*, vol. 4, no. 1, 1944, pp. 3–22, esp. pp. 3–9.

49 Seurat's use of white is greater in the study he made for the painting (fig. 55), where unmixed touches of the colour cover much of the top layer.

50 Gustave Kahn, *Les Palais nomades*, Paris: Tresse et Stock, 1887. This was lot 57 in the sale at Sotheby's, Paris, 15 December 2010: *Rimbaud, Verlaine, Mallarmé and their Friends: Books, Manuscripts and Photographs from the Poetical Collection of Eric and Marie-Hélène B.*

51 At the *Salon des Indépendants* of 1886, he exhibited *Grandcamp (Evening)* (fig. 7), which has a similar arrangement to *The Roadstead of Grandcamp* (cat. 3). At the 1887 *Exhibition of Les XX* and *Salon des Indépendants*, he exhibited *Mouth of the Seine. Evening* (fig. 26), which broadly mirrors the composition of *The Shore at Bas-Butin (Honfleur)* (cat. 6). And at the 1889 *Salon des Indépendants* and 1890 *Exhibition of Les XX*, he exhibited *The Semaphores and the Cliff* (cat. 16), which reverses the arrangement of *Port-en-Bessin – The Outer Harbour (High Tide)* (cat. 14). On the 1891 *Salon des Indépendants*, see below.

52 Brücke and Helmholtz 1878, p. 187.

53 Draft of a letter from Georges Seurat to Maurice Beaubourg, 28 August 1890, published, for example, in Rey 1921, p. 132; also cited and reproduced in Dorra and Rewald 1959, pp. LXXII and XCIX.

54 Ibid.

55 Huysmans 1887, p. 53.

56 Ibid.

57 Ibid.

58 Fénéon 1889, p. 339.

59 Letter of 9 September 1889, reprinted in *Correspondance de Camille Pissarro 2: 1886–1890*, ed. Janine Bailly-Herzberg, Paris: Valhermeil, 1986, p. 292.

60 Octave Mirbeau, 'Néo-Impressionnistes', *L'Écho de Paris*, no. 3529, 23 January 1894, p. 1.

61 Kahn 1887, p. 229.

62 Ibid.

63 See Smith 1984, pp. 562–65.

64 See Pierre Jacob and Marc Jeannerod, *Ways of Seeing,* Oxford: Oxford University Press, 2003, pp. 239–42.

65 See Simone Gori, Riccardo Pedersini and Enrico Giora, 'How do painters represent motion in garments? Graphic invariants across centuries', *Spatial Vision*, vol. XXI, no. 3–5, 2008, pp. 201–27.

66 See Hubbard 2010, pp. 83–84.

67 See Gombrich 1982, p. 55.

68 Hubbard 2010, p. 87.

69 Ibid., pp. 94–96.

70 Gombrich 1982, pp. 55 and 58.

71 Hubbard 2010, p. 82.

72 Gombrich 1982, p. 55. See also John F.A. Taylor, *Design and Expression in the Visual Arts*, New York: Dover, 1964, pp. 26–67.

73 See Smith 1997, p. 161, for a photograph of the motif.

74 See Braddick 1995, pp. 211–12.

75 Ibid., pp. 210, 217 and 227.

76 James J. Gibson, *The Senses Considered as Perceptual Systems*, Boston: Houghton Mifflin, 1966, pp. 199, 203, 204 and 206.

77 On tidal signal flags, see Figuier 1870, p. 527; and Baker 1877, pp. 16–17.

78 See Alan Lee, 'Seurat and Science', *Art History*, vol. X, no. 2, June 1987, pp. 203–26, esp. pp. 215–16; and John Gage, 'The Technique of Seurat: A Reappraisal', *The Art Bulletin*, vol. XLIX, no. 3, Fall 1987, pp. 448–54, esp. p. 452.

79 Ambroise Vollard, *Souvenirs d'un marchand de tableaux*, Paris: Albin Michel, 1937, p. 177.

80 Podro 1991, p. 163.

81 Braddick 1995, pp. 207 and 209–11.

82 Fénéon 1889, p. 339.

83 Fénéon 1887, p. 139.

84 See also Willats and Durand 2005, p. 321, which does not distinguish between 'individual' style and the general style of a 'school'.

85 On these structures, see *Origines: Genéalogie Association Gravelines*, *Numéro Spécial: Georges Seurat (1859–1891)*, no. 84, September 2018, pp. 15–17; and Ellen W. Lee, 'Seurat at Gravelines: The Last Landscapes', in Lee 1990, pp. 24–59, at p. 29. The signal mast should not be confused with the much larger semaphore near the lighthouse in Petit-Fort-Philippe, which is mentioned in Baker 1877, p. 533. The marine administration building, constructed around 1880, now has a new roof closely modelled on the M-shaped original with irregularly spaced windows.

86 See Figuier 1870, p. 526, and Baker 1877, pp. 16–17.

87 On this semaphore, see Baker 1877, p. 407.

88 See Figuier 1870, p. 527; and Baker 1877, pp. 16–17 (and pp. 529–35 for a detailed description of the harbour).

89 On exemplification (as opposed to representation), see Nelson Goodman, *Languages of Art*, Indianapolis and New York: Bobbs-Merrill, 1968, pp. 85–95.

90 See Baker 1877, pp. 16–17.

91 Ibid., pp. 446–47.

RICHARD THOMSON

During Georges Seurat's all-too-brief decade of creativity, the sea – as it has been throughout human culture – was a subject of fascination. The historian Jules Michelet's *La Mer*, published in 1861 and reprinted in 1885, noted how it was at the foot of cliff walls that one could best appreciate 'the tide, the breathing, one might say, the pulse of the sea'.[1] Such pantheism was flatly contradicted by Eugène Mouton's 1885 volume on physiognomy in nature, humanity and art, which dismissed the 'literary amplifications' of 'poets and indoor sailors', stating that, after a while by the sea, one realised that 'all that poetry is simply water in very great quantity'.[2] If that blunt disagreement was not so overtly articulated in painting, nor could hardly have been, it is nevertheless significant that Seurat chose to paint the time-honoured subject during a period of aesthetic change, and that his pioneering experimentation with touch, colour and surface took place during a decade when artists were, as ever, fascinated with painting marine motifs and when searching for new forms of expression for an age-old subject was a challenge for the avant-garde artist, just as it might be a matter of record for the more descriptive painter.

The 1880s was the decade that saw naturalism – the direct and detailed description of the everyday world – as the dominant aesthetic in French culture. It was in the ascendant in contemporary literature and given credence by the politics of the Third Republic, now in its second decade, which laid stress on *liberté*, *égalité* and *fraternité*, civic virtues that naturalism inherently articulated: anything might be represented, everybody could respond to it, and it was shared social experience.[3] Naturalism thrived not only in the visual arts but very emphatically in literature. Two prominent naturalist novelists of different generations – Gustave Flaubert and Guy de Maupassant – were from Normandy and the Channel coast features in their work. While the leading naturalist novelist of the decade, Émile Zola, may have been from Aix-en-Provence, his 1884 novel *Joie de vivre* was based on a stay at Grandcamp on the Calvados shore during August and September 1881. Up-to-the-minute modern writing sought to engage with the social and psychological experience of living by the seacoast, whether as a native of the region or a visiting tourist.

By the closing decades of the nineteenth century, the Channel coast of Normandy and the Pas-de-Calais had long been attracting artists from different parts of France. The coastline offered a rich variety of motifs, both natural – extensive beaches and dramatic cliffs – and man-made, whether the noble buildings of past centuries that had stimulated the fascination for the picturesque since the Romantic era or the industrial harbours, fishing ports and resorts with their hotels and casinos that had burgeoned in recent decades. Such diversity drew summer tourists – indeed the chic Paris magazine *La Vie moderne* dedicated its 17 July 1886 issue to Dieppe – and, with them, artists who joined with local painters such as Eugène Boudin (1824–1898) in depicting the sites of the Channel coast. Lucien Quintard (1849–1905) and Jules Bastien-Lepage (1848–1884), for example, hailed from Nancy and Damvillers in north-eastern France but sought motifs at Grandcamp and Honfleur respectively. The motives of such artists were varied; Bastien-Lepage did not show his Normandy work at the Paris Salon but Quintard did, no doubt hoping for sales, perhaps from fellow visitors who could recognise his coastal sites. Seurat, a Parisian, may well have followed the established path to the

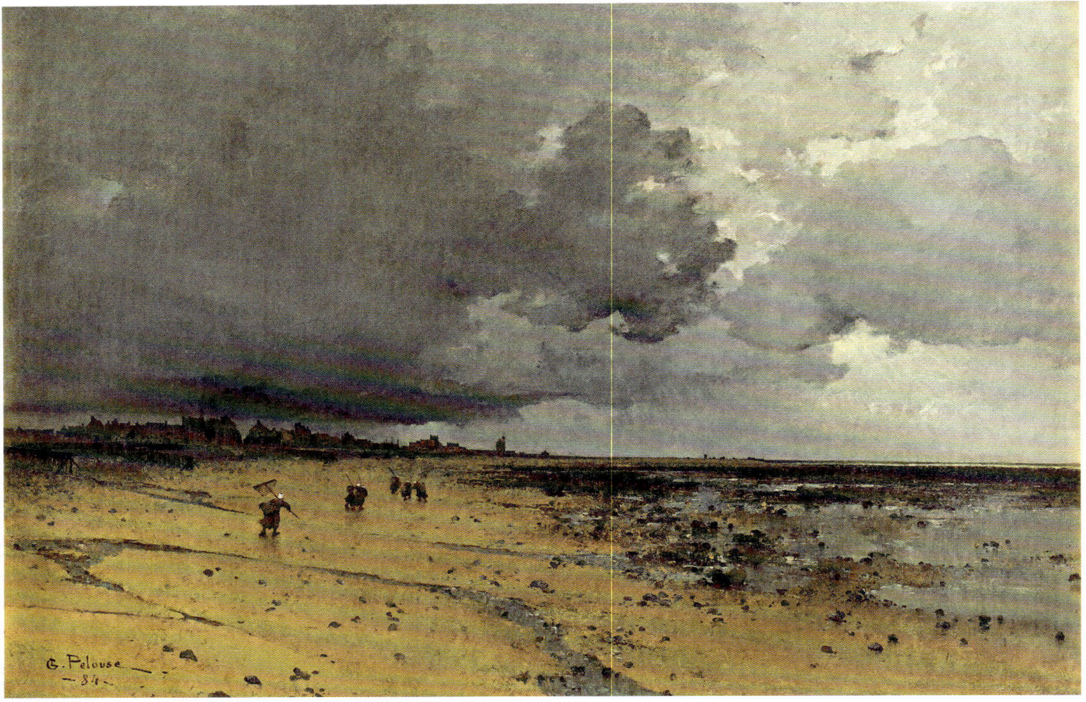

34. Léon-Germain Pelouse (1838–1891), *Grand-camp, Low Tide*, 1884, oil on canvas, 97 × 147 cm, Musée des Beaux-Arts, Carcassonne

Normandy coast to extend his range as a painter of natural scenes from the relatively proximate landscapes of the forest of Bondy and Fontainebleau.

Grandcamp

It is unlikely that Seurat was drawn to Grandcamp in 1885 by Zola's recent novel, which, in any case, used a fictive name for its location. However, the coastal village, far away from any substantial town, had drawn the Lerolle family for a holiday in 1854, when their son Henri, later to become an important painter and collector, was six.[4] Two artists from towns north-west of Paris, Léon-Germain Pelouse (1838–1891) from Pierrelaye and Léon-Gustave Ravanne (1854–1904) from Meulan, worked there in the 1880s. At the Salon of 1884, Pelouse showed *Grandcamp, Low Tide* (fig. 34), which was bought by the wealthy Languedocien businessman Bruno-Casimir Courtejaire for the developing Musée des beaux-arts in far-away Carcassonne.[5] Pelouse's quintessentially naturalist canvas shows the beach at low tide, an expanse of sand and rocks, with fisherfolk making their way to the distant village as the heavily clouded sky threatens a storm. The subject is hardly the tiny figures nor Grandcamp itself, a commune not blessed with an impressive harbour or picturesque buildings, but rather the description of natural phenomena – coastline and weather – and of vast space. The coast at Grandcamp, stretching westwards towards the Cotentin peninsula across the joint estuary of the rivers Douve and Taute, is flat and featureless, rising to cliffs and sites such as the Bec du Hoc only to the east.

Most painters who came to work there seem to have been drawn by that consistent open interplay between flat shore with buildings along the beach and the unbroken sea. This was the solution adopted by Ravanne, in a painting from perhaps 1881 (fig. 35), and by Eva Gonzalès (1849–1883), who had worked there a few years earlier (see, for example, *View of Grandcamp, Study*, c. 1877–78, private collection). It was followed by Quintard's submission to the Salon of 1887, *À Grandcamp (Calvados)* (unlocated but known through an engraving in the catalogue to the Salon).[6] In the meantime, Seurat, during his visit in the summer of 1885, had come up with that same solution.

Three of Seurat's Grandcamp canvases were among his submissions to the *Eighth Impressionist Exhibition* in May 1886, and it is noteworthy that at least four critics – George Auriol in *Le Chat noir*, Gustave Geffroy in *La Justice*, 'Labruyère' in *Le Cri du peuple* and Octave Mirbeau in *La France* – much admired them while registering their mood as 'melancholy'.[7] Mirbeau went further, comparing the 'penetrating melancholy' of Seurat's seascapes to the work of Jean-Charles Cazin (1841–1901), whose paintings of his native Pas-de-Calais also relished broad vistas, subdued tonalities and unpeopled shores (see, for example, *Equihen on the Cliff, Low Tide*, c. 1883, National Gallery of Art, Washington, D.C.).[8] It is interesting that astute critics used the language of mood to discuss Seurat's seascapes from the start. This was several months before Jean Moréas would publish the 'Symbolist Manifesto' in the French newspaper *Le Figaro* on 18 September, encouraging writers to cultivate emotion, suggestion and mood in their work, and promoting a subjectivity at odds with the dominant aesthetic of frank naturalist description. From the outset, it seems, Seurat's treatment of seacoast scenes – subdued in colour, unpeopled and sparse, even banal in motif – coincided with an emergent aesthetic.

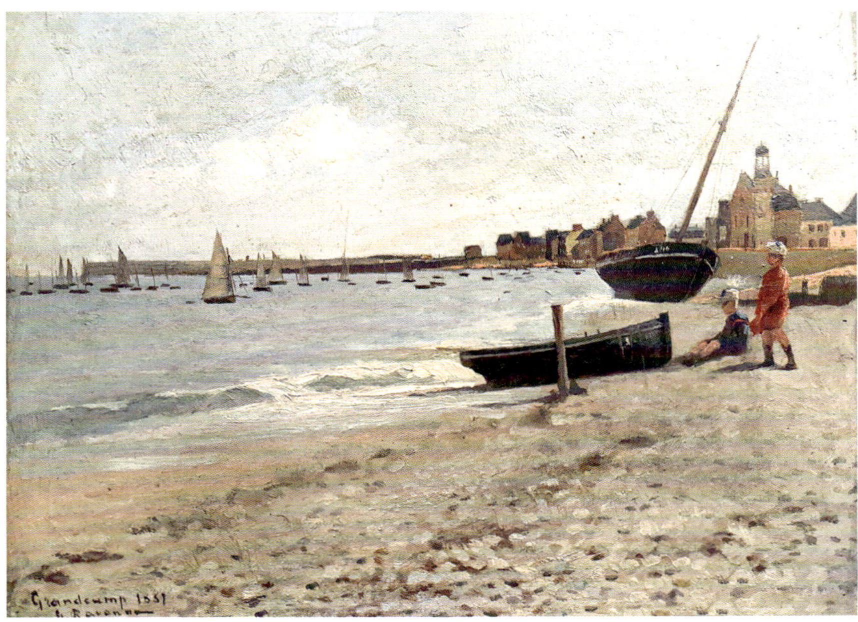

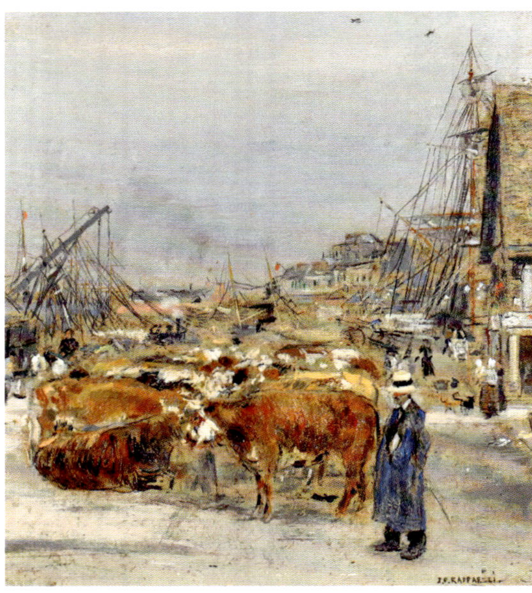

36. Jean-Francois Raffaëlli (1850–1924), *The Boarding of Cattle Destined for England*, 1880, oil on wood panel, 22.9 × 20.3 cm, Leighton Fine Art

Honfleur

For his second visit to the Channel coast, Seurat chose Honfleur, where he worked from late June to mid-August 1886. The contrast with Grandcamp could not have been greater. Not only was Honfleur a busy port but it was also a town with a long history and distinguished buildings. Its location on the south side of the Seine estuary as it debouches into the sea made Honfleur an important port from the eleventh century onwards, initially well placed for trade across the Channel to England and the North Sea. Over the last three hundred years, transatlantic trade had also developed. Commercial prosperity brought important structures, such as the late fifteenth-century Church of Saint Catherine in the town centre and, on the high ground of the Côte de Grâce to the north, the early seventeenth-century Notre-Dame de Grâce, as well as the portside *Lieutenance*, an eighteenth-century construction incorporating some of the medieval fortifications. Seurat ignored all that history in favour of actuality. Honfleur was a thriving port. Its traffic had doubled in the last decade, rising from 440,000 tons in 1874 to 882,000 tons in 1884.[9]

In Seurat's day, Honfleur remained a destination for artists. The leading naturalist painter Bastien-Lepage worked there briefly around 1880; one of his canvases of the inner port, or *bassin*, was shown at his posthumous exhibition at the École des Beaux-Arts in Paris in the spring of 1885.[10] At his one-man-show held in Paris in 1884, Jean-François Raffaëlli (1850–1924) exhibited a 'Set of six painting on Honfleur', mixing portraits of local seamen, a panorama of the town from the Côte de Grâce, a view of the historical *Lieutenance* and a painting of cattle being held on the quayside prior to be loaded for export to Britain (fig. 36).[11] It attracted foreigners too, with the Swede Richard Bergh (1858–1919) working there in 1881, painting its narrow medieval alleys.[12] During the 1880s and 1890s the Belgian Alfred Stevens (1823–1906), long settled in France, regularly painted along this coast, typically compositions looking directly out to sea. Honfleur also had a local community of artists. Louis Alexandre Dubourg (1821–1891) was born there and became a well-established painter of the town, the surrounding countryside and marine subjects. Boudin, although also born in Honfleur, had a more peripatetic career but consistently painted in his native region. Adolphe-Félix Cals (1810–1880), born in Paris, had moved to Honfleur in 1871, buying a house there two years later and painting both seascapes and characters from the town's population.[13]

Visiting Honfleur would have completely changed Seurat's limited experience of the Channel. Its motifs of varied kinds – not only distant vistas but also a surrounding landscape with cliffs and higher ground, a picturesque and historical town, and modern harbour – had been exploited by local and visiting artists for decades. However, in his responses, Seurat, while in all likelihood not knowingly following other painters' examples, made choices of motifs that showed a degree of consistency. Repudiating the picturesque and absorbing the modern, a canvas like *The 'Maria' (Honfleur)* (cat. 10) shows Seurat in naturalistic mode, focusing on the actuality of a steamship built at Port Glasgow in 1871 and moored at the Jetée du Transit constructed between 1865 and 1868, with railway tracks on the quayside added to ease the movement

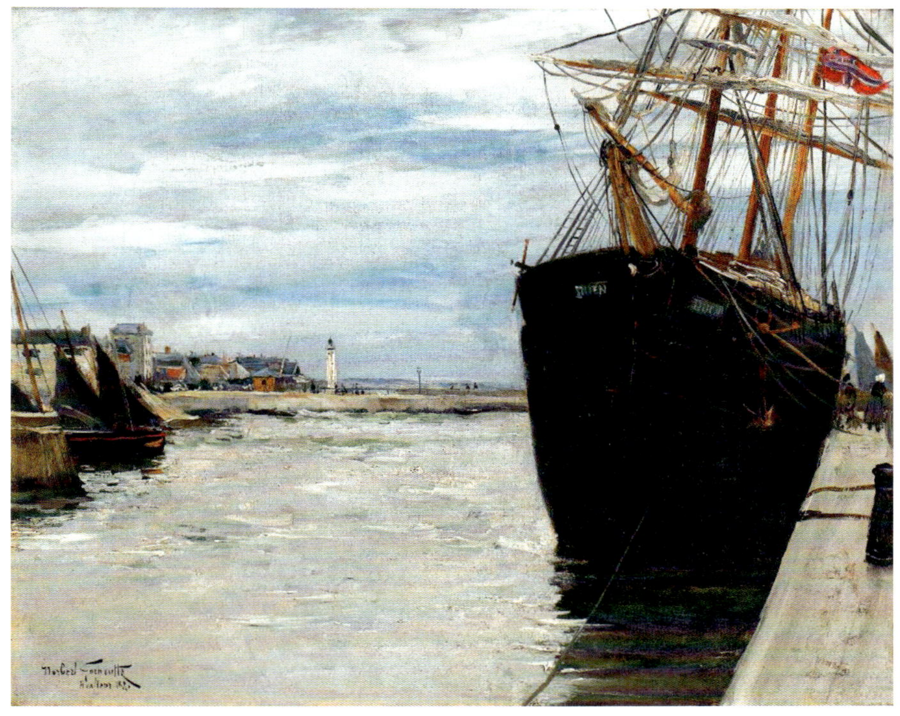

of goods in response to the modernising Plan Freycinet of 1879.[14] The emphasis on the hard surfaces of the metal hull and stone quay, the cluttering of the sky with masts and rigging, and the sharp perspective along the dockside corresponds quite closely to the way an artist subscribing to the naturalist aesthetic such as Norbert Goeneutte (1854–1894) had painted a similar motif (fig. 37).

Honfleur's port facilities had been quite consistently developed throughout the nineteenth century, as a proud text by an anonymous local applauded in 1867.[15] Nine years later, an official volume written by Eugène Arnoux and published by the Ministère des Travaux Publics listed in detail the development of the structures and facilities of the port. It had been substantially rebuilt in mid-century, with the Jetée de l'Est constructed between 1839 and 1842. Between 1861 and 1867, the jetties had all been rebuilt in stone. Such progress was registered by artists. In 1865, the Dutchman Johan Barthold Jongkind (1819–1891) depicted the view out to sea, with the tide high and the steep perspective up the new Jetée de l'Ouest giving a sense of momentum to the vessel departing the harbour entrance, while the hard edges of the construction emphasise human control over nature (fig. 38). This more modern character recurs in other paintings of the late 1860s or 1870s. For example, *Boats in the Port of Honfleur* by Henri Cassinelli (1833–1926), another local painter, represents a busy traffic of steam and sailing vessels making their way in and out of the harbour entrance (fig. 39). To the rear right can be seen both the tower constructed in 1843 to indicate the tide and the signal

38. Johan Barthold Jongkind (1819–1891),
The Jetty at Honfleur, 1865, oil on canvas,
33.5 × 43.3 cm, Van Gogh Museum, Amsterdam
(Vincent van Gogh Foundation)

39. Henri Cassinelli (1833–?), *Boats in the
Port of Honfleur,* 1860s, oil on wood panel,
23 × 32 cm, Musée Eugène Boudin, Honfleur

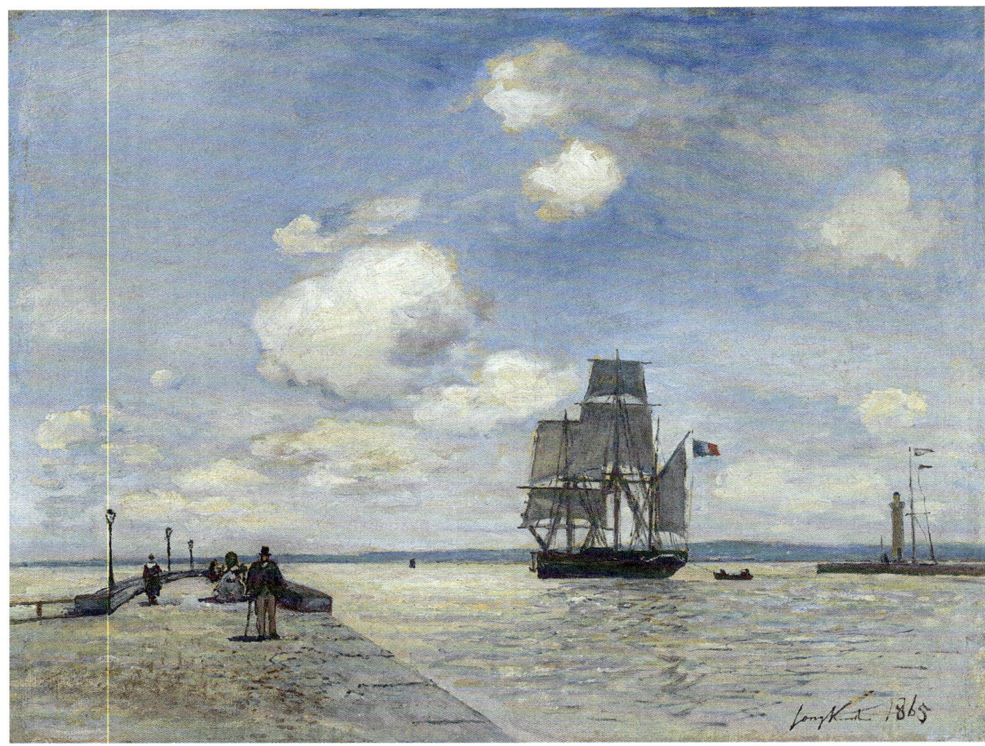

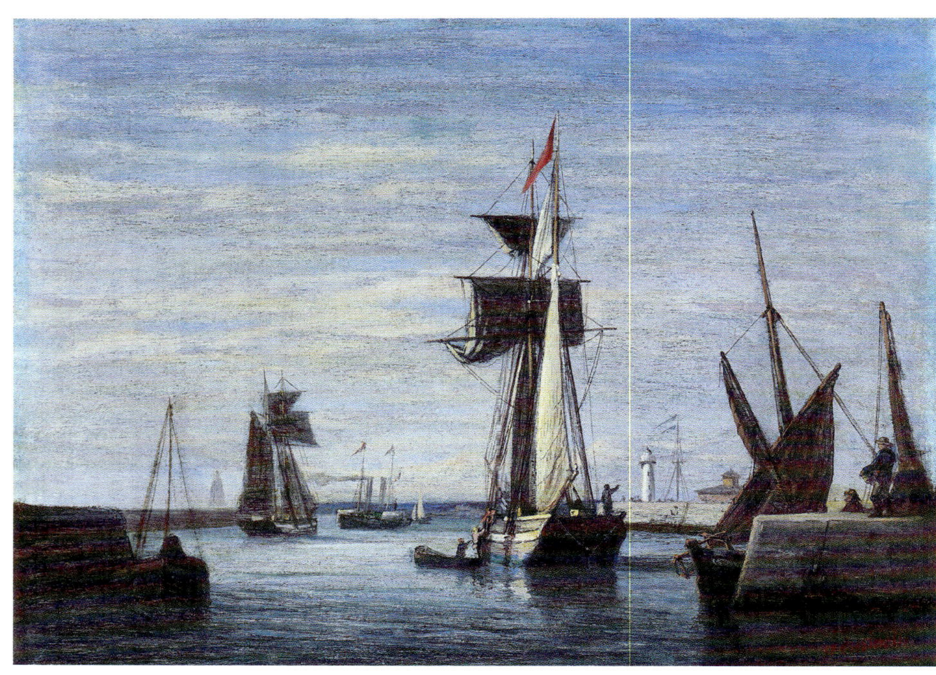

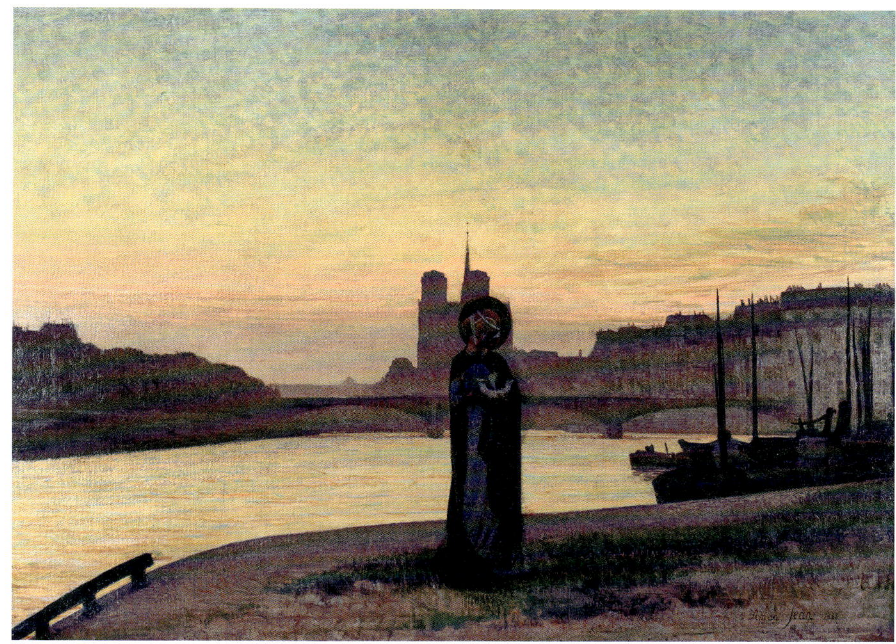

40. Edmond Aman-Jean (1858–1936), *Saint Geneviève before Paris*, 1885, oil on canvas, 74 × 101 cm, Musée des Beaux-Arts de Brest métropole

mast erected in 1857 to show the water level in the channel leading into the harbour.[16] A canvas by Dubourg shows a similar scene, with the solid stone quays dominating the seaway (*Honfleur, Boats at the Entrance of the Port,* Musée Eugène Boudin, Honfleur). All these paintings demonstrate French and foreign artists' awareness of the modernising momentum necessary to sustain the economic viability of a port such as Honfleur.

Two decades on, Seurat's *Entrance of the Port of Honfleur* (cat. 8) also recognised the potential of this strong and lively motif, although he may not have been aware of the use of this vista by previous artists. However, there is a hitherto unrecognised parallel that might be mentioned. Seurat's painting has a similar design – firm foreground plane with a solid central feature, open middle ground across the water and identifiable buildings in the distance – to *Saint Geneviève* by his friend from student days Edmond Aman-Jean (1858–1936), a 1885 painting exhibited at the official Paris Salon the following year, which opened not long before Seurat left for Honfleur (fig. 40). Was this curious compositional conjunction just a coincidence, an excursus with the same design? Seurat dismissed pious Aman-Jean's figure of Saint Geneviève and the distant cathedral of Notre-Dame – and replaced them with the welcome of the lighthouse and the security of the bollard. There may have been a tacit repudiation of his friend's piety in the conversion of his composition into the banality of the Channel port.

Seurat followed this modern and even technocratic momentum when he painted the lighthouse on the shore to the west of Honfleur (cat. 5). It had been erected next to the sixteenth-century hospital building between 1853 and

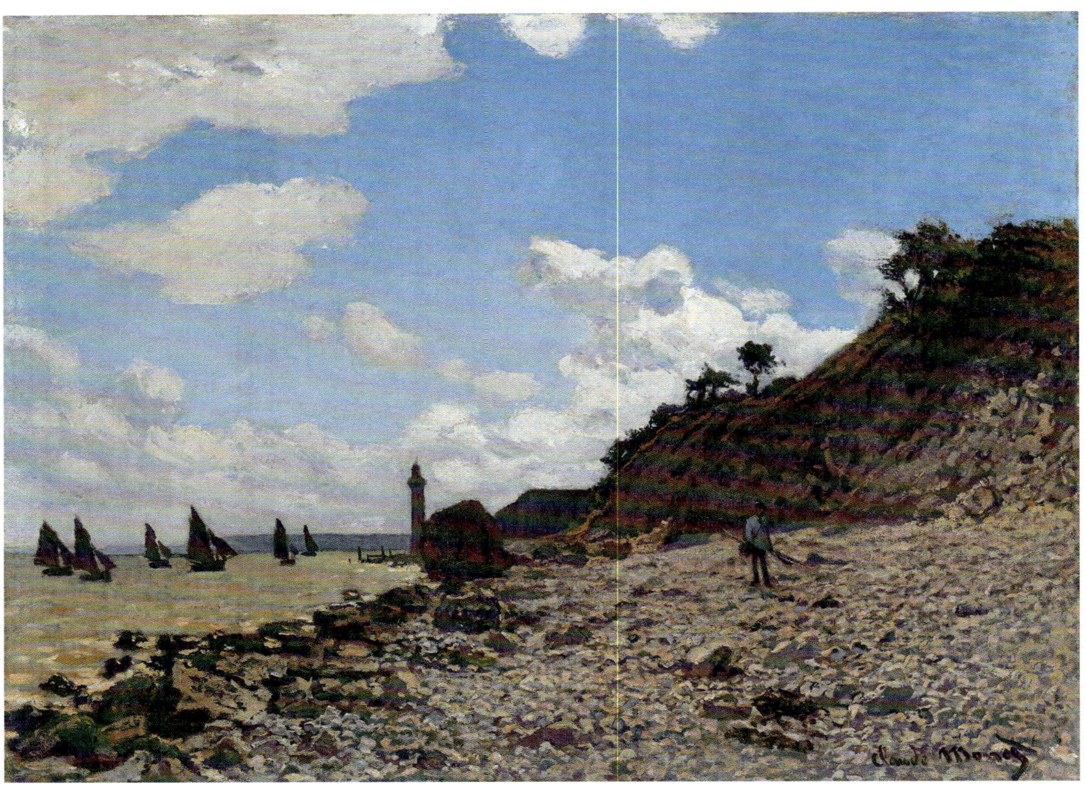

41. Claude Monet (1840–1926), *The Beach at Honfleur*, c. 1864–66, oil on canvas, 59.7 × 81.3 cm, Los Angeles County Museum of Art

42. Eugène Boudin (1824–1898), *The Lighthouse at Honfleur*, c. 1864–66, oil on wood panel, 26.7 × 39.8 cm, private collection

43. Stanislas Lépine (1835–1892), *The Lighthouse at Honfleur*, c. 1874–77, oil on canvas, 18.2 × 30 cm, Musée Eugène Boudin, Honfleur

44. Alexandre Defaux (1826–1900), *The Lighthouse of the Hospital*, *Honfleur*, c. 1880, oil on wood panel, 17.5 × 40.5 cm, private collection

1857. The lighthouse's reliance on mirrors to increase the light given by its lamps used a system devised by the physicist Augustin Fresnel, a fact proudly announced in Michelet's *La Mer* as he described the chain of lighthouses in the Seine estuary guiding vessels from America to the great transatlantic port of Le Havre.[17] In his 1888 novel *Pierre et Jean* Maupassant wrote admiringly of the reliable rhythm of the identifiable lights of the Bay of the Seine: 'I am Trouville, I am Honfleur, I am the river at Pont-Audemer.'[18] Once again, the motif – not just of the lighthouse but specifically of the view from the west looking up the estuary of the Seine with the hospital building to the right – had been used by other artists. In 1864, Monet had painted it from further away, bringing in more of the sloping cliff to the right and including a number of fishing boats out to sea (fig. 41). At the same moment, Boudin had also painted it from closer in (fig. 42). In the following decade, Cals tackled the motif from a similar distance as Monet (1873, Musée Eugène Boudin, Honfleur), while Stanislas Lépine (1835–1892) came closer, setting the vertical of the lighthouse illuminated by sunlight against the dark, angular cluster of the hospital (fig. 43). Not long before Seurat painted the lighthouse and the hospital, the experienced landscapist Alexandre Defaux (1826–1900) took on a similar view in a small but panoramic format that emphasised the busy workyard in the foreground, in all its ramshackle naturalism (fig. 44). In

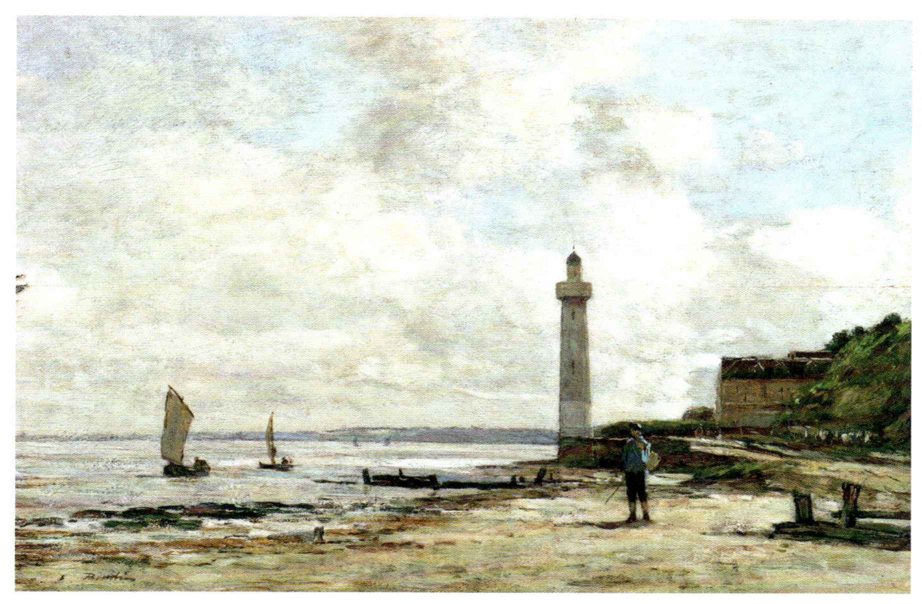

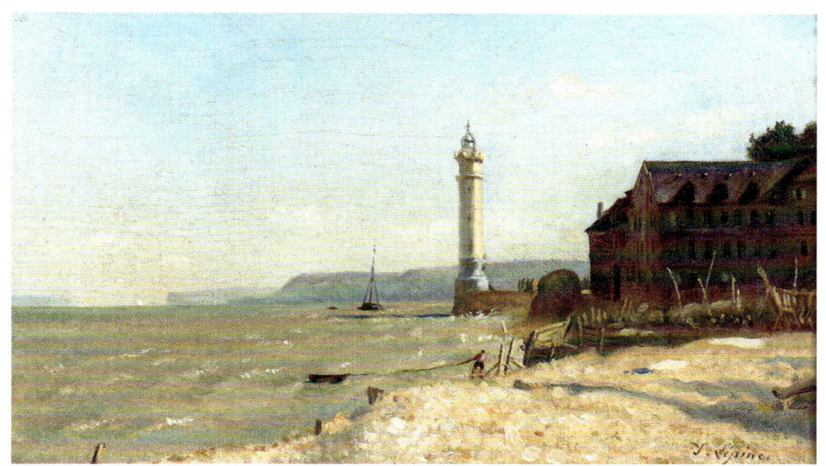

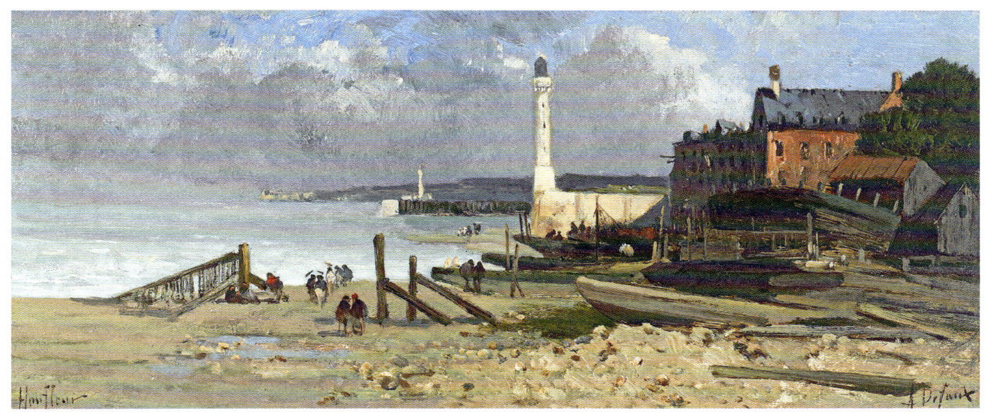

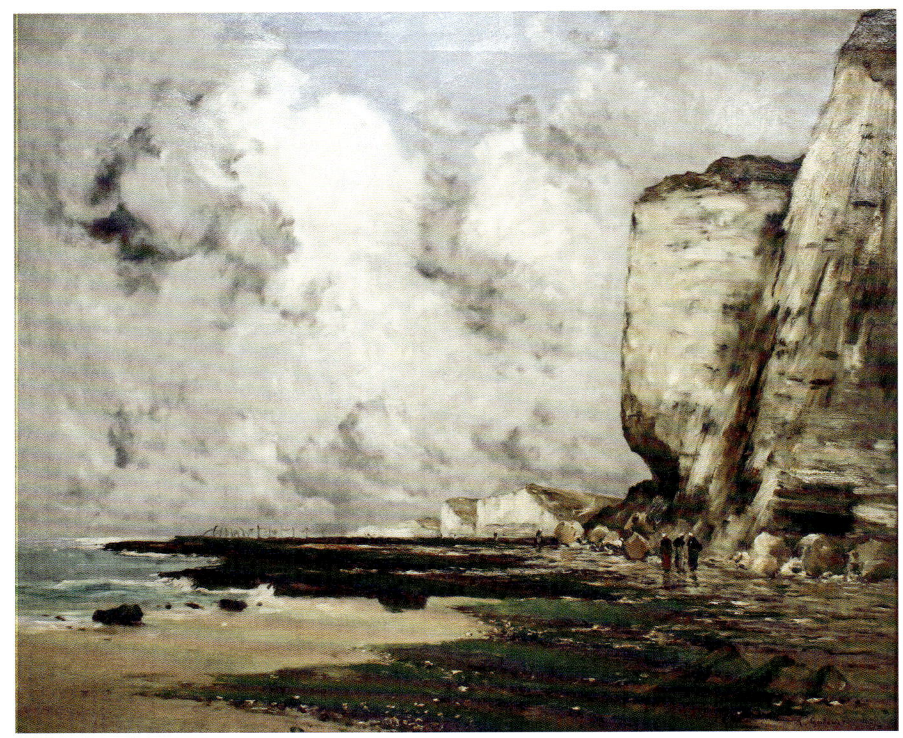

45. Antoine Guillemet (1843–1918), *The Cliffs of Puys at Low Tide*, 1877, oil on canvas, 87 × 103.5 cm, Château-Musée, Dieppe

1886, Seurat – who may well not have been aware of any such predecessors – selected a vista similar to Lépine's but one that made more of the contrasting architectural features, albeit tidying Defaux's clutter. He emphasised the distant quay and, beyond it, the coastal ridge to create a strong horizontal against which to set the vertical of the lighthouse, creating a reverse L shape on the left of his composition while the right featured a variety of different forms – the angularity both of the hospital roof and a nearby wooden frame, plus a circular wheel.

If Seurat's campaign at Honfleur chiefly concentrated on modern motifs, he did seek some more natural options. In *The Shore at Bas-Butin* (cat. 6), some breakwater posts on the beach and distant shipping scarcely intrude into a composition in which the chalk face of the cliff and its skirting of grasses tumbling down to the beach contrast with the calm, flat distance of the sea beyond. It was a type of composition common among naturalist painters in their topographically precise depictions of the coastal wall along the Channel. Antoine Guillemet (1843–1918) had used it for a painting exhibited at the Salon of 1877 (fig. 45) and Élodie La Villette (1848–1917) also did so for similar canvases of accurate environmental observation (see, for example, *View of the Cliffs from the Beach of Yport*, undated, private collection). The other canvas amongst Seurat's Honfleur works without insistent modernity is *Mouth of the Seine. Evening* (fig. 26). The painting, looking down the Seine estuary along its south bank westwards in the dying light of day's end, sets the shingle beach

Detail of cat. 6

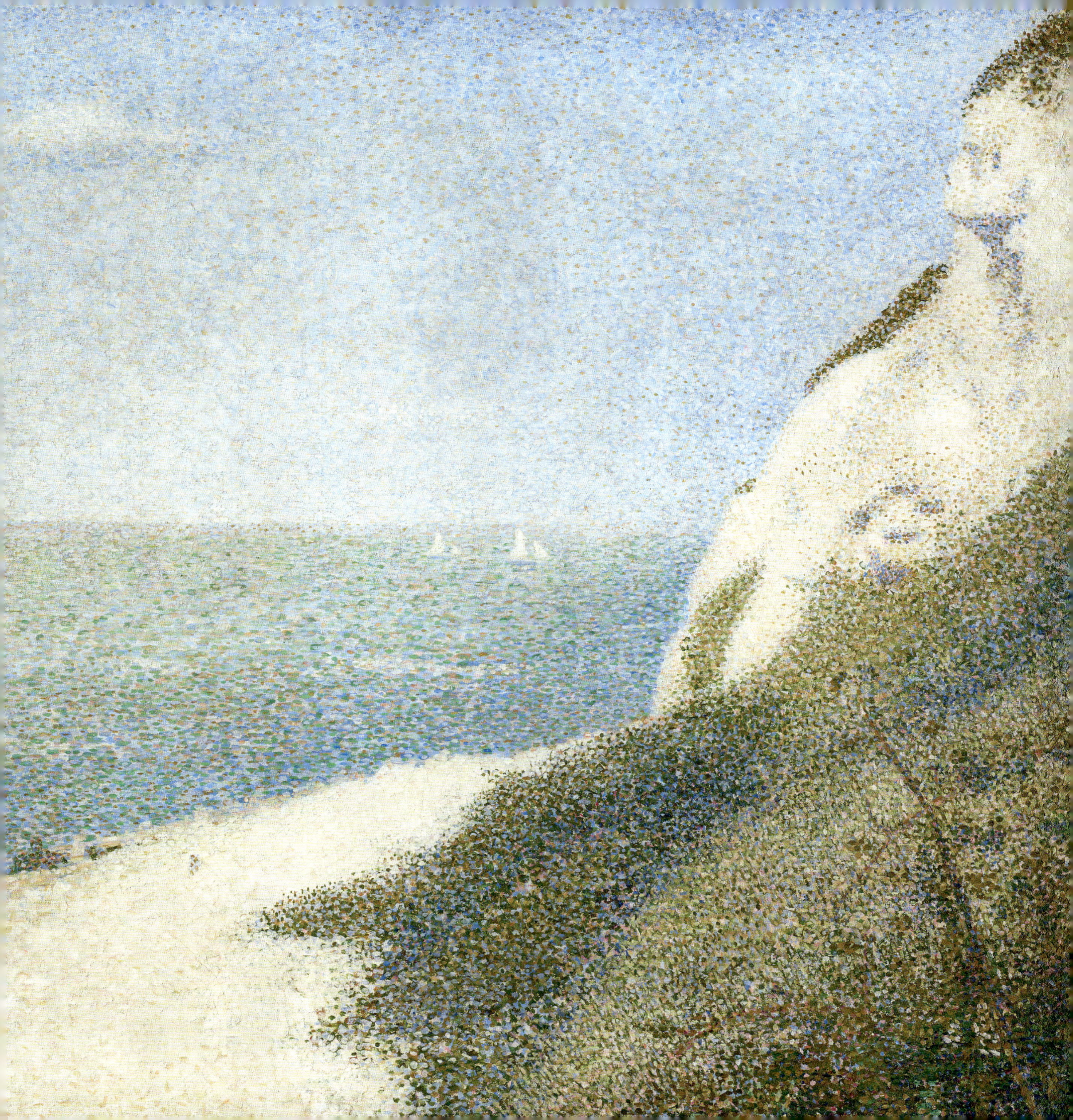

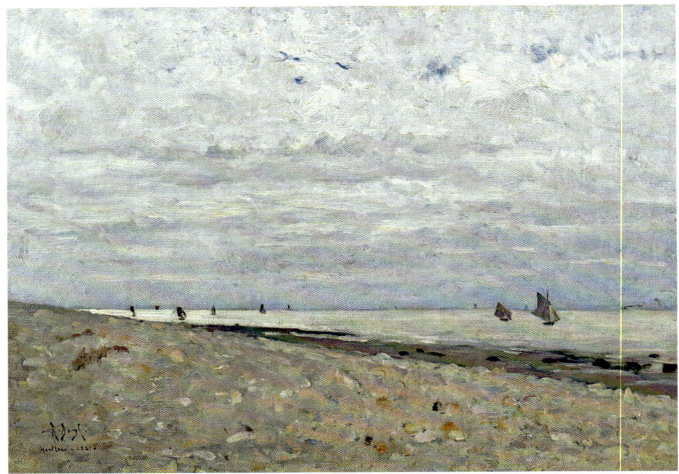

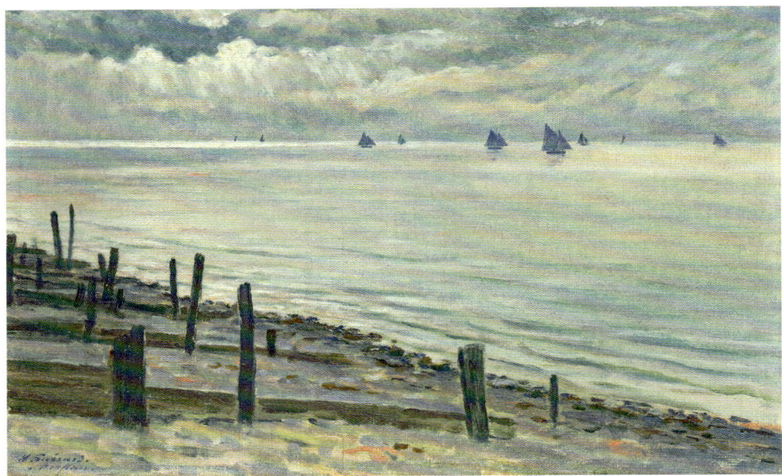

46. Richard Bergh, *Sea Landscape off Honfleur*, 1881, oil on canvas, 38 × 53 cm, Stockholm, Nationalmuseum

47. Henri Guérard (1846–1897), *Honfleur*, 1887, oil on canvas, 48 × 30 cm, courtesy of Gillis Goldman Fine Art, Brussels

and the solid regularity of its dark breakwaters against the vast translucency of the vista over the still water, the last rays shining bright on the flat sea and the distant horizon echoed by long, regular banks of cloud. This was a moment that attracted other painters, with Cals writing in a letter of June 1873 – the year he purchased his house in Honfleur – that he enjoyed painting the evening light: 'that deep and sweet hue, which is not yet night and which is no longer day'.[19] The view was one that attracted other artists during the following decade, Bergh in 1881 (fig. 46) and Henri Guérard (1846–1897) in 1887 (fig. 47), both painting scenes of open vastness similar to Seurat's.

Long after Seurat's death, his fellow Neo-Impressionist painter Charles Angrand remembered how, in the mid 1880s, they attended *soirées* at their friend Paul Signac's studio on the boulevard de Clichy along with another '*Néo*', Albert Dubois-Pillet, the novelist Paul Adam and the poet Henri de Régnier.[20] This might explain why Seurat had chosen to visit Honfleur in 1886, as Régnier had been born there and may have suggested it – although such a long-established site for marine painting hardly needed recommendation. More significant may be that, in 1886, Régnier published his second collection of verse, *Apaisement*. Coming out in the year Moréas published the 'Symbolist Manifesto', Régnier's poetry belonged to this new aesthetic of suggestion and allusion. One of the poems was *Heures marines*, which includes the lines:

> *Un souffle languissant se lève, qui circule*
> *À travers la chaleur tiède du crépuscule.*
> *Dans la nuit sonne un bruit de lointaines enclumes;*
> *C'est la mer basse qui gémit son chant puissant;*
> *Et voici le sommeil qui vient, assoupissant*
> *Les souvenirs cuisants et chargés d'amertumes*
> *Des dolentes cités où longtemps nous vécûmes.*[21]

A languid breath is raised, which circulates
Through the warm heat of the dusk.
In the night sounds the noise of distant anvils;
It's the low sea that groans its powerful song;
And here is sleep coming, dozing away
Sour memories charged with the bitterness
Of the sad cities where we've lived so long.

The theme of the calming effect of the sea on the world-weary city-dweller
may have resonated with Seurat, and a canvas such as *Mouth of the Seine.
Evening* might best be understood not only as a painting using the newly
developed Neo-Impressionist technique to register the subtle light of the dying
day over the expanse of the serene surface of the sea but also as a work that
engaged with the emergent Symbolist sensitivity to the nuanced expression
of emotion. This painting was among the seven canvases Seurat showed at
the *Salon des Indépendants* in February 1887. In his review of the show in *La Vie
moderne*, Gustave Kahn, himself a poet in the Symbolist movement, wrote of
how Seurat's work was in concord with that of such young writers.[22] Indeed,
Kahn's sparse, suggestive words about this painting – 'extreme land, extreme
light; a vast serenity fades' – chose language that harmonised with Seurat's
subtle and expansive marine.[23]

Port-en-Bessin

If we do not know what motivated Seurat to work at Grandcamp in 1885 and
Honfleur in 1886, it seems likely that it was Signac who recommended Port-
en-Bessin, having worked there in the three successive summers of 1882, 1883
and 1884. This small fishing port some ten kilometres north of Bayeux, Seurat
would have been told, offered cliffs, with the views they presented, to both east
and west, as well as an active and recently modernised harbour. It was not so
historical and picturesque as Honfleur, and had a convenient combination of
natural features and modernity that Grandcamp had not offered. On his visits
to Port-en-Bessin, Signac had chosen a variety of motifs. These included the
small twelfth-century church (now destroyed) and the Tour Vauban, built
in 1694 by the architect Benjamin de Combes as an artillery tower to defend
the port at a time when Anglo-Dutch fleets threatened the northern French
coasts.[24] But Signac also painted the iron and glass fish market constructed on
the central jetty of the harbour in 1879 (fig. 48).[25]

Adolphe Maugendre (1809–1895), a professional topographical lithographer
from Le Havre, had made a panoramic view of Port-en-Bessin in the early
1860s (fig. 49). In it can be seen the low conical Tour Vauban just above
the boats drawn up on the beach and, in the foreground to the right, the
semaphore used to communicate information about weather conditions to
vessels out at sea as well as to send messages along the coast from port to port.
Maugendre's print usefully records the state of the harbour two decades before
Seurat worked there. In the meantime, Port-en-Bessin had been modernised.
Two protective jetties had been built and completed in 1864. However, the
winds proved too strong to provide adequate protection in stormy weather

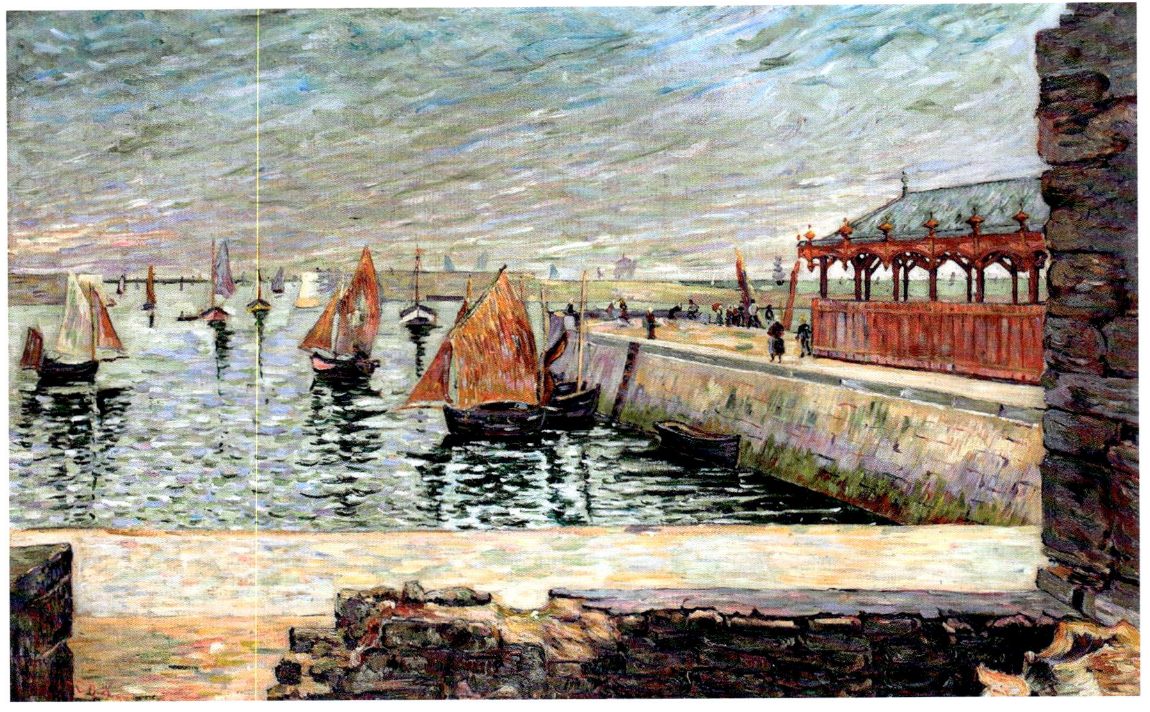

48. Paul Signac (1863–1935), *Port-en-Bessin. The Fish Market,* 1884, oil on canvas, 60 × 92 cm, private collection

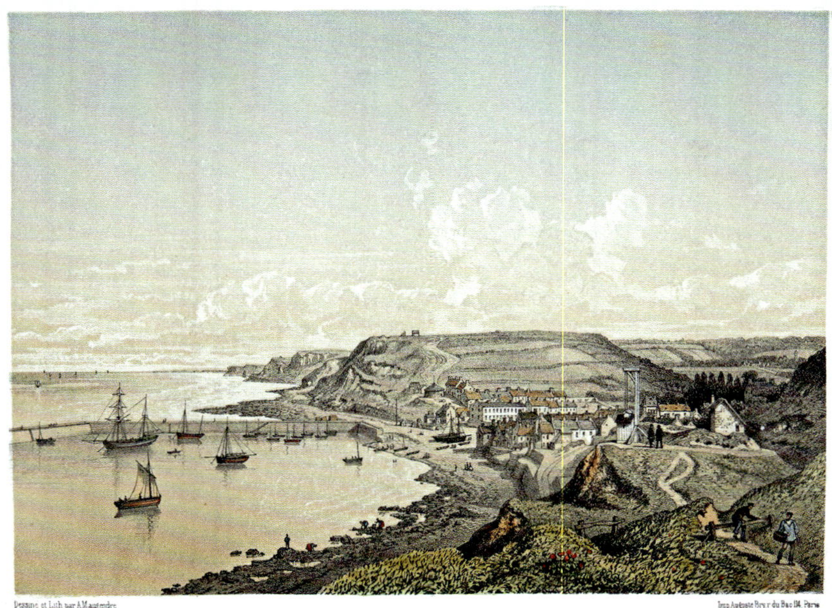

49. Adolphe Maugendre (1809-1895), *Port-en-Bessin*, chromolithograph, published in *Bayeux et ses environs*, 1862–65, Paris: Renou et Maulde, c. 33.5 × 25 cm, private collection

and, in 1866, the municipal council decided an interior port was required. However, it was not for a decade, until 17 March 1876, that the state Ministère des Travaux Publics took on the project to create a 75-metre-long channel to an interior *bassin* 150 × 50 metres in format. This work was completed in 1880 and, in July that year, a swivelling bridge was in place across that interior waterway to ease access between both sides of the little town. However, Port-en-Bessin's fishing fleet was growing and a second interior *bassin* was needed, on which work began in late 1882, with an excavating machine that had been used for digging the Suez Canal brought in to help in 1883.[26]

It is perhaps unsurprising that, when Seurat worked at Port-en-Bessin during the summer of 1888, he was responding directly to this modernisation. *Port-en-Bessin – The Outer Harbour (High Tide)* (cat. 14) takes essentially the same view as Maugendre's chromolithograph, looking eastwards over the harbour. The painting discreetly shows Seurat's continued lack of interest in the picturesque, as the Tour Vauban is registered but hardly featured at the start of the track up the far cliff. By contrast, his commitment to modernity is to the fore, with the fish market built from industrial materials at centre and a fishing boat making its way from the inner *bassins* through the outer harbour to the sea. For Seurat's response to Port-en-Bessin was far more programmatic in its commitment to the modernity of the small port than the younger Signac had been in previous years. His paintings of the inner harbour looking seawards, *Port-en-Bessin – A Sunday* (cat. 11) and from an outer jetty looking landwards, *Port-en-Bessin – The Outer Harbour (Low Tide)* (cat. 13),

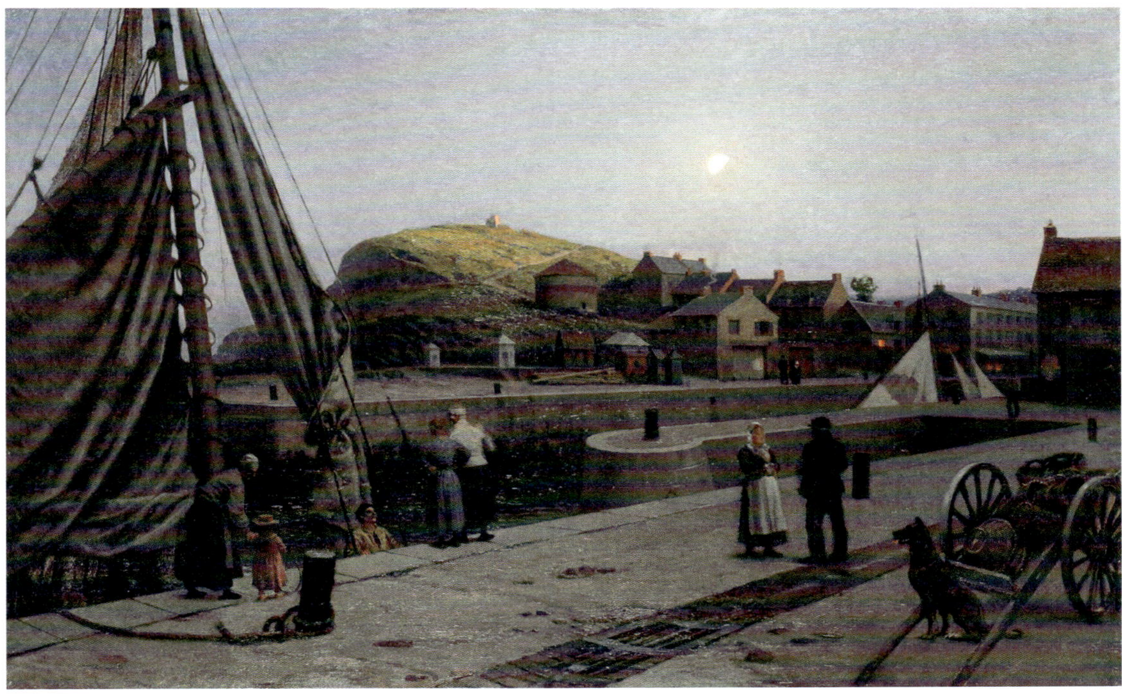

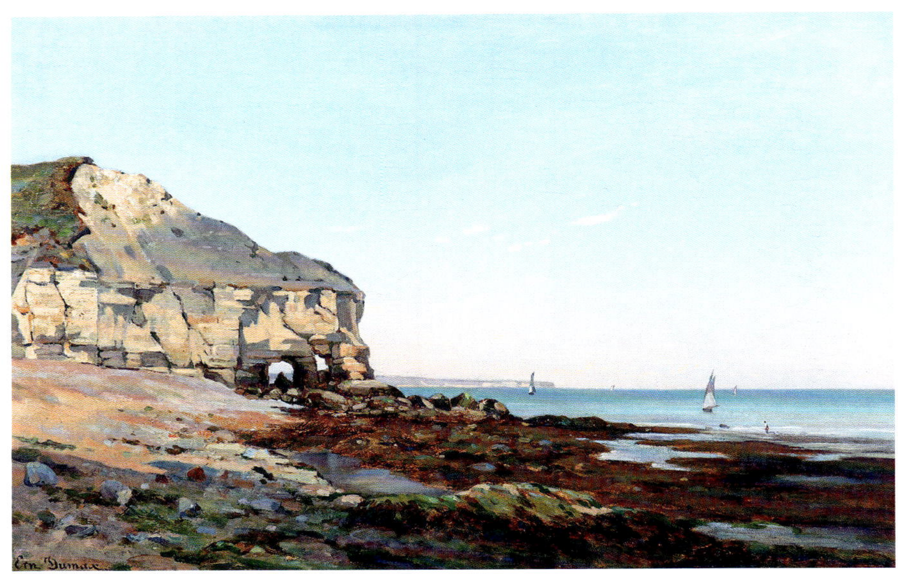

systematically explore the new facilities. Seurat's focus on the new features in the port is evident in *Port-en-Bessin – The Bridge and the Quays* (cat. 12), with its swing bridge constructed eight years previously. This canvas includes an unusual amount of staffage for Seurat's port paintings, whether at Port-en-Bessin or elsewhere. The same channel from the outer harbour to the inner *bassins* had been painted by the painter and civil engineer Eugène Marion (1850–1913) prior to the provision of the swing bridge, so around 1879–80 (fig. 50). It is notable that Marion not only contrasted the seventeenth-century Tour Vauban in the background with the new construction in the foreground but also featured more local people and specified their roles and interchange more closely than Seurat did. Nevertheless, it was at Port-en-Bessin that Seurat most specifically painted the population – the customs officer, the woman carrying a basket, the inquisitive child. Marion was appointed *ingénieur en chef des ponts et chaussées du Pas-de-Calais* in 1893, so had professional experience of public works. Perhaps his role as a civic functionary assumed republican credentials and his paintings record both state investment in Port-en-Bessin and the *égalité* and *fraternité* between its citizens, which inherently assumed an ethos that Seurat did not feel so committed to promote.

In *The Semaphores and the Cliff (Les Grues et la percée)* (cat. 16), Seurat painted the westward view from Port-en-Bessin. Even in a canvas of the tumbling terrain atop the cliffs looking towards bands of clouds in the evening light above the calm sea, he included modernity, with the posts of the semaphore in the upper left-hand corner. These were presumably '*Les Grues*' – the French word for crane or lifting equipment – of the title. '*La Percée*' would seem to refer to the spit of rock sticking out into the sea in the mid-distance. The rock-strewn beaches of this stretch of coast had been painted

52. Albert Siffait de Moncourt (1858–1931),
View of Le Crotoy in the Middle Ages, c. 1885,
Church of Saint-Pierre, Le Crotoy

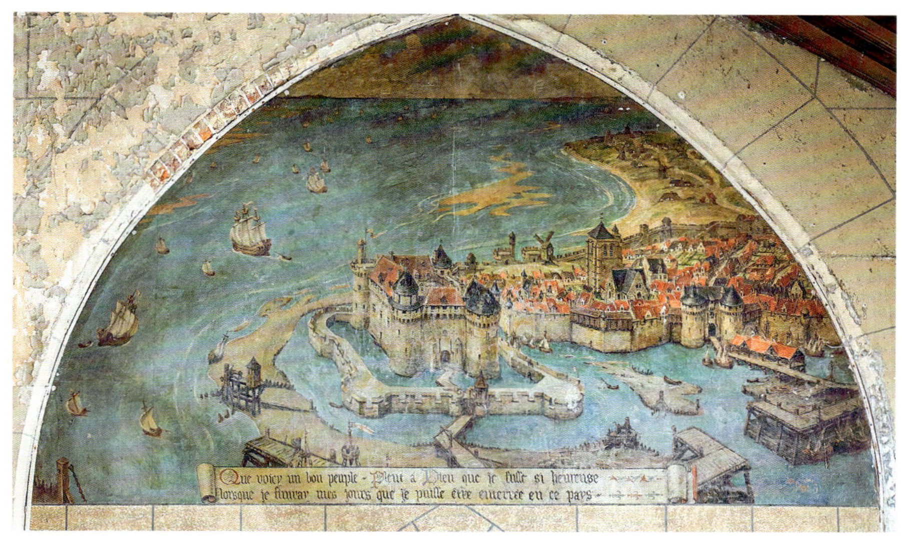

some years previously by Ernest-Joachim Dumax (1811–1900), in a canvas which had entered the collection of John and Josephine Bowes at Barnard Castle by 1885 (fig. 51). Dumax's canvas is painstakingly naturalistic in its depiction of the rock formation and the rocky, seaweed-strewn beach, a great contrast with the stylised undulations of Seurat's composition. However, the comparison demonstrates Seurat's limited engagement with the natural world, even though the geological and paleological attractions of the cliffs around Port-en-Bessin with their ammonites and fossils had been amusingly handled in Chapter 3 of Flaubert's comic novel *Bouvard et Pécuchet*, published posthumously in 1881.[27]

Le Crotoy

Le Crotoy was not much frequented by artists, unlike Saint-Valéry-sur-Somme across the bay of the river Somme. Louis Braquaval, a wealthy Lillois and painter, bought a house in Saint-Valéry in 1895, where Edgar Degas came to visit and made views of the open waterway. Boudin had painted briefly at Le Crotoy in 1890. However, the old medieval town had perhaps more contemporary renown because the novelist Jules Verne, whose wife, Honorine, was from nearby Amiens, had visited in 1865. He had been struck by the way the high and low tides dramatically altered the vista and wrote to his publisher, Hetzel, in May 1867 of his delight with 'this charming little hole of Crotoy' where there is 'sand, nothing but sand and untouched dunes'.[28] Two years later, Verne rented a house there, bought a boat, the *Saint-Michel*, and settled in Amiens in 1871. His best-selling novel *20,000 Leagues under the Sea* (1871) used his experience of sailing off Le Crotoy.[29]

It seems that Seurat may first have visited the Bay of the Somme region around 1882, when he and his friend Aman-Jean went to Rue, just five kilometres north of Le Crotoy. There, they would have called in on Albert

Siffait de Moncourt (1858–1931), who came from a distinguished local family. Siffait de Moncourt seems to have been a fellow student of theirs at the École des Beaux-Arts, although there is no documentary evidence of him having been in the studio of Henri Lehmann.[30] That connection may have drawn Seurat back to the region in 1889. During the intervening years, Siffait de Moncourt had painted a decoration for Le Crotoy's Church of Saint-Pierre, a medieval building that had fallen into disrepair and was rebuilt between 1850 and 1865, retaining the original clock tower. Seurat would surely have seen his friend's 1885 canvas in an ogival format representing an aerial view of Le Crotoy in the Middle Ages, placed above a sculpture of Joan of Arc who had briefly been imprisoned in the town (fig. 52). Adopting the style of a fifteenth-century manuscript illumination, Siffait de Moncourt reimagined the port as it would have been in her day, with its castle and fortified harbour, making a feature of the waterline as it snakes around the castle in an arching S-shaped rhythm. Seurat's *Le Crotoy (Upstream)* (fig. 13) – in which the towers of Saint-Pierre constitute a central feature – also responded to the bay's curving shore, setting the irregular skyline vista of the town's towers and roofs against a great sweep of shoreline that scoops upwards from the lower left corner of his composition to the centre of the right edge. That regularity of placement adds emphasis to the ensemble, giving linear and spatial animation to the expansive open foreground.

Gravelines

It may have been Aman-Jean or Siffait de Moncourt, better acquainted with northern France, who recommended that Seurat paint in Gravelines in 1890. Once again, Seurat showed himself uninterested in the historical town, with its star-shaped fortifications, constructed by the Marquis de Vauban in the decades following the town's definitive cession to France in 1659. Seurat turned his back on this, consistent with the lack of interest in the picturesque that had characterised his responses to Honfleur and Le Crotoy. Rather, he was drawn by the strongly perspectival canalisation of the river Aa, first built in 1737–40 and improved between 1862 and 1872.[31] By opting to paint along the man-made stone channel leading out to the sea between Petit- and Grand-Fort-Philippe, Seurat more consistently than ever confirmed his commitment to the modern in his landscape work.

He may have been nudged towards selecting such motifs by the canvases Signac had brought back from his visit to the Breton port of Portrieux in 1888, five of which he had exhibited at the Salon des Indépendants in March–April 1890. In these paintings Signac, who would have arrived in his own sailing boat, focused on the features of the harbour in which he had moored – the long straight quays, the regular stonework, the imposing verticality of the lighthouse and the masts of the docked vessels (see, for example, fig. 53). He was recording the actuality of the port, the practical features that made it safe, sheltered and efficient. Seurat, of course, was not a sailor, unlike his friend. But he responded with enthusiasm to the regularity of the Gravelines channel. One reason for this – to judge from his choice of motif – was its emphatic practicality: the evident course of travel and so direction of the gaze,

53. Paul Signac (1863–1935), *Portrieux. The Masts, Opus 182,* 1888, oil on canvas, 46 × 55 cm, private collection

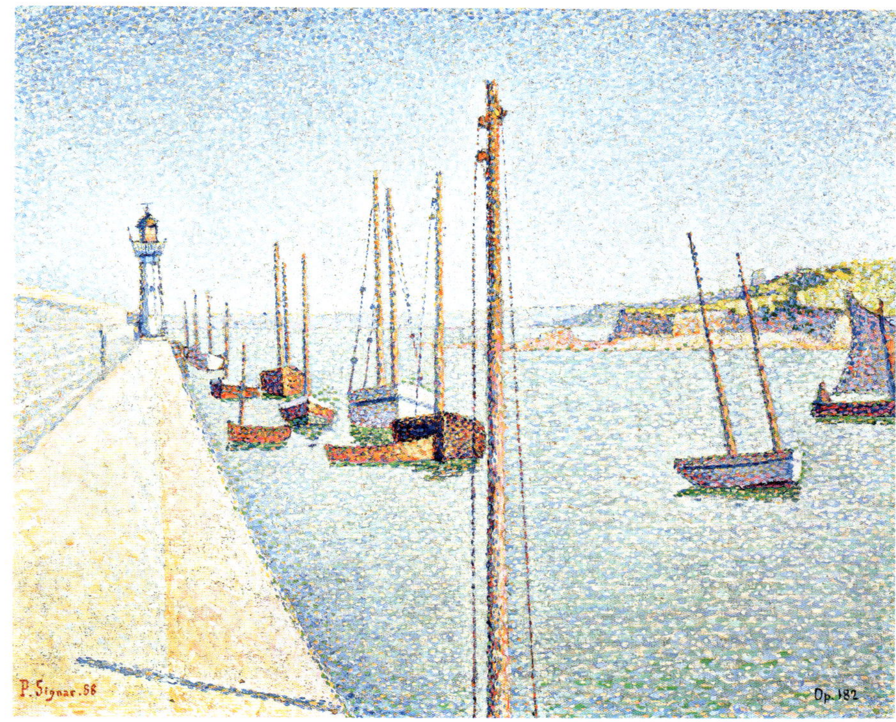

and also the usefulness of the verticals, whether stumpy mooring bollards, high masts for signal flags, or the dominant lighthouse to signal destination and shelter.

That is not to say that Seurat's Gravelines paintings lacked aesthetic principles and decisions. Here was the satisfactory search for aesthetic harmony in the actuality of modern marine painting. *The Channel of Gravelines: Petit-Fort-Philippe* (cat. 20) is emphatic in this regard. The boats, all moored and still, make horizontal accents in the middle ground, while a nearby bollard echoes the solid vertical of the distant lighthouse. But the main compositional feature is the curve of the quay across the foreground, its pale stone edge echoed by the shadow cast on the still water of the channel and repeated on the very right edge of the canvas, so its warm, pale reach pulls the gaze smoothly into the pictorial distance.

Seurat essayed another aesthetic gambit while at Gravelines. This allied composition and colour more closely to mood and, as such, once again showed his affinities with the Symbolist aesthetic. In 1883, Cazin, an artist a generation older than Seurat who hailed from this Pas-de-Calais region, had exhibited *The Dead Town* (fig. 54) at the private Cercle Volney exhibition in Paris.[32] Representing the large market-place of Montreuil-sur-Mer, it shows the town at dusk, with the sun low in the sky behind clouds, lamps lit in the windows, and the vast open space devoid of people, their daily activities suggested by the stationary carriage, and the only movement a runnel of water across the

54. Jean-Charles Cazin (1841–1901), *The Dead Town* (*La Ville morte*)*, 1883, oil on canvas, 71 × 91 cm, private collection, London

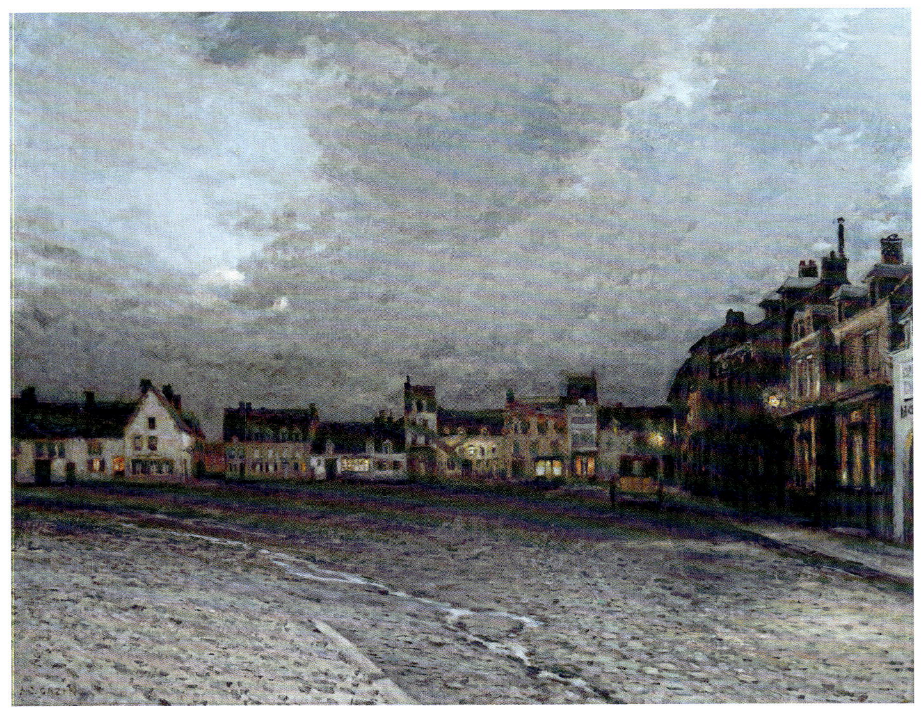

cobbles and the massing clouds above. The painting enraptured the artist Odilon Redon (1840–1916). He wrote in his private journal about 'the calm of evening and dusk'; 'there's all the silence of deep countryside, the emptiness of a rural evening, the gloomy torpor of stillness' – a response that, with its stress on mood and suggestive association, prefigures the Symbolist aesthetic.[33] One wonders whether the recollection of Cazin's *The Dead Town* was in Seurat's mind as he painted *The Channel of Gravelines: An Evening* (cat. 22). His canvas also depicts the dying light of day and an expansive open space between artist/ spectator and habitation, although the fishing boat making for the open sea gives a sense of gentle activity that the parked coach in Cazin's canvas quietly denies. The pennant flying on the distant mast serves a similar purpose to the lit windows in *The Dead Town*, showing human agency without visible human presence. Equally, *The Channel of Gravelines: Grand-Fort-Philippe* (cat. 18) may represent daytime, but its spacious foreground, distant houses and stationary calm also recall Cazin's *The Dead Town*, which had been shown again the previous year at the Universal Exhibition in Paris.[34] Despite their different styles – naturalist or Neo-Impressionist – and distinct motifs, both Cazin's and Seurat's paintings evoke a similar mood of calm and community, a moment of repose and reflection in a constantly changing world.

By making such comparisons with his contemporaries of different generations and creative temperament, the achievement of Seurat's marines comes into rich context. The sites he chose were not necessarily new, but the gradual development of both his Neo-Impressionist technique and his very personal sensibility can be charted in the motifs he chose – sometimes shared, sometimes individually selected – and the means by which he adapted composition, touch and colour to bring locales and vistas into concord with his emergent aesthetic. Naturalist contemporaries may often have shared these, but naturalism itself was a flexible aesthetic, and their compositional and even – in the case of Cazin – suggestive possibilities offered stimulus to the progressive development of Seurat's Neo-Impressionism and its Symbolist subtlety.

1   Michelet 1980, p. 32.
2   Eugène Mouton, *La Physiognomie comparée. Traité de l'expression dans l'homme, dans la nature, et dans l'art*, Paris: Paul Ollendorff, 1885, p. 543.
3   Richard Thomson, *Art of the Actual. Naturalism and Style in Early Third Republic France, 1880–1900*, New Haven and London: Yale University Press, 2012, pp. 1–79.
4   Aggy Lerolle, *Henry Lerolle, Paris 1848–1929*, Paris: Wapica, 2022, p. 20.
5   Jean-François Mozziconacci, *Répertoire des peintures du XIXe siècle, Collections du Musée des beaux-arts de Carcassonne*, Carcassonne, 1990, vol. 5, no. 181, p. 79.
6   *Salon de 1887. Catalogue illustré*, Paris, 1887, no. 1970, p. 253.
7   George Auriol, 'Huitième exposition', *Le Chat noir*, 22 May 1886, p. 708; Gustave Geffroy, 'Hors du Salon. Les Impressionnistes', *La Justice*, 26 May 1886, pp. 1–2; 'Labruyère', 'Les Impressionnistes. II', *Le Cri du peuple*, 3rd year, no. 942, 28 May 1886, pp. 1–2, at p. 2, and Octave Mirbeau, 'Exposition de peinture (1, rue Laffitte)', *La France*, 21 May 1886, pp. 1–2, at p. 2.
8   Thomson 2024.
9   Darragon 1984, p. 272.
10 Marie-Madeleine Aubrun, *Jules Bastien-Lepage, 1848-1884. Catalogue raisonné de l'œuvre*, Paris, 1985, no. 468.
11 *Catalogue illustré des œuvres de Jean-François Raffaëlli, suivi d'une étude des mouvements de l'art moderne et du beau caractériste*, exh. cat., 28bis avenue de l'Opéra, Paris, 1884, no. 58.
12 Hans Henrik Brummer, ed., *Richard Bergh ett Konstnärskall*, exh. cat., Prins Eugens Waldemarsudde, Stockholm, 2002, no. 1, p. 140.
13 *Adolphe-Félix Cals, 1810–1880*, exh. cat., Musée Eugène Boudin, Honfleur, 1990, p. 10.
14 Darragon 1984, p. 266.
15 *Histoire de Honfleur, par un enfant de Honfleur*, Honfleur: Charles Lefrançois, 1867, pp. 253, 260, 264, 266 and 268.
16 Eugène Arnoux, *Port de Honfleur. Ministère des Travaux Publics. Ports maritimes de la France. II. Du Havre au Becquet*, Paris: Imprimerie nationale, 1876, pp. 293–94, 297 and 314.
17 Michelet 1980, pp. 65–66.
18 Guy de Maupassant, *Romans*, Louis Forestier ed., Paris: Gallimard, 1987, vol. I, p. 737.
19 Quoted in Arsène Alexandre, *A.F. Cals, ou le bonheur de peindre*, Paris: Georges Petit, 1900, p. 114.
20 Coquiot 1924, p. 39.
21 Henri de Régnier, *Premiers poèmes*, Paris: Mercure de France, 1920, 11th edn, p. 78.
22 Smith 1984, p. 569.
23 Kahn 1887, p. 230.
24 Cachin 2000, nos. 15, 21, 25, 66 and 68. See G. Villers, 'La Tour Vauban à Port-en-Bessin (Calvados)', *Bulletin archéologique du Comité des travaux historiques et scientifiques*, 1899, pp. 122–25.
25 Cachin 2000, no. 64, and Allard 2014, p. 7.
26 Allard 2014, pp. 7–10.
27 Gustave Flaubert, *Bouvard et Pécuchet*, Paris: Alphonse Lemerre, 1881, pp. 105-08.
28 Daniel Compère, 'Avec Jules Verne en bateau le long de la côte', *Nord*, vol. 80, no. 2, 2022, pp. 43–52, at p. 44.
29 Eline Erzilbengoa, 'L'Histoire du Dimanche – Jules Verne et Le Crotoy ou le coup de foudre de l'écrivain pour la baie du Somme qui lui inspira Vingt Mille Lieues sous les mers', *France Info 3 Hauts-de-France*, 9 January 2022: https://france3-regions.franceinfo.fr/hauts-de-france/somme/l-histoire-du-dimanche-jules-verne-et-le-crotoy-ou-le-coup-de-foudre-de-l-ecrivain-pour-la-baie-de-somme-qui-lui-inspira-vingt-mille-lieues-sous-les-mers-2405209.html
30 Benoît Blanc and Laura Gall, *Albert Siffait de Moncourt & l'éloge du patrimoine*, Montreuil-sur-Mer: Éditions des amis du musée et du patrimoine montreuillois, 2012, p. 31.
31 A. Plocq, 'Port de Gravelines', *Ministère des Travaux Publics. Ports maritimes de la France. I. De Dunquerque à Étretat*, Paris: Imprimerie nationale, 1874, pp. 137 and 148.
32 Thomson 2024, p. 285.
33 Odilon Redon, *À soi-même: Journal (1867–1915)*, Paris: José Corti, 1961, pp. 152–53.
34 F.-G. Dumas, ed., *Exposition Universelle de 1889: catalogue illustré des Beaux-Arts*, Lille: L. Danel, 1889, no. 277.

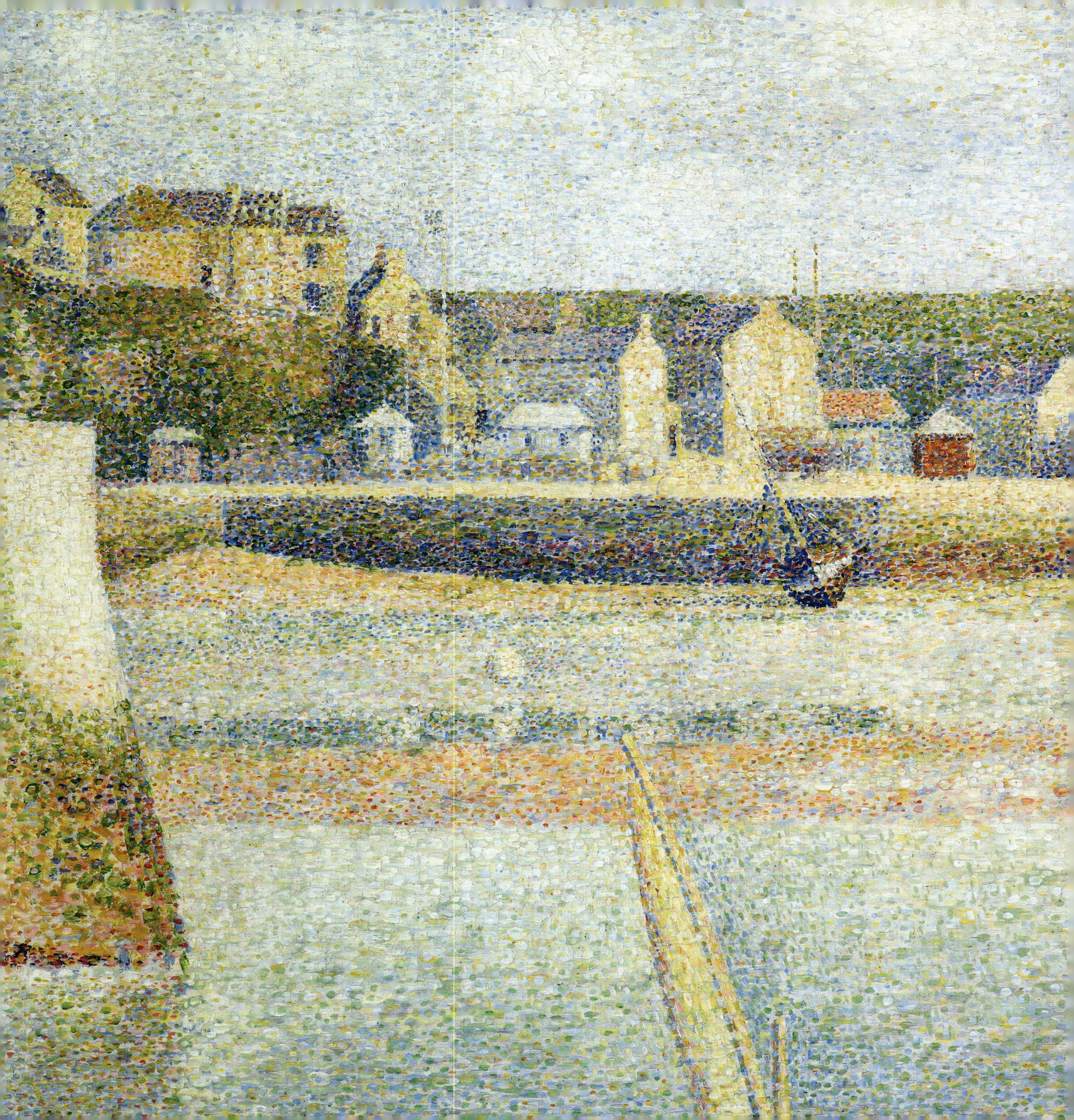

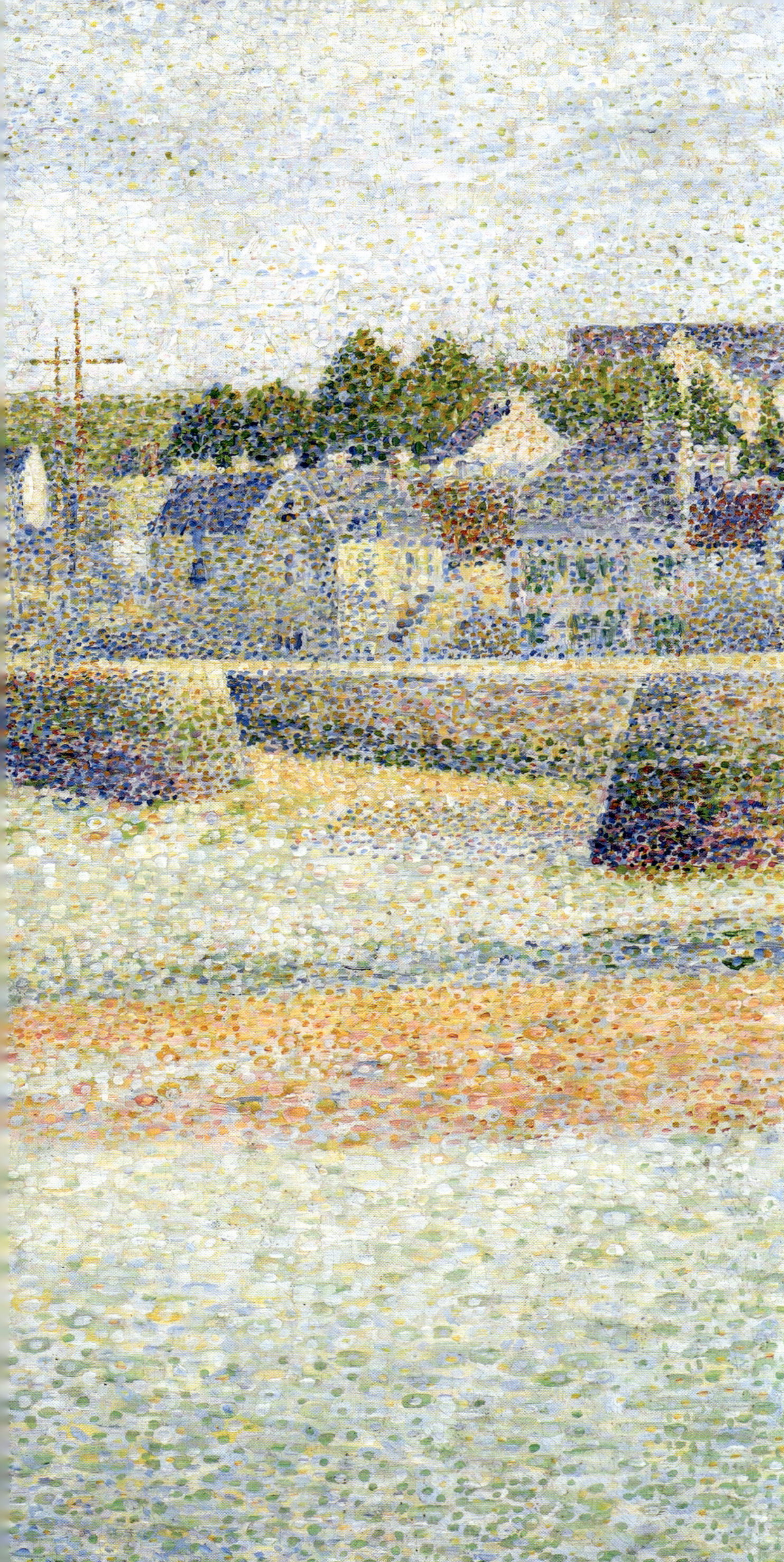

Catalogue

KAREN SERRES

NOTE TO THE CATALOGUE

Numbers

Each work is identified by the number assigned to it in the two catalogue raisonnés of Georges Seurat's work: Dorra and Rewald 1959 (DR) and Hauke 1961 (H).

Provenance

The names of dealers and auction houses are in brackets, to differentiate them from private collectors.

List of exhibitions in Seurat's lifetime

Also noted are the exhibitions in which each work was included during Seurat's lifetime and the title given by the artist. Its direct English translation is used throughout. The entries follow the sequence in those early catalogues.

1886 New York	*Works in Oil and Pastel of the Impressionists of Paris*, American Art Galleries, New York, opened on 10 April and transferred on 25 May to the National Academy of Design, until June
1886 Paris (Impressionists)	*Eighth Impressionist Exhibition*, 15 May–15 June
1886 Paris (Indépendants)	*Second Salon des Indépendants*, 21 August–21 September
1886–87 Nantes	*Exposition des Beaux-Arts*, 10 October 1886–15 January 1887
1887 Brussels	*Fourth Exhibition of Les XX*, 5 February–5 March
1887 Paris	*Third Salon des Indépendants*, 26 March–3 May
1888 Paris (Jan.)	Exhibition of the *Revue indépendante*, January
1888 Paris (Feb.)	Exhibition of the *Revue indépendante*, February
1889 Brussels	*Sixth Exhibition of Les XX*, 13 February–13 March
1889 Paris	*Fifth Salon des Indépendants*, 3 September–4 October
1890 Paris	*Sixth Salon des Indépendants*, 20 March–27 April
1891 Brussels	*Eighth Exhibition of Les XX*, 7 February–8 March
1891 Paris	*Seventh Salon des Indépendants*, 20 March–27 April

1

Le Bec du Hoc (Grandcamp)

1885, reworked c. 1888–89
Oil on canvas
64.5 × 81.5 cm
Tate

DR 153
H 159

Exhibitions
1886 Paris (Impressionists) (*Le bec du Hoc [Grand-Camp]*)
1886 Paris (Indépendants)
1887 Brussels
1888 Paris (Feb.)

Provenance
Camille Laurent, Belgium, by 1892, at least until 1904;
Georges Famenne, Brussels, by 1908; private collection,
Berlin; Julius and Lina Kocherthaler, Hamburg and
Madrid; with or through [Alfred Flechtheim, Berlin
and Düsseldorf]; Kenneth Clark, London, 1935; acquired
from him by the National Gallery, London, through
[Marlborough Fine Art, London] with grant-in-aid,
1952; transferred to Tate, 1953

'La Pointe du Hoc', also known as 'Le Bec du Hoc' after its beak-like shape, was a rocky formation a few kilometres east of the fishing village of Grandcamp, the site of Georges Seurat's first summer campaign on the Channel coast, in 1885. The promontory fills the space of the canvas, its tip just breaking the horizon line. Above it, a flock of birds barely fit in the remaining sliver of sky, while triangular sails are dotted in the distance. The indication of an agitated sea, a rare occurrence in Seurat's oeuvre, can be found in the scumbles of thicker white paint, representing breaking waves. The water is otherwise rendered in short horizontal strokes of blue, green and lavender, enhanced by vertical dashes of complementary yellow to indicate the shimmering reflection of the sun. The scene is set in the afternoon, with the sunlight shining on the west face of the Bec du Hoc, casting its east side in shadow. Seurat has rendered the low vegetation and rocky terrain with short strokes in a criss-cross pattern (called '*balayé*'), followed by the addition of thick dots. The painted border was added several years later over the existing paint, slightly constraining the scene. Seurat not only applied the dark blue, red and orange dots on the perimeter but also reworked the adjacent areas to create a harmonious transition between them. He may also have reworked other sections at that time, for example adding thinner dots to the shadows.[1]

The setting of a dramatic cliff against a vast expanse of sea inevitably brings to mind the Normandy paintings of Claude Monet (1840–1926), most notably his views of the cliffs of Pourville from 1882. Seurat would have seen these works exhibited in Paris the following year. Unlike Monet's compositions, however, Seurat's painting offers no recession. Despite its modelling with colour, the Bec du Hoc appears flat, applied on to its background and rising – majestic and slightly oppressive – before the viewer's eyes rather than projecting into the sea.

Le Bec du Hoc (Grandcamp) was exhibited four times in Seurat's lifetime and always admired. Commenting on Seurat's work in the *Eighth Impressionist Exhibition* in 1886, the critic Gustave Geffroy describes 'three beautiful seascapes brought back from Grandcamp. One of them, in particular: *Le bec du Hoc*, beautifully captures the wild appearance of the rock and the melancholy of the sea.'[2] Sadly, it is no longer possible to get a sense of the dramatic formation. It was famously the site of one of the earliest D-Day landings on 6 June 1944, as American troops targeted the German bunker built where Seurat had once stood. Heavy bombing and ongoing erosion have forever changed the view.

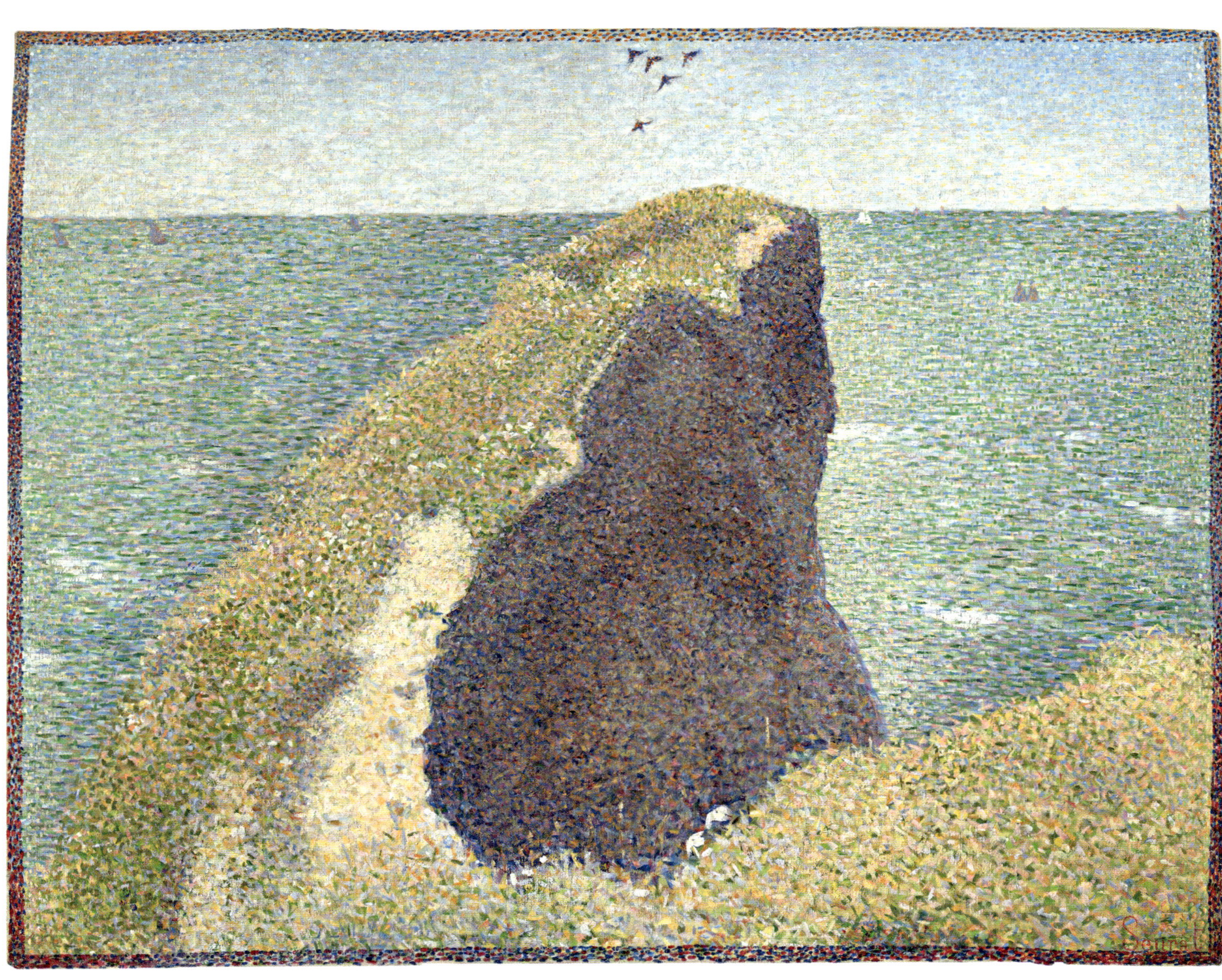

2

Study for *Le Bec du Hoc (Grandcamp)*

1885
Oil on wood panel
15.6 × 24.5 cm
National Gallery of Australia, Canberra
Purchased with proceeds from *The Great Impressionists*
exhibition, 1984

DR 152
H 158

Exhibitions
1886 New York (part of a group of '12 Studies, framed
together')
1887 Paris

Provenance
Probably by inheritance to the artist's partner, Madeleine
Knobloch (d. 1903), Paris, 1891; acquired by Jean de Greef,
Auderghem (Belgium), February 1892, and held until no
later than 1894; Alfred Tobler, Berlin; [Bernheim-Jeune,
Paris] by 1920; Charles Hall Thorndike (1875–1935), Paris;
private collection, Paris; private collection, Switzerland;
[Galerie Schmit, Paris], 1983; acquired from [Alex. Reid
& Lefevre, London] by the National Gallery of Australia,
November 1984

Of the nineteen known oil sketches painted by Georges Seurat on the Channel coast, twelve date from his stay in Grandcamp in 1885. He may have been using them to try out compositions or, as he would write to Paul Signac the following year, 'to acclimatise myself' to a new site.[3] This beautiful sketch is a study for one of the five large canvases Seurat painted that summer, *Le Bec du Hoc (Grandcamp)* (cat. 1). It shows the elements of Seurat's composition already firmly in place, with the diagonal of the promontory rising from the lower left-hand corner and its tip covering the horizon. The elongated 'marine' format of Seurat's oil sketch has reduced the sky to a mere strip, whereas the squarer canvas gives it more space. The final work also does away with the darker areas behind the Bec du Hoc (sometimes identified as the beach below at low tide),[4] enhancing its dramatic setting floating over the sea.

The lively criss-cross brushstrokes found in the large painting to render the rock formation are already present here, as are the horizontal dashes of blue, green and lavender to depict the water. As he did in almost all his oil sketches (called '*croquetons*' at the time), Seurat left areas of the wood support visible, using its darker colour as an additional tone in his colour scheme. A strong vertical grain is visible, forcing the paintbrush to skip over it and creating accidental reserves. We know that Seurat sometimes intentionally roughed up the surface of his small panels to create these effects (see, for example, cat. 7 and fig. 55) and that is probably also the case here.

Study for Le Bec du Hoc (Grandcamp) was, along with *Boats, Grandcamp* (now known as *Three Boats and a Sailor*, private collection), the first seascape ever exhibited by Seurat. Both sketches were part of a group of '12 Studies, framed together' and included in the exhibition *Works in Oil and Pastel of the Impressionists of Paris*, which opened at the American Art Galleries in New York on 10 April 1886.[5] Also included in the exhibition were two other oil sketches, framed separately, and *Bathing, Asnières* (fig. 2). The exhibition was the brainchild of the Parisian art dealer Paul Durand-Ruel, who had gathered almost 300 works by Impressionist and Post-Impressionist artists in an attempt to penetrate the American art market (Durand-Ruel and his sons would open a permanent branch in New York the following year). The works did not sell and were returned to Seurat in late November.[6] The oil sketches were still framed together when Seurat's studio was inventoried after his death and must correspond to the 'framed panels' on the list of works that Seurat's partner, Madeleine Knobloch, asked to be allocated to her in the division of his estate.[7] She must have prevailed as the framed sketches were still together at Seurat's posthumous exhibition at Les XX the following year but then sold individually.

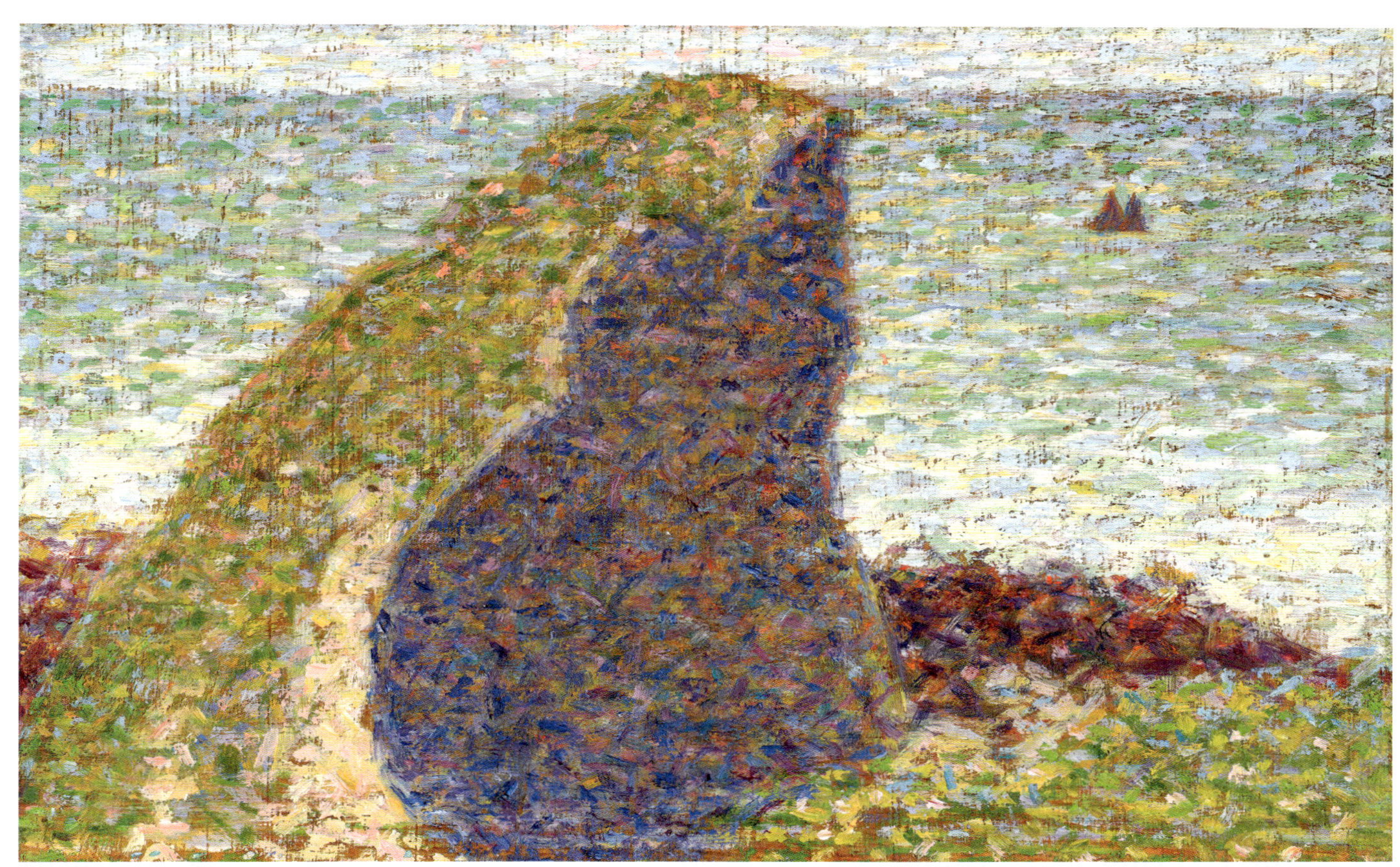

3

The Roadstead of Grandcamp

1885
Oil on canvas
65.4 × 81.2 cm
Private collection

DR 154
H 160

Exhibitions

1886 Paris (Impressionists) (*La rade de Grand-Camp*)
1886 Paris (Indépendants)
1887 Brussels
1888 Paris (Jan.)

Provenance

By inheritance to the artist's mother, Ernestine Seurat (née Faivre; 1828–1899), Paris, 1891; by descent to her son, Émile Seurat (1846–1906), Paris, 1899; [Bernheim-Jeune, Paris], by 1904 and until at least 1925; probably acquired from them by [Alex. Reid & Lefevre, London], by 1928; jointly owned with [Knoedler & Co., New York] from 1929; acquired from them by [Étienne Bignou, Paris], December 1934; possibly acquired from them by Lady Edith Chester Beatty (née Dunn; 1886–1952), London, May 1936; by inheritance to her husband, Sir Alfred Chester Beatty (1875–1968), Dublin, 1952; acquired from him by [Paul Rosenberg, New York]; acquired from him by Peggy (1915–1996) and David (1915–2017) Rockefeller, April 1955; their sale, [Christie's, New York], 8 April 2018, lot 18; acquired there by the present owner

Moving away from the dramatic cliffs and the Bec du Hoc (cat. 1), Georges Seurat positioned himself at shore level in Grandcamp to represent this passing fleet of boats. Their uniform hull and sails could indicate that they are not fishing vessels but racing sailboats taking part in a regatta. This was an unusual subject matter for Seurat but perhaps influenced by similar paintings by Claude Monet (1840–1926) depicting leisure summer activities on the Channel. The composition, however, recalls that of *Le Bec du Hoc (Grandcamp)*. The wall and shrubs in the foreground, rising into a triangle in the centre, boldly block the expected view of open water. As he had done for the Bec du Hoc, Seurat rendered the vegetation in the present painting using short strokes of green and orange, turning to purple, blue and black in the shadows. A dusting of small red dots, added as a final layer, animate the surface. The water is depicted using thicker horizontal brushmarks of yellow, white and green, darkened to purple and blue to create the shadow of passing clouds overhead.

When the Grandcamp paintings were unveiled in Paris in 1886, Seurat's seascapes were widely commended for rendering with great accuracy the subtle light of northern France. The critic Félix Fénéon, who would become a staunch supporter, noted that

> Mr Seurat's seascapes, calm and melancholy, expand and, reaching the distant drops of sky, lap away monotonously ... a sequence of sails assert themselves as scalene triangles – The Roadstead of Grandcamp .... His type of painting does not care for any sweetness of colour nor showy execution and appears austere, with a bitter, salty flavour.[8]

The perception of an austere atmosphere and 'salty' air in these works, as well as their 'penetrating melancholy', remained a constant in the reception of Seurat's seascapes.[9]

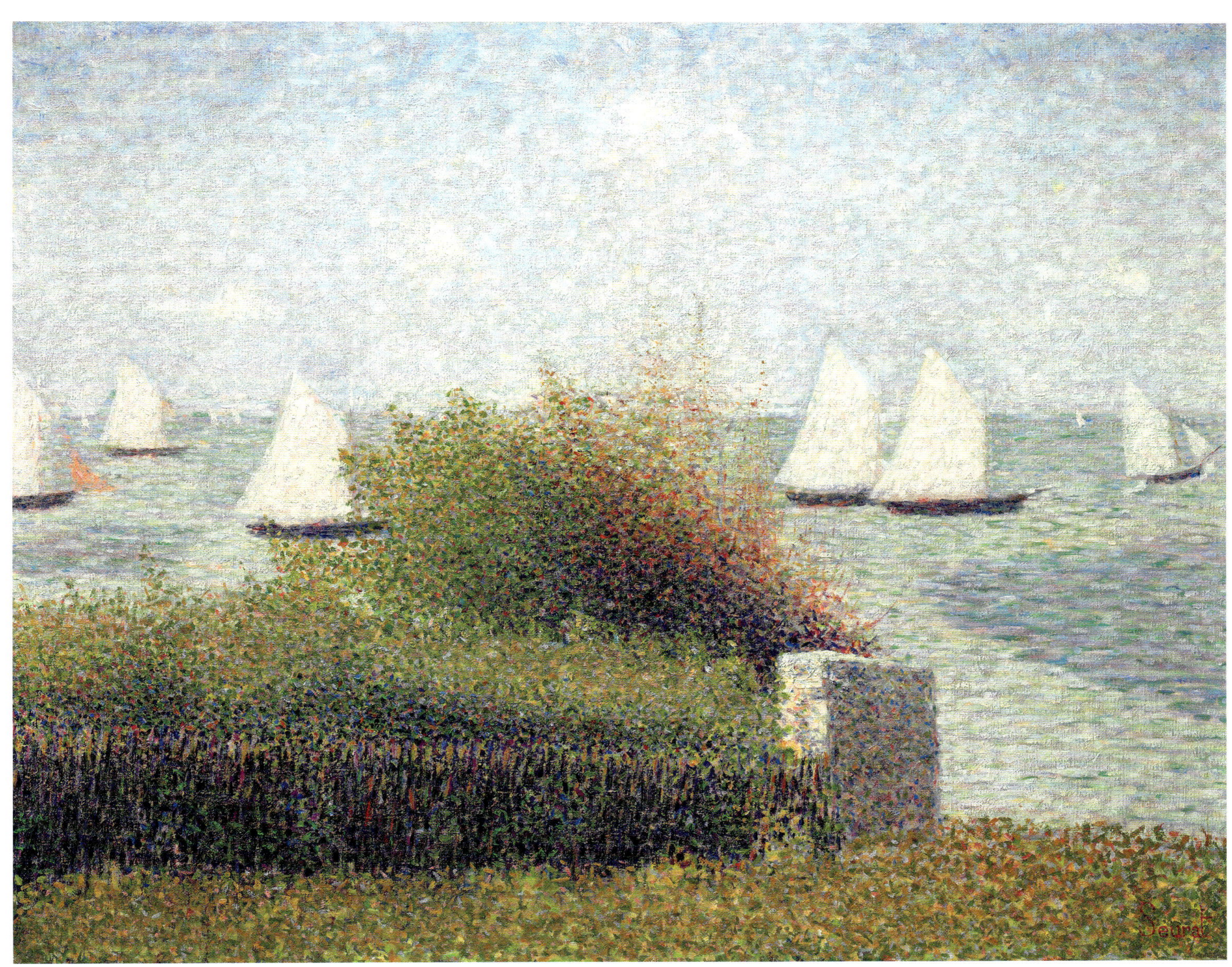

4

Marine at Grandcamp

1885
Oil on wood panel
16.5 × 25.7 cm
Courtesy of Bailly Gallery, Geneva and Paris

DR 146
H 147

Provenance

[Léonce Moline, Paris]; Charles Hall Thorndike
(1875–1935), Paris; Robert (1920–2008) and Nadine
(née Lambiotte, d. 2025) Schmit, Paris, since at least 1983;
their sale, [Sotheby's, Paris], 8 December 2021, lot 14

The application of paint in this lively oil sketch is much looser than in *Study for Le Bec du Hoc (Grandcamp)* (cat. 2) and must constitute an initial study of the motif. The brushstrokes are thicker and rely more heavily on the dark tone of the wood support for contrast. The sketch shows Georges Seurat at his freest and most experimental. The site could be that of the Pointe du Hoc viewed from the west at low tide. It would explain the sweeping curve of the coastline and the jutting out into the sea of the cliff in the middle distance. A nuanced difference in the rendering of the short touches at the top of the composition and the greater use of white show that Seurat had placed the horizon line very high, as he had done in his views of the Bec du Hoc.

Such studies were made on site with the use of a '*boîte à pouce*', a small travel box that held panels on the inside of the lid and paint materials in the bottom (see fig. 8). Seurat used such panels to depict scenes around Paris and the Channel coast, as well as to make preparatory sketches for his large figural works. Upon visiting Seurat's studio, the painter Charles Angrand was struck by the sight of, 'in closely spaced frames, many of those small studies from a travel paint box, which he said were his greatest joy.'[10] One hundred and sixty-three were inventoried in his studio after his death and *Marine at Grandcamp* was given the number 129, inscribed on the back of the panel.

The signature in the lower left was not added by Seurat himself nor at the time of the inventory but is a stamp created by the Parisian dealer Léonce Moline, probably in 1895. The art historian Robert L. Herbert has noted that this was done without any intent to deceive but was meant to mark works that had entered his stock, probably from Madeleine Knobloch, and were being exhibited in Moline's gallery in February that year.[11] At least twenty sketches (including fig. 55) and eleven drawings bear the stamp. A ghostly capital S in the lower right-hand corner of *Marine at Grandcamp* indicates that the stamp may have been initially applied in that corner but moved to a more visible spot.

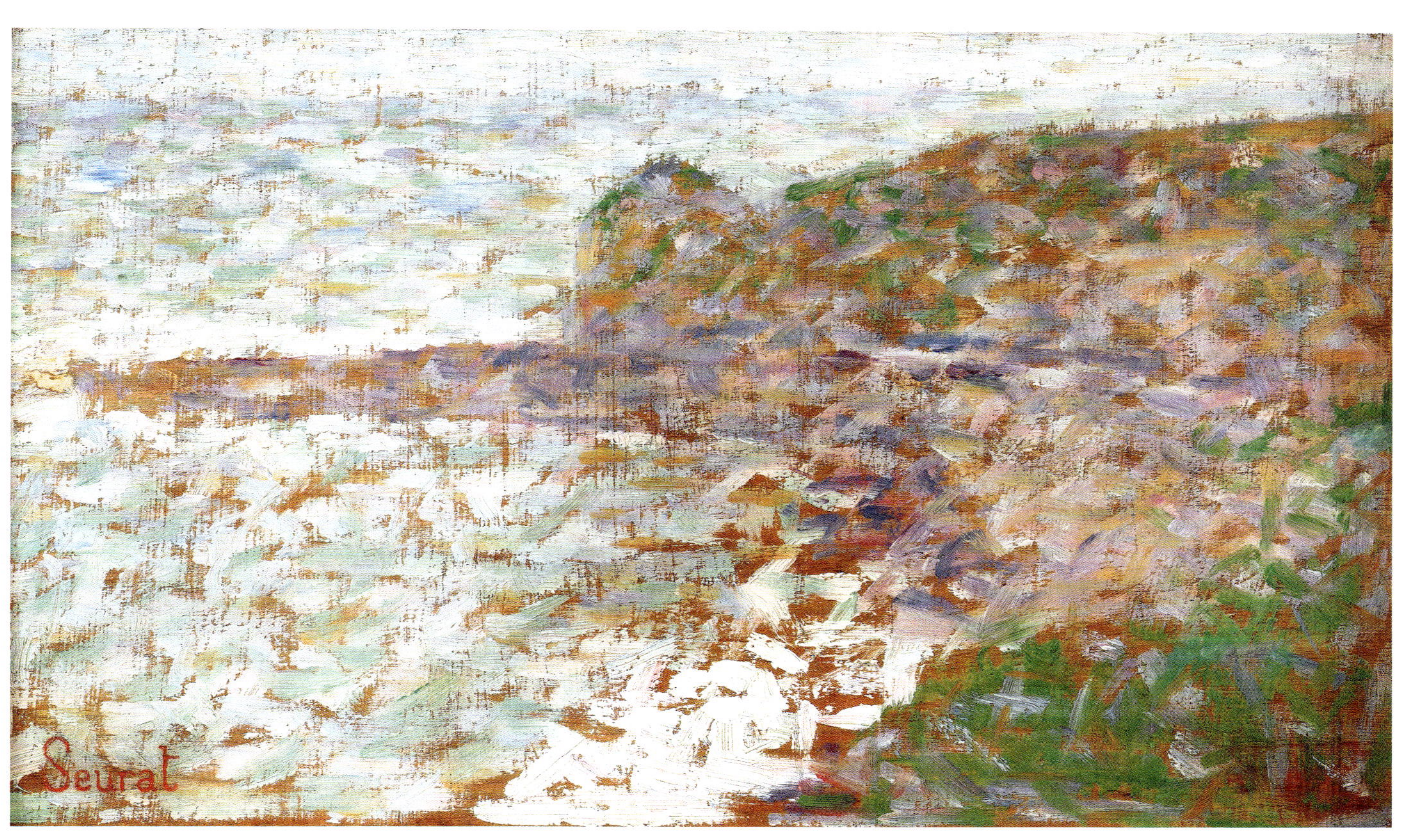

The Hospice and the Lighthouse of Honfleur

1886
Oil on canvas
66.7 × 81.9 cm
National Gallery of Art, Washington, D.C.
Collection of Mr and Mrs Paul Mellon

DR 168
H 173

Exhibitions

1886–87 Nantes (*L'hospice et le phare de Honfleur*)
1887 Brussels
1887 Paris

Provenance

Acquired from the artist by Émile Verhaeren (1855–1916), probably February 1887 and held until at least 1905; Curt von Mützenbecher, Wiesbaden, by 1907 and until at least 1908; [Bernheim-Jeune, Paris] from 1909 until 1913; probably acquired from them by Richard Goetz (1874–1954), Paris, 1913; his property sequestered by the French state during the First World War; sale of his sequestered property, [Hôtel Drouot, Paris], 23 February 1922, lot 181; acquired there by 'Grunewald' (perhaps the Swedish artist Isaac Grünewald, who probably returned it to Goetz); acquired from Goetz by [César de Hauke, New York] through [Alfred Gold, Berlin], June 1929; on joint account with [Alex. Reid & Lefevre, London] and [Jacques Seligmann et Cie., New York and Paris], 1931; acquired from [Alex. Reid & Lefevre, London] by Lady Edith Chester Beatty (née Dunn; 1886–1952), London, 1934; by inheritance to her husband, Sir Alfred Chester Beatty (1875–1968), Dublin, 1952; acquired from [Arthur Tooth & Sons, London] by Paul Mellon (1907–1999), Upperville, Virginia, 1965; gifted by him to the National Gallery of Art, 1983

For his second stay on the northern coast of France, in the summer of 1886, Georges Seurat settled in Honfleur, on the estuary of the Seine. Generations of artists before him had visited the town, attracted by its medieval streets and picturesque port, which, despite recent enhancements, had escaped the heavy industrialisation of its neighbour across the river, Le Havre. The striking site of Honfleur's lighthouse and hospital had also been inspiring painters for decades before Seurat made it his own. During his eight-week stay in Honfleur he resided west of town, on the rue de Grâce, a steep street in the back hills that offered views of the lighthouse as well as the Beach du Butin below (see cat. 6).

In the present painting, most of the foreground is occupied by a wide shore into which vegetation has started to creep. On the right, the expanse shows signs of use as a makeshift dockyard, with a wheel and sawhorse to the right, and the hull of a small boat further afield.[12] The area was perhaps used by the occupants of the hospital in the background, which also functioned as a care home and took in mariners in their old age. Built in the sixteenth and seventeenth centuries, the building had been remodelled over time but finally closed in 1977. The lighthouse itself was a more recent addition, erected only from 1853 on a small granite jetty and inaugurated in 1857. Standing 25.5 metres tall, it was meant to meet the demands of increasing traffic on the estuary of the Seine, but closed in 1908.

As in the case of *The Shore at Bas-Butin (Honfleur)* (cat. 6), a preparatory *croqueton*, or oil sketch, for the present painting survives (fig. 55) and

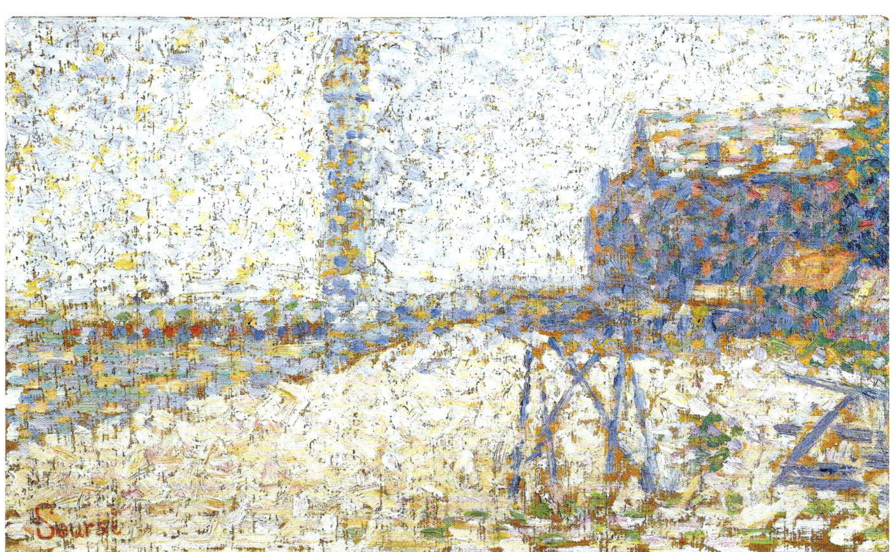

55. *Study for The Hospice and the Lighthouse of Honfleur*, 1886, oil on wood panel, 15.8 × 25 cm, private collection

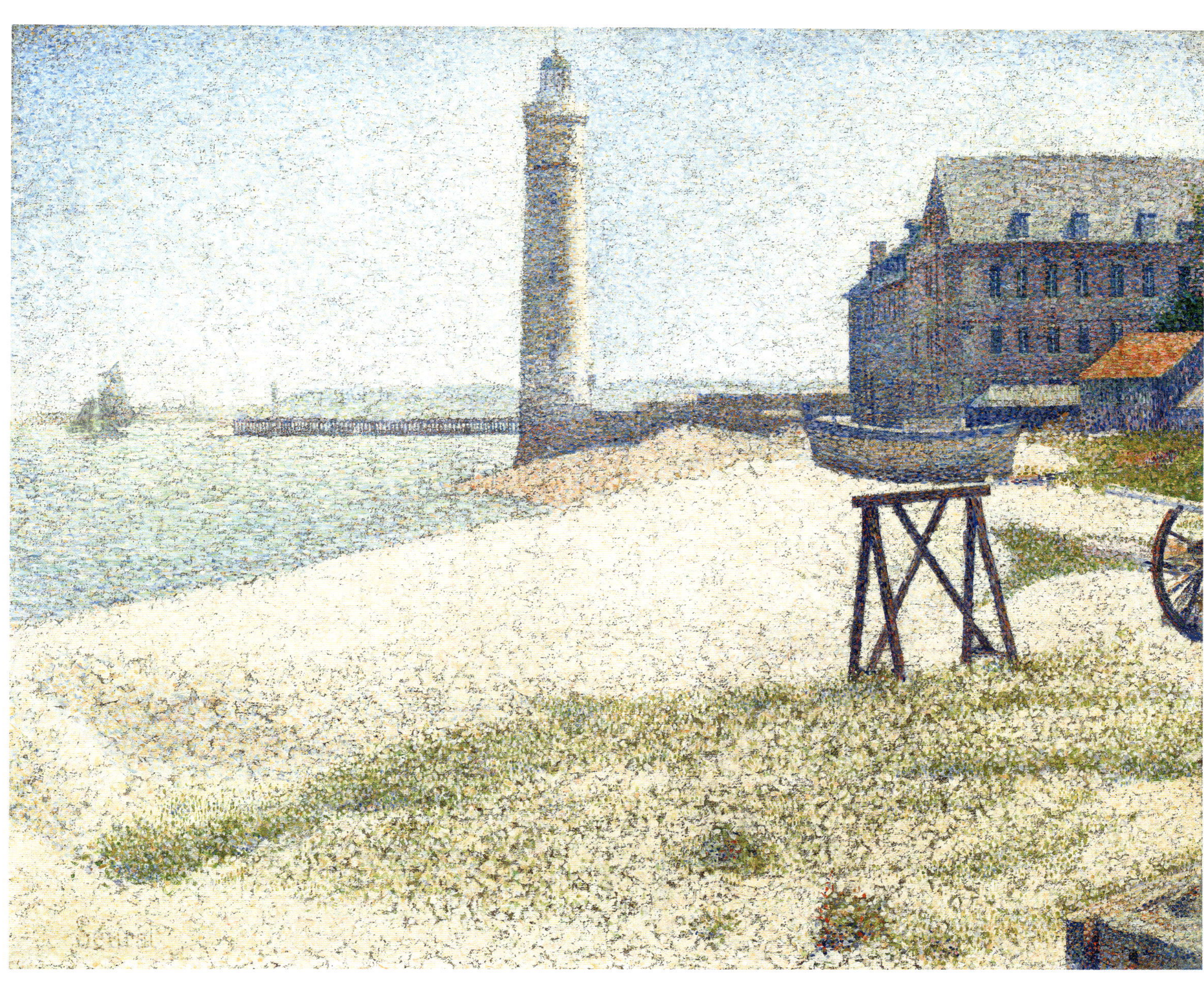

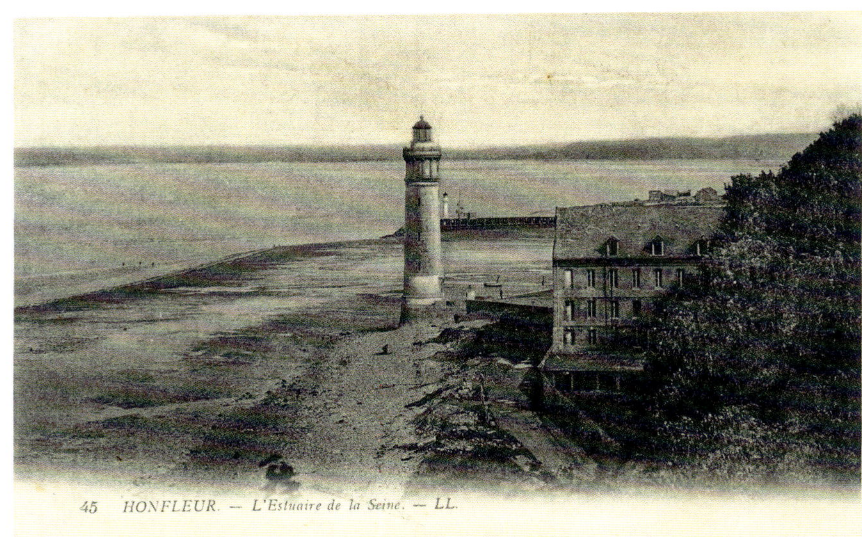

56. Postcard of Honfleur, 'The Estuary of the Seine', late 19th century, private collection

shows the elements of the composition already in place. Seurat decided to push the top of the lighthouse to the very edge of the composition, a point of tension retained in the final canvas. Similarly, he confined the hospice to the upper right-hand corner, creating an open area in the foreground, instead of broadening the sky as one might expect. Contemporary postcards indicate that the site had already become picturesque and popular in the late nineteenth century (fig. 56) but Seurat's approach differs markedly from these photographs and the work of previous artists, where the lighthouse is cast as a symbol of the coast and set at the centre of a vast expanse of beach, sea and sky (fig. 41–44). By shifting the placement of these elements, Seurat turned a traditional scenic view into a daring composition.

The Honfleur paintings are particularly revealing of a moment of transition in Seurat's technique. An x-ray of *The Hospice and the Lighthouse of Honfleur* shows a flurry of criss-cross brushstrokes as an initial layer, later covered by a 'skin' of irregular thick dots, often applied once the first layer had had time to dry.[13] Despite this thickly layered surface, the white priming has been left visible in certain areas, as part of the colour scheme and to reinforce the edges of some of elements. As Seurat later wrote to the Belgian poet and critic Émile Verhaeren, who would purchase the painting, he worked on it for two and a half months.[14]

Seurat's paintings of Honfleur were admired by Belgian and French critics, who were by now better acquainted with the Neo-Impressionist style. One of them noted:

Messrs Seurat and Signac have here [at the 1887 *Salon des Indépendants*] around twenty paintings in their familiar style, but some of which are very beautiful, provided you view them from the suitable distance and with the obligatory blink of the eyes. The Lighthouse of Honfleur, by Mr Seurat is a painting of a delicate clarity, of a rare transparency. Here and there, skilfully placed details reveal the bold touch of an artist who is at the same time very delicate, as in the flash … of a red roof vibrating in the sun. The technique used in this painting no longer has the charm of mystery. Mr Seurat multiplies small, closely spaced touches, pearls of colour, which give his canvas, when seen up close, the appearance of a tapestry. But this technique, which has replaced the juxtaposition of flat colours, of raw patches, is only as good as the artist's talent …. Mr Seurat has a lively and subtle view of landscape, especially of the sea, and he appreciates, when painting it, the strength and effect of a colour with a precision that gives his hand assuredness and lightness.[15]

The reception had been equally warm in Brussels the previous month, at the *Fourth Exhibition of Les XX*. As Verhaeren recounted, 'visitors, all the while rejecting the painter's major submission [*A Sunday on La Grande Jatte*, fig. 3], allow themselves to be drawn to his small landscapes: Marines and Ports. Two canvases found buyers …. Never has anyone been able to render with such precision details within grandeur. The *Bec du Hoc* and the *Lighthouse of Honfleur* are at once meticulous and vast.'[16] Verhaeren does not disclose that he was one of the two buyers, having acquired the present painting, which he praised in his review. A letter from Seurat to Verhaeren, dated late February or early March 1887, reveals their negotiation:

> … *The Lighthouse* took two and a half months to complete, while *The Quay* [*Corner of a Harbour*; fig. 18] only eight days. I told you this when I ceded it to you. I considered it as a large sketch. We will find an agreement on a discounted price. *The Lighthouse* is yours. By that I mean that I will not sell it in Paris but it must be sent back to me for the exhibition at the Indépendants (from 25 March to 5 May). I am very poor in paintings. I have absolutely nothing but my last three landscapes exhibited in Brussels …. I absolutely need for my exhibition before 14 March *The Lighthouse*, *The Shore* and *The Setting Sun*. That is all that worries me at present.[17]

Verhaeren, like the collector Henri Van Cutsem, who had acquired *The Shore at Bas-Butin (Honfleur)* under the same conditions, therefore had to wait a few additional months for his painting.

6

The Shore at Bas-Butin (Honfleur)

1886
Oil on canvas
65.5 × 82 cm
Collection of the Musée des Beaux-Arts de la Ville de Tournai
DR 165
H 169

Exhibitions

1886–87 Nantes (*La grève du Bas-Butin [Honfleur]*)
1887 Brussels
1887 Paris

Provenance

Acquired from the artist by Henri Van Cutsem (1839–1904), Brussels, probably February 1887; bequeathed by him to the Musée des Beaux-Arts de la Ville de Tournai, 1904, with the sculptor Guillaume Charlier (1854–1925), Brussels, retaining a life interest

An open, sandy path draws the viewer out to sea. Along the shore, the water is deep blue, rendered in dabs of pure pigment, but turns to emerald green as it recedes. Our sweeping view is interrupted by the tall white cliff on the right, which closes off the composition and establishes a strong diagonal to counterbalance the horizon line. The sense of wilderness, created by the dense vegetation growing freely on the sand and cliff, is curtailed by signs of human intervention in the landscape. A set of small breakwater posts, designed to prevent the erosion of sand and gravel, line the edge of the shore. In the distance, a cargo steamship – its flatness emphasising the horizon – and a strip of land remind us that we are not looking towards the open sea but across the busy estuary of the Seine. Georges Seurat painted this view from the Beach du Butin or Bas-Butin, located slightly west of Honfleur, not far from where he was staying.

The Shore at Bas-Butin (Honfleur) was one of seven canvases begun during Seurat's summer in Honfleur in 1886, the most productive of his seascape campaigns. While all the paintings were started during his stay on the Channel coast, they were completed in his Parisian studio in autumn and winter 1886–87 (with the exception of *Corner of a Harbour (Honfleur)* [fig. 18], a 'large sketch' from August 1886 Seurat considered finished given that the boat depicted had left port). By October 1886, *The Shore at Bas-Butin (Honfleur)* was ready to be displayed and was sent to the *Exposition des Beaux-Arts* in Nantes.[18] Seurat and a few fellow Neo-Impressionists had been invited to the event only thanks to the intervention of Camille Pissarro. Their new style was widely derided as formulaic, with the kindest critic noting in the local newspaper *Le Phare de la Loire* that 'Mr Seurat, a researcher, has here a *Lighthouse at Honfleur* [cat. 5] and a *Shore at Bas-Butin*, which inform us about the advantages and disadvantages of the formula, "the division of tone".'[19] The two paintings were more favourably received when they were shown in exhibitions in Brussels in February 1887 and in Paris the following month. One critic wrote: 'M. Seurat sees a golden, very golden light. His *Lighthouse of Honfleur* and his *Shore at Bas-Butin* are of an exquisite refinement. It is impossible to achieve a greater luminosity with greater harmony'.[20]

Seurat's work held a special appeal for Symbolist writers and poets, many of whom doubled as art critics and did much to promote his art. The novelist Paul Adam (1862–1920), one of the earliest proponents of the movement, described Seurat's work at the *Third Salon des Indépendants*, presenting the artist as

the prodigious conjuror of seas with endless herds of waves, and quiet shores. In a restful blue, a soft green, the immense floating expanses rise towards the curve of the clouds and the overcast skies. Thus [is] *The Shore at Bas-Butin* so tenderly dusted of its golden sands, in which a sea of changing shades of

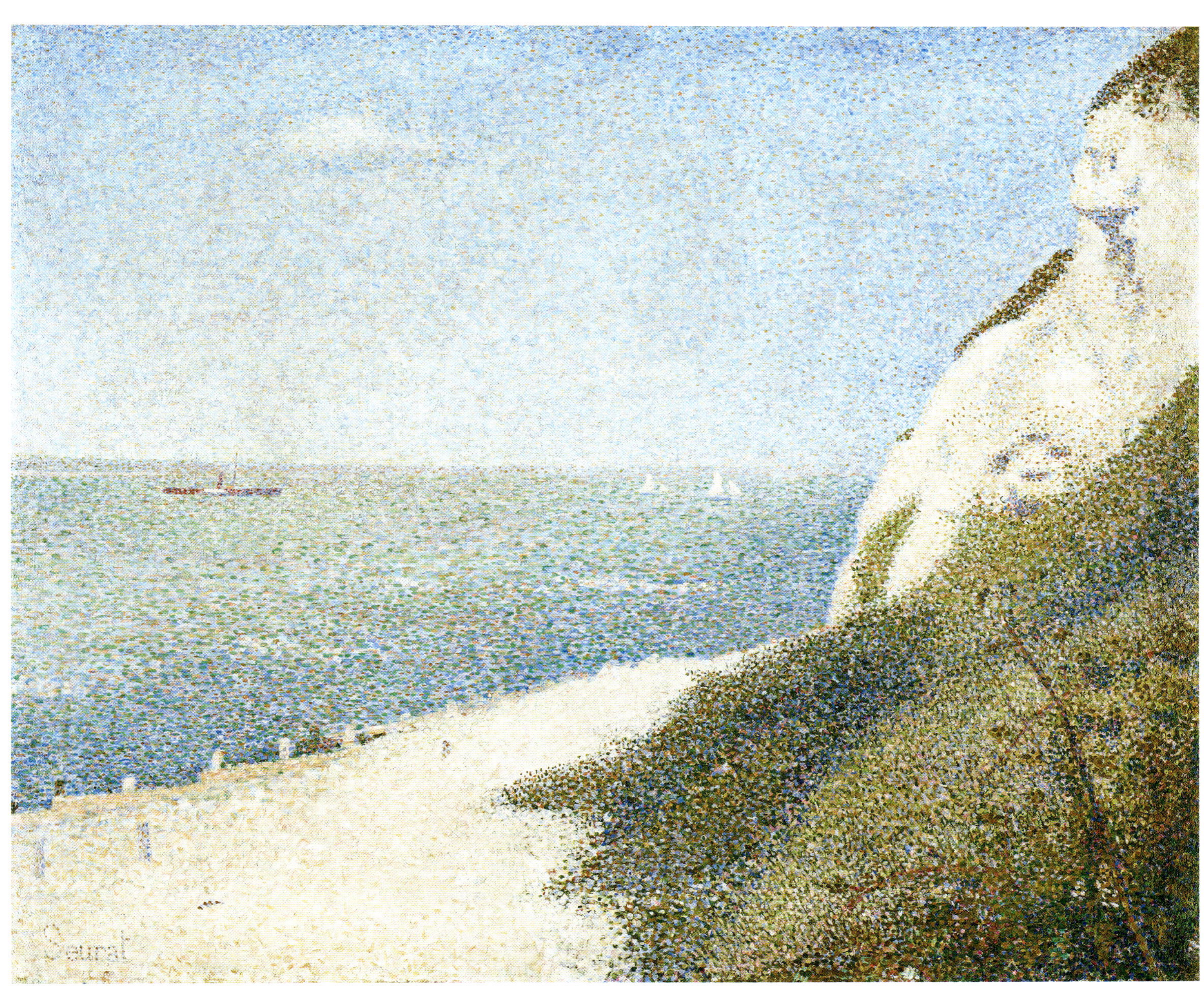

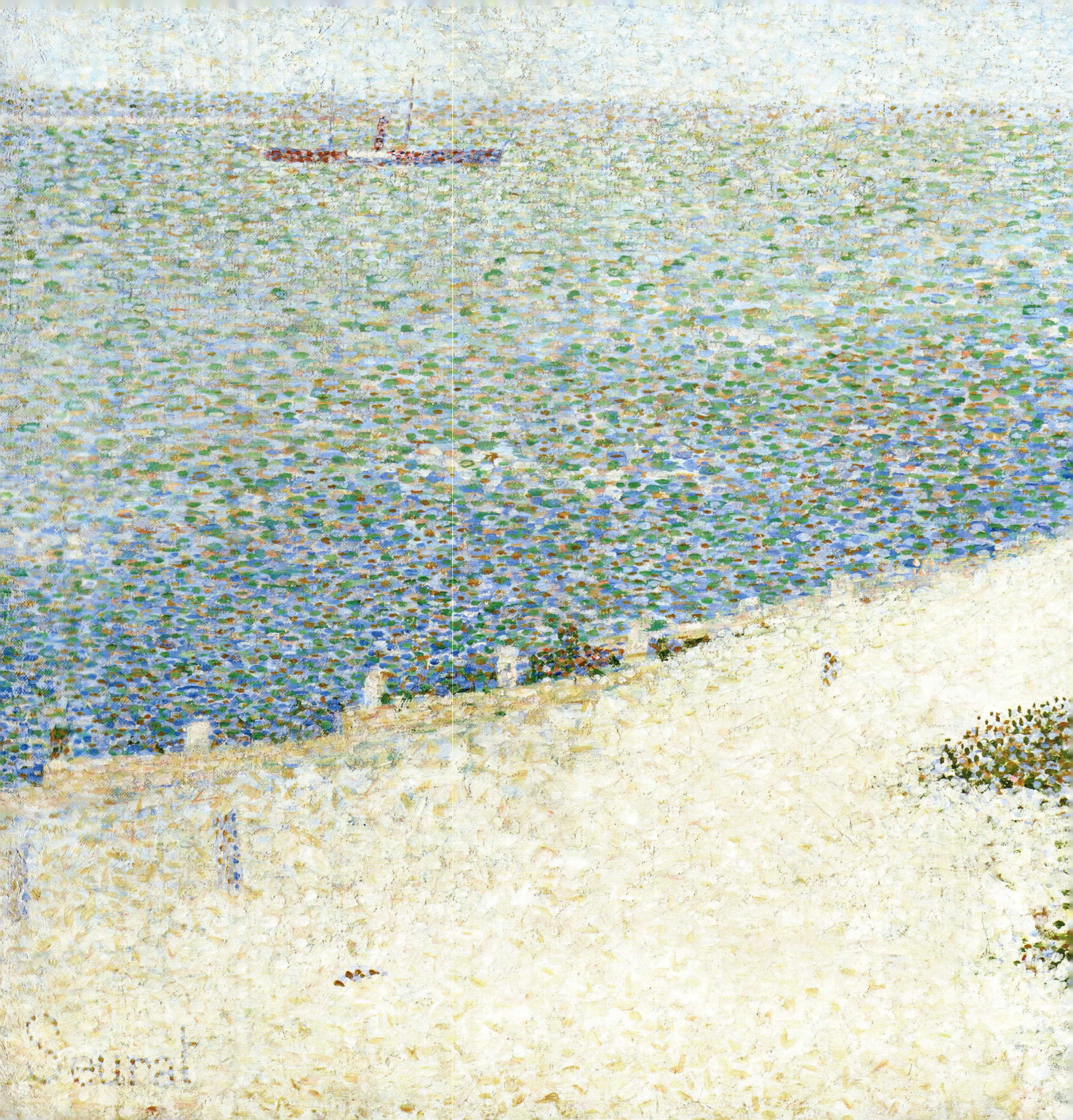
Seurat

malachite and emerald, lapis too, pours forth; while the firmament pulses, like a large jewellery box filled with tiny gems. Over there, thin and sly, a steamboat speeds by, coquettishly adorned with quick colours.[21]

The present painting is one of only three canvases recorded as sold by Seurat during his lifetime (the others are cat. 5 and 13). In the catalogue of the *Salon des Indépendants* in March 1887, it is listed as belonging to 'Van Cutsem'. Henri Van Cutsem, a Belgian painter and wealthy patron of the arts, had bought the work the previous month, when it was shown in Brussels. This constituted a very rare acquisition of one of Seurat's works by someone outside his immediate circle and cemented the importance of Belgian collectors for the recognition of Neo-Impressionism. Reminiscing about Seurat in 1934, Paul Signac stated that 'In his lifetime, he sold only two canvases, one in 1887, at the Exhibition of Les XX, in Brussels … *The Bec du Hoc*, *Grandcamp* to M. Van Cutsem, for the sum of 300 francs.'[22] Signac misremembered the painting but we can perhaps assume the price was correct. For the *Exposition des Beaux-Arts* in Nantes a few months earlier, Seurat had valued the painting at 800 francs.[23] Van Cutsem bequeathed his art collection to the city of Tournai, adding to its already rich holdings, and a museum by the famed architect Victor Horta was opened there in 1928.

7

Study for The Shore at Bas-Butin (Honfleur)

1886
Oil on wood panel
17.1 × 26 cm
Baltimore Museum of Art
Bequest of Saidie A. May

DR 164
H 168

Provenance
[Étienne Bignou, Paris]; acquired from [Bernheim-Jeune, Paris] by Saidie Adler May (1879–1951), New York, 1925; bequeathed by her to The Baltimore Museum of Art, 1951

Georges Seurat did not paint canvases such as *The Shore at Bas-Butin (Honfleur)* (cat. 6) directly from life. Rather, he ventured out to the different sites with a travel paint box, whose lid could turn into a miniature easel for small wooden panels. The bottom of the box held a palette, paint tubes and other materials. This allowed Seurat to experiment on site and paint discreetly, an ideal set-up for a reserved artist exploring a new region.

The present sketch shows that Seurat had already identified his preferred composition, with the strong diagonal of the cliff cutting across the scene. The patches of vegetation are also in place. The sketch shows a much looser brushwork and a greater variation in the use of colour than the finished canvas, with the heavier presence of dots of orange, for example, contrasting with the blue of the sea. The warm brown colour of the wood support is left deliberately visible in several areas, as part of the colour scheme. In addition, paint has skipped over textured areas of the support, which was probably intentionally toothed to achieve this effect. The passing steamship on the left, embodying the heavy traffic in the Seine estuary, was retained in the final canvas, but the single large sailboat, which is more in proportion with the rest of the composition, was replaced by two smaller, toy-like boats.

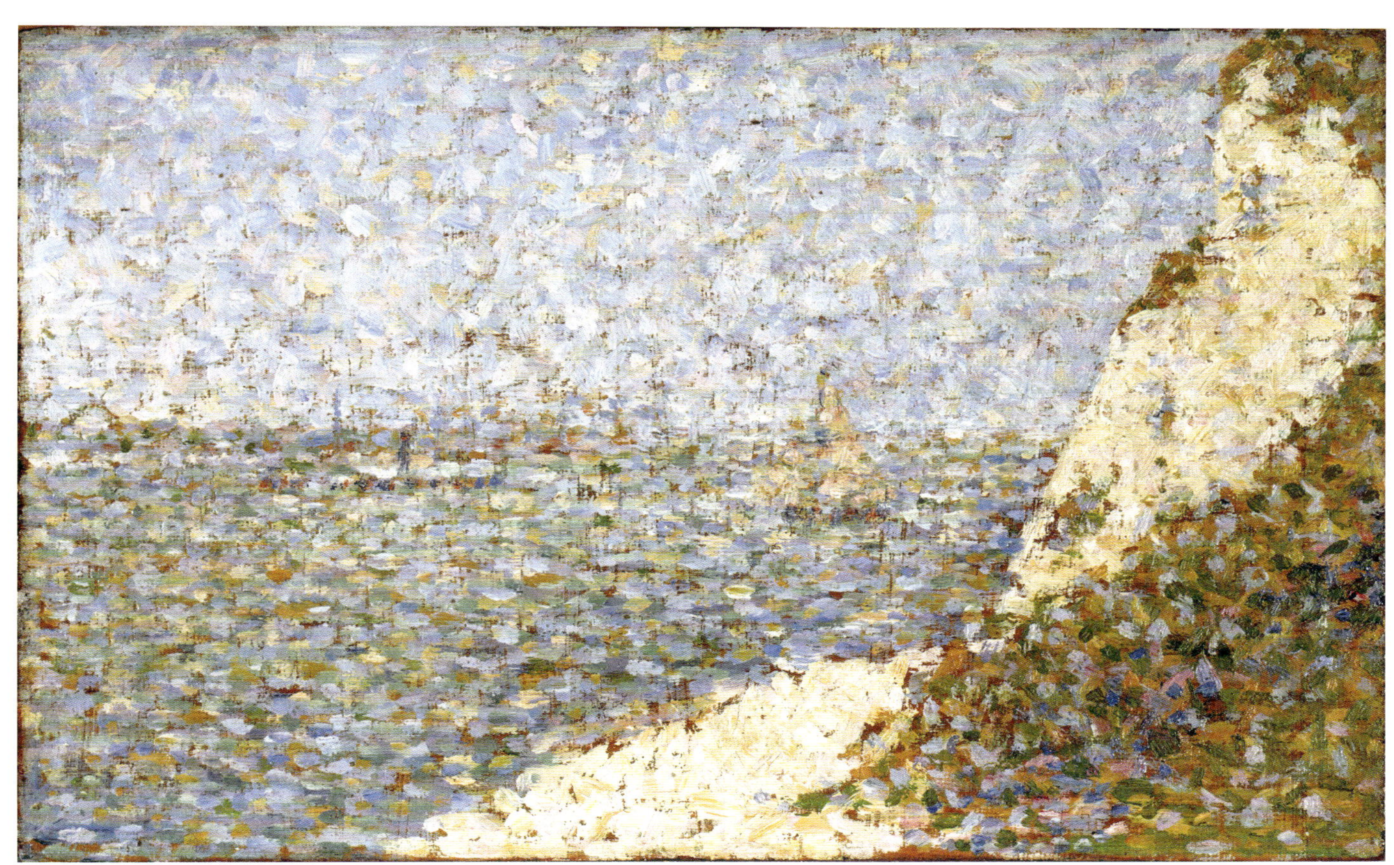

8

Entrance of the Port of Honfleur

1886, reworked c. 1890
Oil on canvas
54.3 × 65.1 cm
The Barnes Foundation, Philadelphia
DR 162
H 171

Exhibitions

1887 Paris (*Entrée du port d'Honfleur*)

Provenance

Probably gifted by Georges Seurat to Félix Fénéon (1861–1944), Paris, by March 1887; returned by him to Seurat (in exchange for *Front-Facing Model*), 1890; probably by inheritance to the artist's partner, Madeleine Knobloch (d. 1903), Paris, 1891; Karl Ernst Osthaud (1874–1921), Hagen; [Alfred Flechtheim, Berlin]; Rolf de Maré (1888–1964), Stockholm and Paris; [Alex. Reid & Lefevre, London]; acquired from [Étienne Bignou and Georges Keller, Paris] by Albert C. Barnes (1872–1951), Merion, Pennsylvania, November 1934

Georges Seurat painted this view of Honfleur standing on the central Jetée du Transit and looking out towards the narrow opening of the port as boats entered and exited its shelter. To the left is the end of the wooden pier of the Jetée de l'Ouest. To the right are key port structures for navigators: the 36-metre-tall tide signal mast indicated the depth of the water by positioning black balls on its vertical axis (giving the level in metres) and on the horizontal crossbar (for centimetres). At night, the shorter lighthouse ('*feu des marées*') took over, emitting red and white light pulses to informing approaching ships of current tide levels.[24] A contemporary postcard places us in the same spot as Seurat, revealing how carefully he rendered what were to him unfamiliar surroundings (fig. 57). Such postcards are particularly useful in enabling us to recapture the area in the late nineteenth century, as the landscape of Normandy has since undergone major changes, through industrialisation, the defences erected during the Second World War and the destruction in its wake. They, and works by other artists depicting the same site (see fig. 29, 30, 38 and 39), reveal, by contrast, the particularities of Seurat's approach. Instead of emphasising open vistas, Seurat flattened his composition and focused on the port entrance. He crowded the narrow channel with sailboats, steamships, buoys and masts, symbols of the intense activity and industry of Honfleur.

In contrast to Seurat's other paintings from that summer, which present strong diagonals, *Entrance of the Port of Honfleur* is composed of a series of horizontal bands. The edge of the quay in the foreground is echoed by the water line and the range of low cliffs beyond. The iron mooring-post strikes a dark note in an otherwise luminous composition. Its shadow suggests that

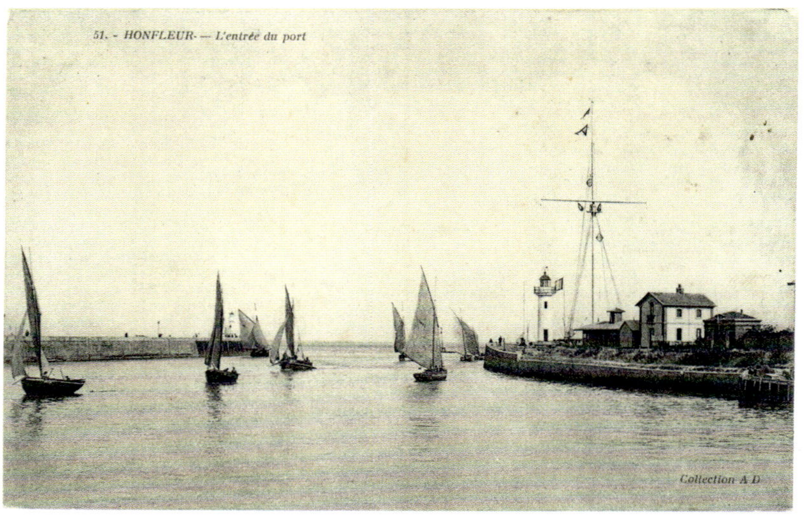

57. Postcard of Honfleur, 'The Entrance of the Port', late 19th century, private collection

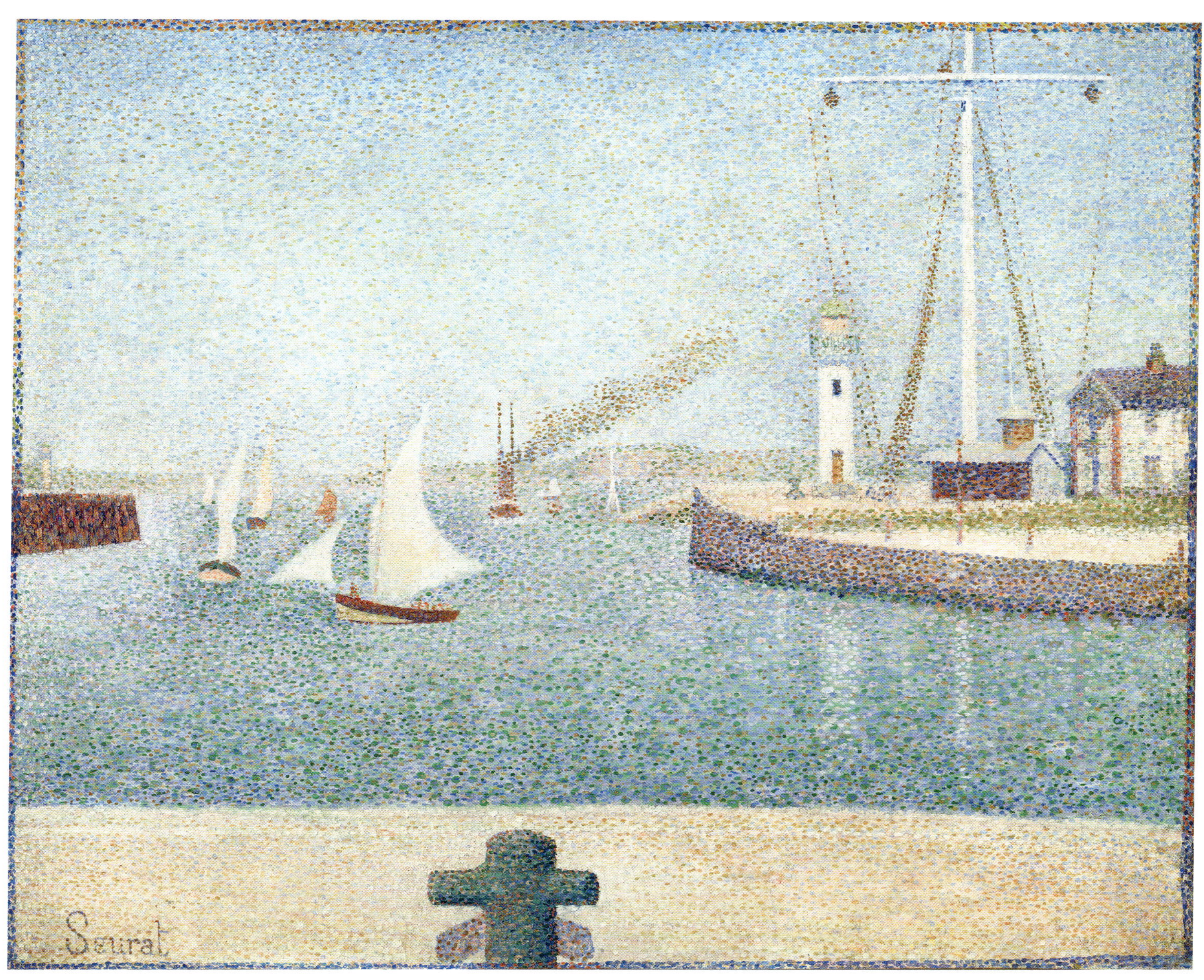

Seurat

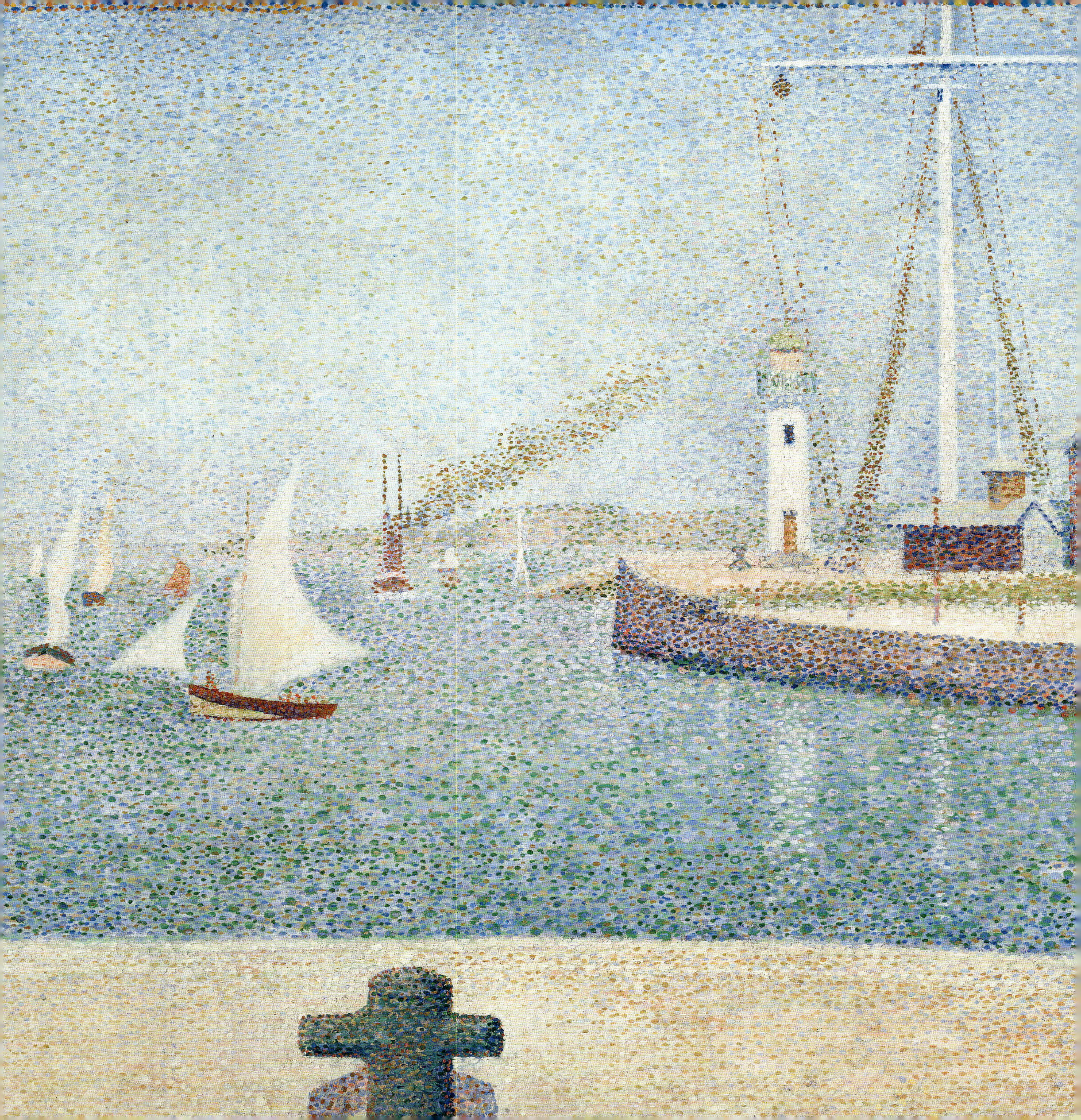

Seurat set the scene in the early afternoon, with the sun high in the sky.[25] As in *The Shore at Bas-Butin (Honfleur)* (cat. 6), the water is rendered in larger dots of dark blue close to the edge and fades into lighter blue and emerald green in the distance. The long white reflections of the lighthouse and mast animate its surface.

When the painting was first exhibited at the *Third Salon des Indépendants* in March 1887, it already belonged to the writer and critic Félix Fénéon, no doubt gifted by the artist to one of his earliest and most vocal advocates.[26] An intriguing feature of the painting is its coloured perimeter, composed of an open weave of coloured dots, which let the paint below show through. Painted borders only started appearing in Seurat's work from late 1888 or, most probably, 1889 onwards. Simultaneously, the artist also returned to earlier paintings and reworked them to add borders on top of existing compositions. According to the author and dealer César de Hauke, who wrote one of the main catalogues of Seurat's oeuvre, Fénéon asked, in 1890, to exchange his seascape for the small oil sketch *Front-Facing Model* (1887, Musée d'Orsay, Paris) to which Seurat had recently added a painted border.[27] It is therefore likely that Seurat did the same to *Entrance of the Port of Honfleur* when it returned to his studio at that time.

The present painting was last exhibited in a Seurat exhibition in December 1933, a year before it was acquired by the American collector Albert C. Barnes.[28] One of the most important collectors of modern art of the pre-war era, Barnes came to own six works by Seurat, including the large *Models* (*Poseuses*), which he had bought in 1926. A loosening of the restrictions imposed by Barnes on lending works from his collection enables *Entrance of the Port of Honfleur* to be brought together with its peers in this exhibition for the first time in almost a century. It is also reunited with its related drawing (cat. 9); they were last together in Seurat's studio in 1891.

9

The Port of Honfleur

1886
Conté crayon heightened with gouache on laid paper
23 × 30.5 cm
Private collection, Germany

DR 162a
H 657

Provenance
Charles Vignier (1863–1934), Paris; Eduard von der Heydt
(1882-1964), Zandvoort; [Alfred Flechtheim, Berlin];
[De Hauke and Co, New York], by 1929; [Knoedler Gallery,
New York], before 1943; Grace and Philip Sandblom,
Lund (Sweden), by 1954; sold at [Sotheby's, New York],
7 November 2006, lot 16

This highly finished drawing is reunited in this exhibition with its related painting (cat. 8) for the first time since the dispersal of Georges Seurat's studio in 1891. The artist, an exceptional draughtsman, produced two large drawings during his summer in Honfleur (see also fig. 19). He never deviated from his medium and support of choice, favouring the use of 'Conté crayon' on a very textured type of Ingres paper called Michallet. Patented in 1795, Conté crayon was composed of compressed powdered graphite and carbon black in a clay base. It did not smudge but allowed the creation of a variety of effects, depending on the pressure applied. In the present drawing, Seurat used it masterfully to render a range of tones, from the light foreground of the quay to the grey of the water and sky. Darker elements, such as the bollard, the hull of a moored boat and the wooden west jetty, punctuate the composition. For added contrast, Seurat applied a touch of white gouache to pick out the thin structure of the lighthouse. The heavy texture of the paper meant that the crayon often skipped over its lower ridges, creating reserves of white that Seurat used to animate his surface and render points of light reflecting on the water and clouds.

The final composition of *Entrance of the Port of Honfleur* is already established in the present drawing. A central steamship anchors the scene, in line with the bollard in the foreground. In the drawing, the mooring post breaks the edge of the quay but, in the painting, it remains contained within its light background. Seurat also erased the curve of the foreground and narrowed the opening of the port, giving more prominence to the structures on the right. With most of the elements fixed, the drawing allowed Seurat to explore the tonal contrasts and enhance his understanding of light in the scene. As Paul Signac later wrote, 'Thanks to [Seurat's] perfect mastery of values, one could say that his "white and blacks" [drawings] are more luminous and more colourful than many paintings.'[29]

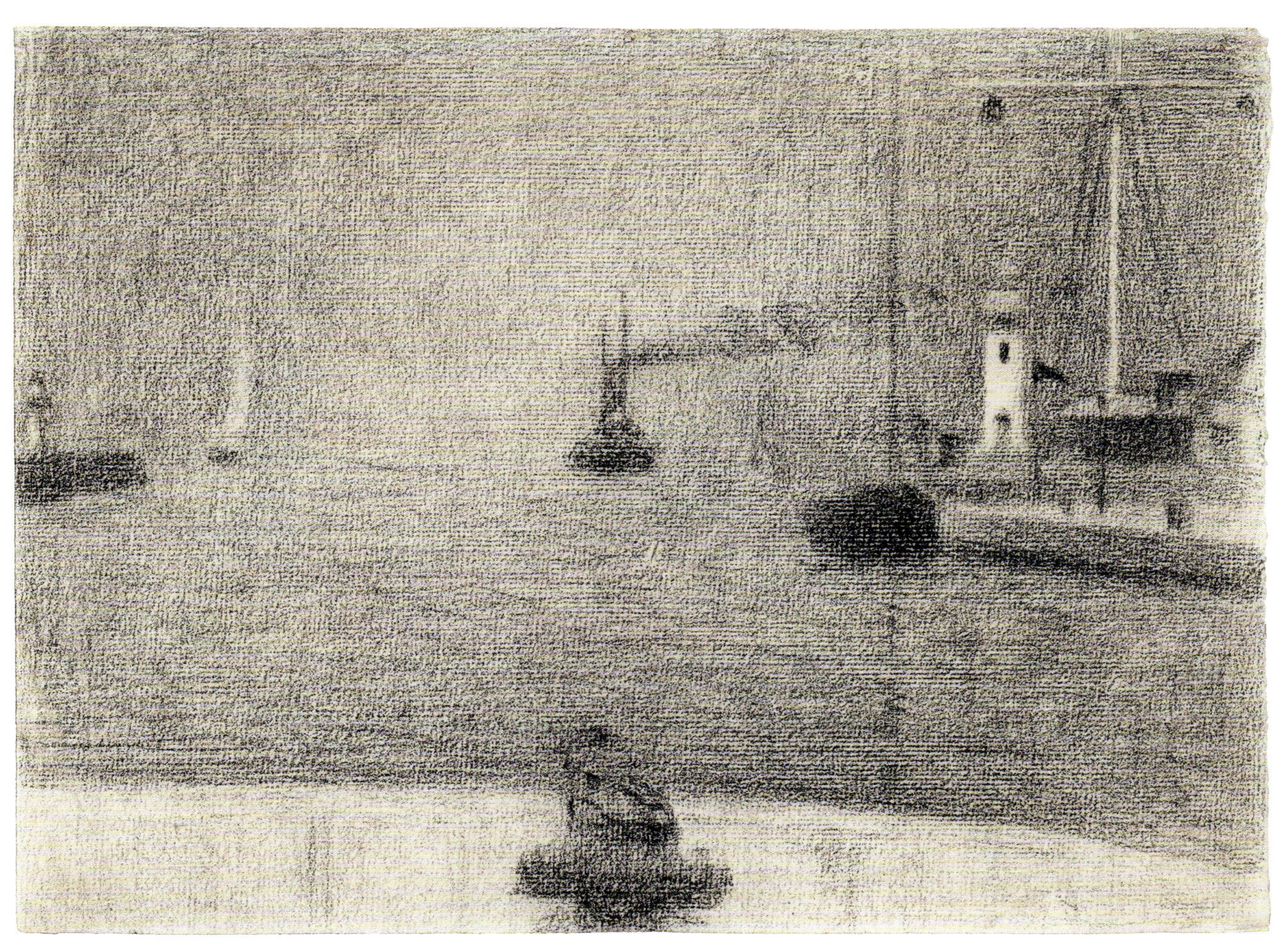

10

The 'Maria' (Honfleur)

1886, reworked c. 1888–89
Oil on canvas
53 × 63.5 cm
National Gallery (Národní Galerie), Prague
DR 169
H 164

Exhibitions
1887 Paris (*La Maria [Honfleur]*)

Provenance
By inheritance to the artist's mother, Ernestine Seurat (née Faivre; 1828–1899), Paris, 1891; Émile Verhaeren (1855–1916), Saint-Cloud, by 1914; acquired from [Galerie Barbazanges, Paris] by the Czechoslovak Republic, 1923

Georges Seurat's exploration of Honfleur in the summer of 1886 involved two unusual works, the present painting and *Corner of a Harbour (Honfleur)* (fig. 18). For these, Seurat turned his back to the sea and depicted ships moored in the port's inner harbours. Devoid of human presence, the quays look abandoned, instead of the busy hubs they were at the time. However, this choice allowed Seurat to focus on the dynamic lines of the rigs, masts, chimneys, mooring posts and rails on the docks to create this striking work.

The 'Maria' was a British ship built in Glasgow in 1871. Operated by the London and South-Western Railway Company, it ran, in Seurat's time, a regular cargo and passenger service between Honfleur and Southampton, with onward rail service to London. The route is advertised by the sign on the warehouse on the right, whose barely discernible lettering reads 'Honfleur to London via Southampton'. The ship was part of the growing trade between France, Great Britain and Scandinavia, which transformed the infrastructure of Norman ports in the nineteenth century.

In contrast to the other dock scene painted by Seurat, which he was forced to abandon when the ship left port after a week, the dependable route of the 'Maria' meant that the painter was sure to find it moored in the harbour every few days.[30] He has carefully rendered its iron hull; its central funnel, the top darkened by coal smoke; its two ancillary masts; and the cranes (called davits) on either side of the ship to lift goods onboard. The route to Southampton was enough of a stalwart of Honfleur port life to warrant a postcard, showing a ship with similar features to the 'Maria' (fig. 58).

In contrast to the flatter composition of *Entrance of the Port of Honfleur* (cat. 8), *The 'Maria' (Honfleur)* has a great sense of depth, thanks to the

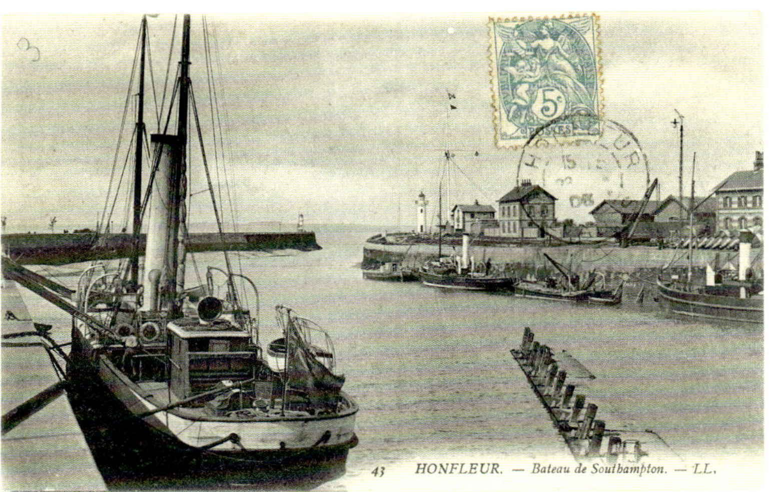

58. Postcard of Honfleur, 'Boat of Southampton', late 19th century, private collection

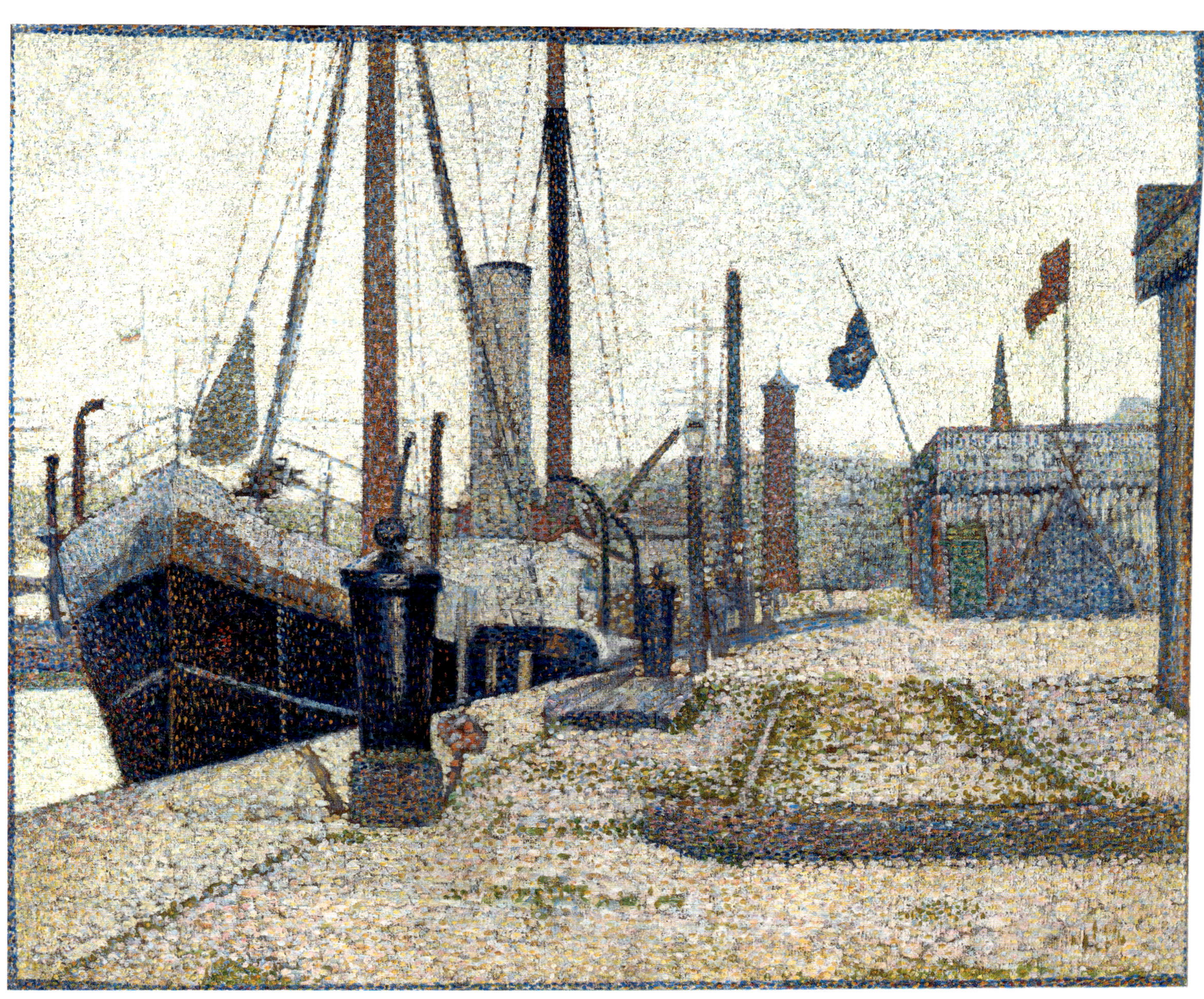

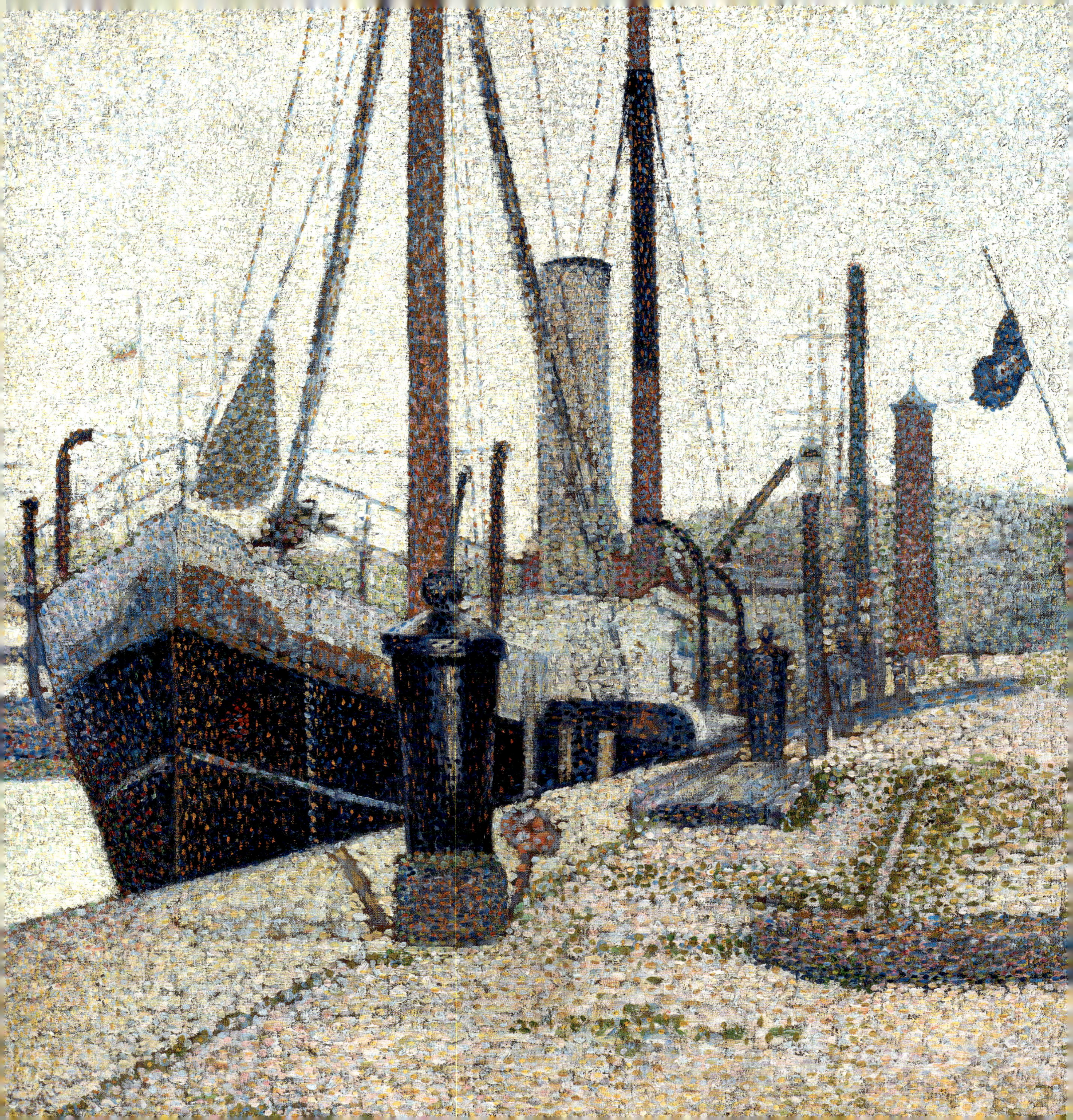

perspectival lines created by the position of the ship, the edge of the quay and the receding rail tracks used to bring merchandise for loading. Even Seurat's signature, in the lower left, follows the perspective and is painted at an angle, a unique occurrence in his oeuvre.

As with the other Honfleur works, the elements in the scene were first rendered in loose planes of colour, which were then covered by a surface of thick dots in a complementary hue. The painted border was added several years later; by then, Seurat had refined his style and was using thinner dots, some of which have floated from the border into the image itself, creating a transition between the two.

The present painting was acquired by the National Gallery, Prague, in 1923 as part of a large purchase of French Impressionist and Post-Impressionist paintings, sculpture and drawings by the new Czechoslovak state. Seurat's painting had been exhibited in Prague, alongside 388 other works, in May of that year at the groundbreaking *Exhibition of 19th- and 20th-Century French Art*, organised by the Mánes Association of Fine Artists (named after the Czech artist Josef Mánes). The works had been sourced from Parisian dealers and the ambitious purchase for the national Modern Gallery of several dozen paintings and sculpture by Post-Impressionist and avant-garde artists, including Paul Cézanne, Vincent van Gogh, Pierre-Auguste Renoir, Pablo Picasso and Georges Braque, as well as Seurat, transformed its holdings.

11

Port-en-Bessin – A Sunday

1888, reworked c. 1889
Oil on canvas
66 × 82 cm
Kröller-Müller Museum, Otterlo

DR 189
H 191

Exhibitions

1889 Brussels (*Port-en-Bessin – Un dimanche*)
1890 Paris

Provenance

Probably by inheritance to the artist's mother, Ernestine
Seurat (née Faivre; 1828–1899), Paris, 1891; acquired from
Henry Van de Velde (1863–1957) by Karl Ernst Osthaus
(1874–1921), Hagen, 1906; acquired from his estate by
Helene Kröller-Müller (1869–1939), The Hague, 1921;
donated by the Kröller-Müller Foundation to the Dutch
state, 1935

After staying in Paris in the summer of 1887, Georges Seurat returned to the coast in 1888. He settled in Port-en-Bessin, located twenty or so kilometres from Grandcamp. The six remarkable paintings he produced there are brought back together in this exhibition for the first time since they were unveiled at the *Sixth Exhibition of Les XX* in Brussels in February 1889.

Scholars have noted how the group could be seen as forming a composite image of the town.[31] As one art historian remarked, 'One could almost describe it as a set of views and counter-views that create an underlying sense of visual control.'[32] Three paintings depict different locations around the small port while the three others were taken from the surrounding hills, with certain features recurring over several works. The sequence seems to start with the present painting, which is listed first of the group in exhibition catalogues during Seurat's lifetime. The painter positioned himself inside the inner basin, looking out towards moored ships bedecked with flags and to the outer harbour and sea beyond. The flutter of the pennants echoes the shape of the scalloped clouds behind them. The French flags indicate that this may not be an ordinary Sunday but a feast day (see fig. 59), although the weekly return to port on Saturday after long days at sea was always cause for celebration.[33] Nevertheless, as in Seurat's other seascapes, the quays remain almost entirely devoid of human presence, although one perceives, in the middle distance, a few stick figures crossing the swivelling steel bridge featured in *Port-en-Bessin – The Bridge and the Quays* (cat. 12).

At its unveiling in Brussels, the present painting made a particular impression on the head of Les XX, Octave Maus, who wrote:

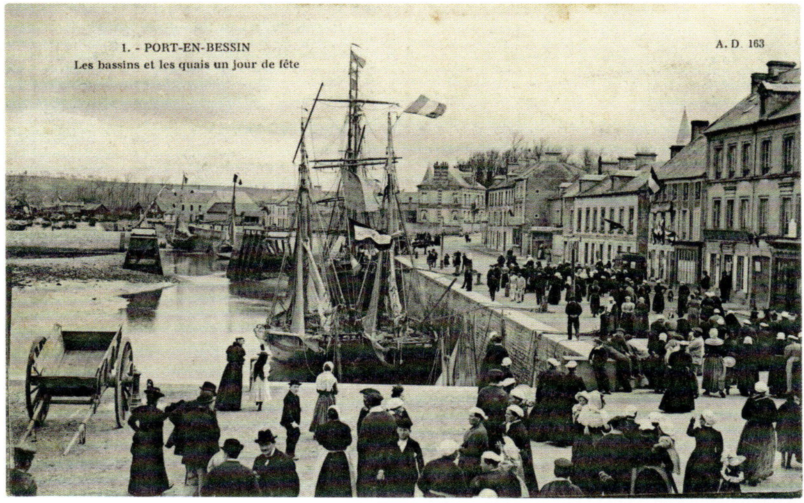

59. Postcard of Port-en-Bessin, 'The Harbours and the Quays on a Day of Celebration', late 19th century, private collection

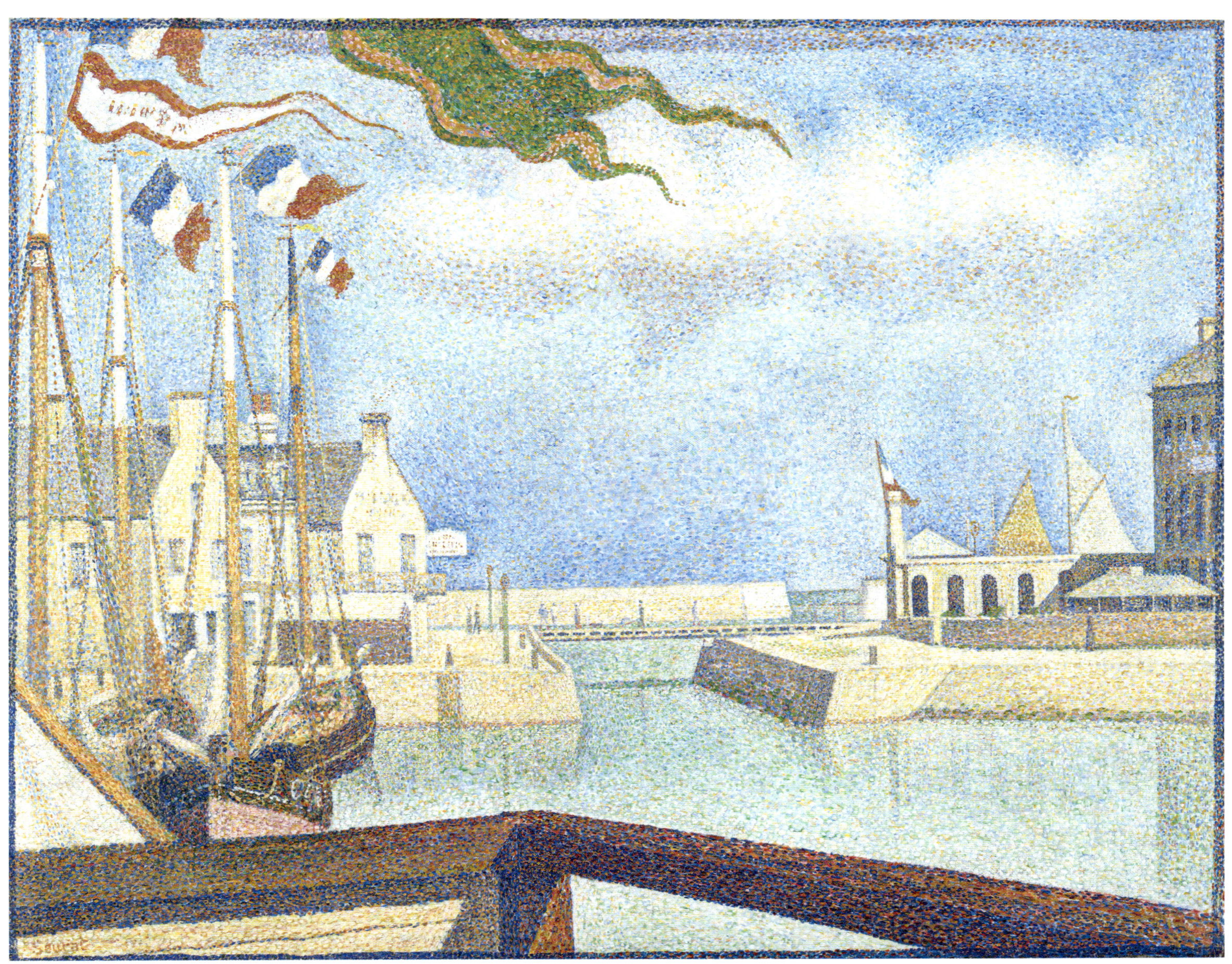

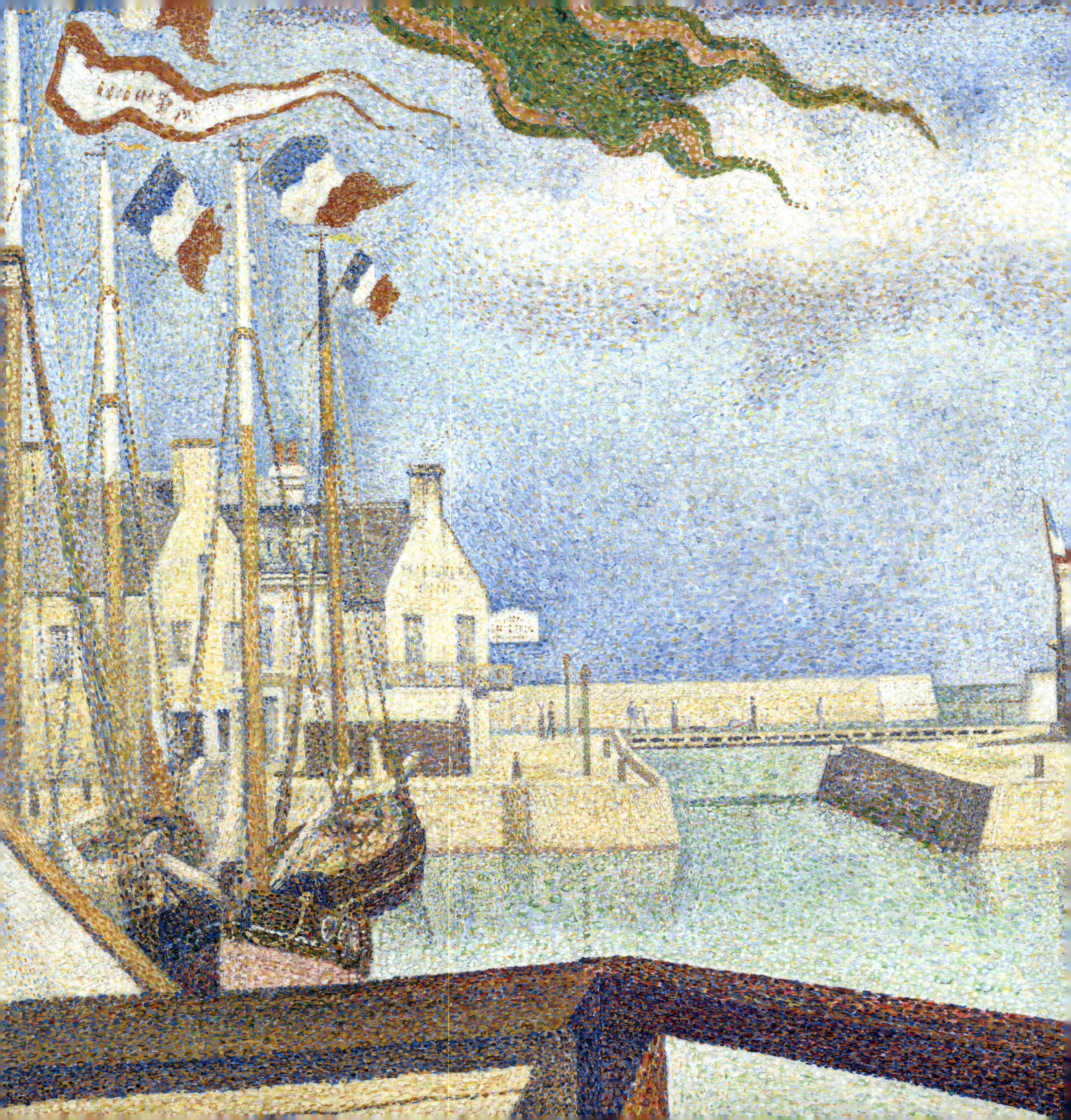

And the eye rejoices in following, alongside the artist, the straight quays,
the jetties, the bridges, the piers, dominated by the grassy mass of the cliffs;
in probing the depth of the green water marbled by the fleeting shadows of the
clouds; in measuring the height of the lighthouses; in searching the distant
horizon of the sea. More than any other canvas, *A Sunday* appealed: it offers,
in the [p]ort strewn with flags, the contemplative impression of hard-won rest,
and the solitude of its quays, and the sweetness of a peaceful day.[34]

Despite this perception of quiet and serenity, the composition is an unusual
combination of sharp angles and abrupt cropping, alongside more whimsical
elements such as the fluttering flags and wave-shaped cloud. The balustrade
in the foreground provides a sense of depth but equally emphasises the flat,
triangular shapes found throughout the work, such as the section of a mast in
the lower left, the sunlit sides of the houses lining the quays and the top of the
sails awkwardly poking out above the low building on the right.

Like the other Port-en-Bessin paintings (with the exception of *The Outer
Harbour (Low Tide)* [cat. 13]), the present work is framed by a painted border,
added on top of the existing composition, probably several months later. It is
mostly composed of tight dark blue dots, with looser additions of red, orange
and green to complement the colours in the adjacent areas of the composition.

12

Port-en-Bessin – The Bridge and the Quays

1888, reworked c. 1889
Oil on canvas
66 × 83.2 cm
Minneapolis Institute of Art
The William Hood Dunwoody Fund

DR 187
H 188

Exhibitions

1889 Brussels (*Port-en-Bessin – Le pont et les quais*)
1889 Paris

Provenance

Perhaps [Galerie Barbazanges, Paris]; Salomon van
Deventer (1888–1972), Wassenaar and The Hague, from
1913 until at least 1937 (owned jointly with [Étienne
Bignou, Paris], by 1934–35; acquired from [Paul
Rosenberg, New York] by [Alex. Reid & Lefevre, London],
1937; acquired from them by Lady Edith Chester Beatty
(née Dunn; 1886–1952), London, 1937; by inheritance
to her husband, Sir Alfred Chester Beatty (1875–1968),
Dublin, 1952; acquired from him by [Paul Rosenberg,
New York], 1955; acquired from him by the Minneapolis
Institute of Art, December 1955

The swivelling steel bridge seen in the distance in *Port-en-Bessin – A Sunday* (cat. 11) takes centre stage in the present work. With the exception of *The Semaphores and the Cliff* (cat. 16), Georges Seurat's Port-en-Bessin paintings focus less on the sea than on the modern infrastructure of the expanding port. The bridge was inaugurated only eight years earlier, to span the entrance to the new basin.[35] Further in the distance are other recent additions: an oil lamp post to light the port at night, a large freshwater fountain and a metallic structure to house the fish market, built in 1879 and depicted by Paul Signac during his 1884 stay (fig. 48). On top of the cliffs is the new semaphore ('*maison des feux*'), inaugurated that September.[36] A contemporary postcard, taken from the same vantage point, attests to the precision with which Seurat rendered his surroundings (fig. 60).

An unusual feature of *Port-en-Bessin – The Bridge and the Quays* are the three figures in the foreground: an officer, head bowed and strolling; a small child facing the viewer (reminiscent of those in the postcard looking at the photographer); and a woman with a pannier on her back. Seurat's Parisian production was full of human presence but this development in his seascapes was not welcomed by critics. Reviewing the *Fifth Salon des Indépendants* in 1889 (where the present painting was the only one shown out of the whole Port-en-Bessin group), Félix Fénéon lamented

one would want the figures walking along the quay of *Port-en-Bessin* to be less stiff: while the appearance of the wandering baby [in English in the original] is charming and authentic, the nebulous customs officer and the woman carrying

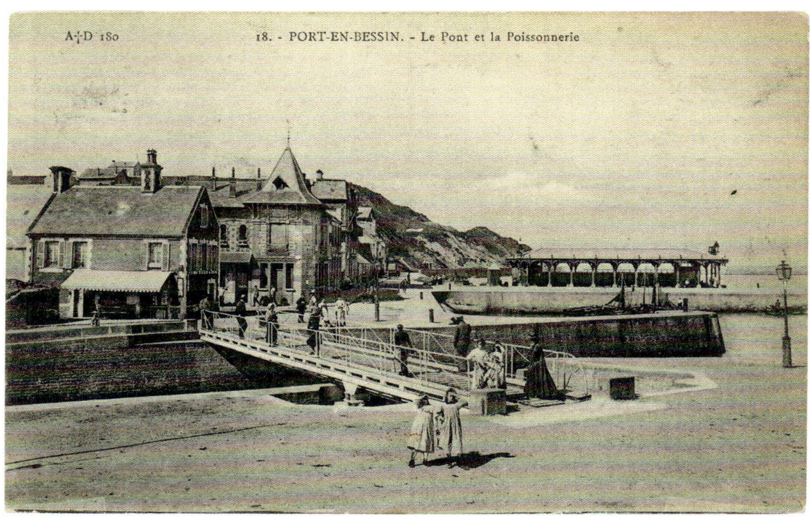

60. Postcard of Port-en-Bessin, 'The Bridge and the Fish Market', late 19th century, private collection

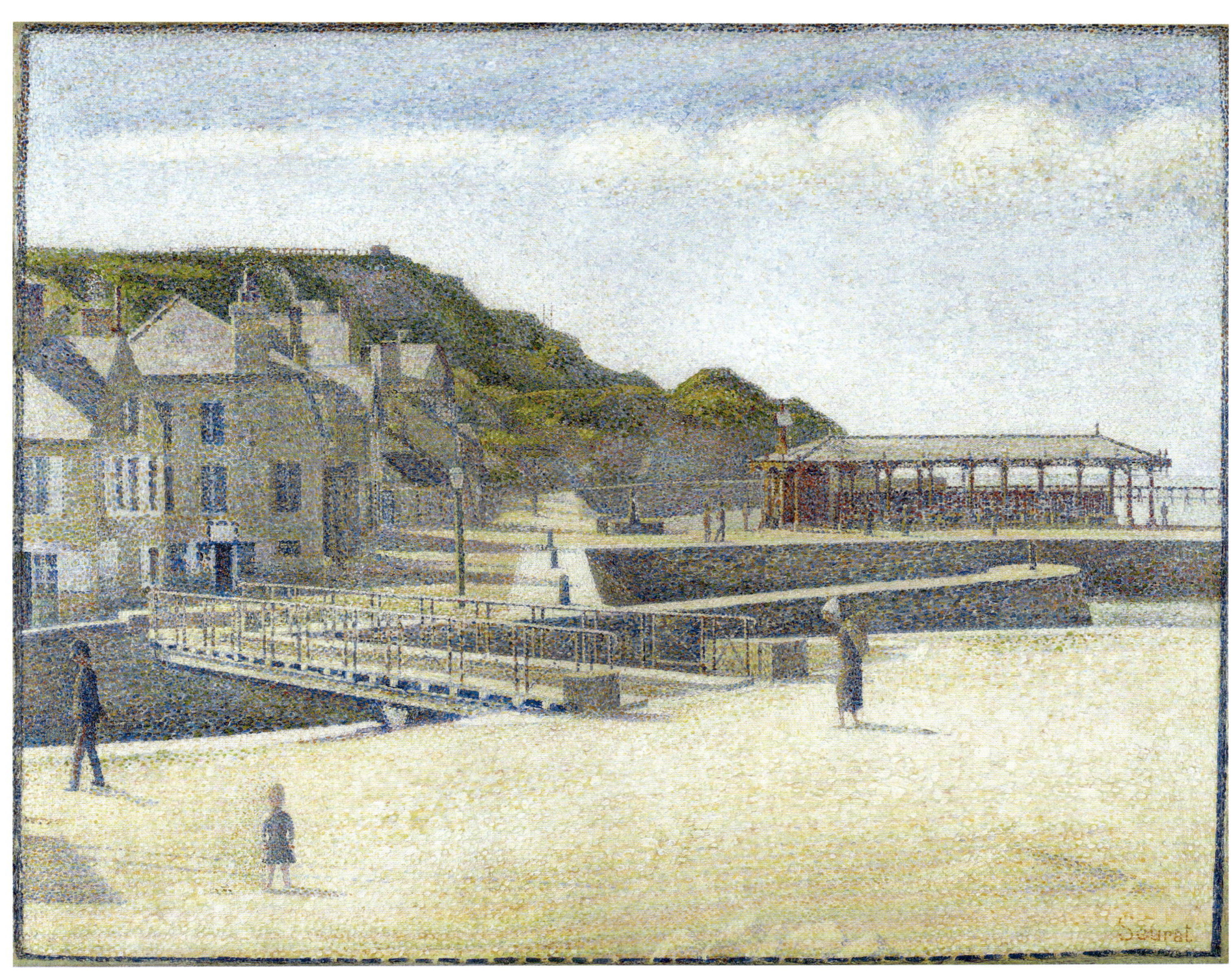

Seurat

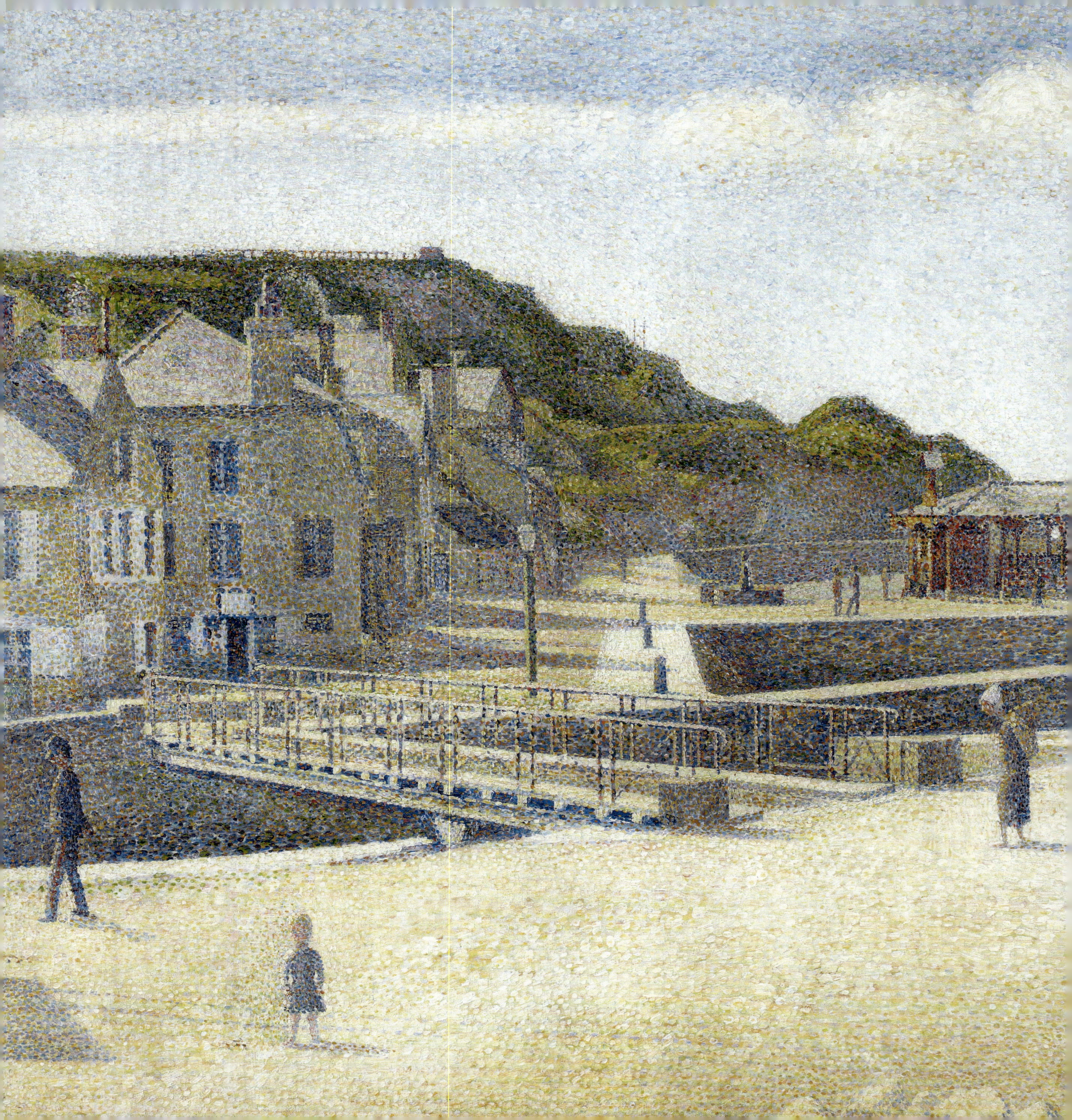

firewood or seaweed remain implausible; that customs officer, we have known
him for the past two years: he was the ringmaster in the *Parade* by the same
Mr Seurat.[37]

As he had in *A Sunday* (cat. 11), Seurat also added a few indistinct figures in the
middle distance, hovering around the fish market and on the quays.

Like all but one of the Port-en-Bessin paintings, *The Bridge and the Quays*
received a painted border that runs over the existing composition and was
added after its completion, probably in early 1889. The border is relatively
simple (compared to what was to come in later paintings) and composed
of large blue marks enlivened by red and orange dots. The border becomes
exclusively dark blue when it meets the light yellow of the foreground in the
lower third of the canvas. Strikingly, the line of Morse code-like horizontal
dashes in the bottom border echoes the openings on the side of the bridge.

13

Port-en-Bessin – The Outer Harbour (Low Tide)

1888
Oil on canvas
54.3 × 66.7 cm
Saint Louis Art Museum

DR 184
H 189

Exhibitions

1889 Brussels (*Port-en-Bessin – L'avant-port [marée basse]*)
1890 Paris

Provenance

G. de La Hault (d. 1901), Brussels and/or Paris, by 1890
and until at least 1892; Théo van Rysselberghe (1862–
1926), Brussels, by 1904 and until at least 1908; Charles
Pacquement, Paris, by 1922 and until at least 1928;
acquired from [George Bernheim, Paris] by [Knoedler
& Co., New York, London and Paris], February 1929;
acquired from them by the Saint Louis Art Museum,
December 1933 or January 1934

Life on the coast of Normandy followed the rhythm of the tide, which dictated when boats could leave and enter port. In the present painting, the outer harbour of Port-en-Bessin is almost entirely dry and a boat rests at an awkward angle on the sand. For his third and final painting at quay level, Georges Seurat positioned himself at the outermost point of the jetty and looked back towards the town and the entrance to the inner port. An indication of the height of the stone jetties is given by the strange element in the foreground, which turns out to be the top of the mast and gathered sail of another boat, moored directly below.

Like many of Seurat's seascapes, *Port-en-Bessin – The Outer Harbour (Low Tide)* is composed of an open space in the foreground, a band of constructions in the middle distance and an expanse of sky beyond. Rather than the sea, the real subject matter of the painting is the complex structure of the port, with its double harbour, inner basins and modern infrastructure. Consisting of geometrical lines and assorted angles, the composition focuses on how the coast was ordered and tamed by modern industry.

Seurat's brush marks here are astonishingly varied, both in their size and shape. The stone structures are rendered with thick dots of light colour, while the shadows are depicted with much finer points of dark blue enlivened by orange and red. Crucially, the dots are not neatly placed side by side, as contemporary optical theory treatises mandated, but overlap to create a rich, dynamic and multicoloured surface. In some cases, a larger disc has been broken up with a dot of complementary hue applied in its centre.

The present painting is the only work from the Port-en-Bessin group without a painted border. As it was possibly sold in February 1889 (at the *Sixth Exhibition of Les XX* where the canvases were unveiled) and was thus out of Seurat's hands thereafter, it could provide the earliest date for when the borders on the other paintings were added. Its purchase is one of only three recorded sales of canvases by Seurat in his lifetime (the other two being cat. 5 and 6).

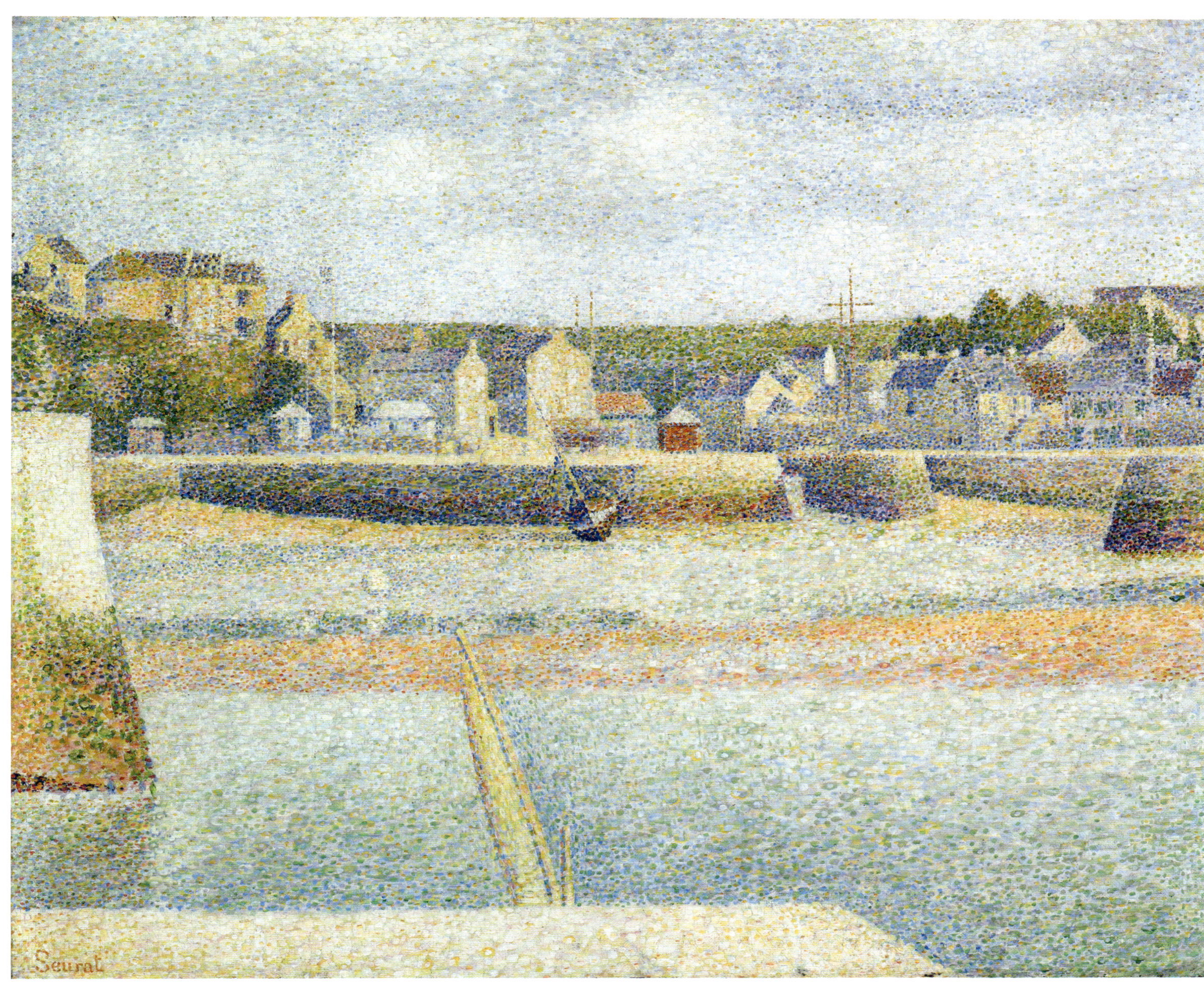
Seurat

14

Port-en-Bessin – The Outer Harbour (High Tide)

1888, reworked c. 1889
66 × 82 cm
Musée d'Orsay, Paris
Acquired thanks to funds from an anonymous
Canadian donation

DR 188
H 193

Exhibitions

1889 Brussels (*Port-en-Bessin – L'avant-port [marée haute]*)
1890 Paris

Provenance

By inheritance to the artist's mother, Ernestine Seurat
(née Faivre; 1828–1899), Paris, 1891; Paul Alexis (1847–
1901), Paris and Marseille, until at least 1900; Alfred
Lombard (1884–1973), Aix-en-Provence, 1923 and until at
least 1951; acquired from [Paul Rosenberg, New York] by
the Musée du Louvre, Paris, January 1952; transferred to
the Musée d'Orsay, Paris, 1977

This view taken from the tall cliffs west of town shows very clearly Port-en-Bessin's unique position, nestled in a recess in the coastline. After depicting three views of the port, Georges Seurat headed to the surrounding hills to complete three further paintings. The present one looks back towards the town and depicts familiar features, such as the fish market and stone jetties of the harbour, already seen in, respectively, *Port-en-Bessin – The Bridge and the Quays* (cat. 12) and *Port-en-Bessin – The Outer Harbour (Low Tide)* (cat. 13). The vantage point is one adopted by earlier artists and favoured by postcard publishers, who emphasised the sweeping view of the Normandy coast, all the way to the estuary of the Seine. In the late 1850s, the topographical lithographer Adolphe Maugendre (1809–1895) had also positioned himself there to produce a view of Port-en-Bessin before the construction of the inner basin, central jetty and other infrastructure (fig. 49). At the time, boats moored directly on the beach. A mere two decades and a half later, the port had been completely transformed.

Despite his precision in rendering the site, Seurat introduced here, as he did in other Port-en-Bessin paintings, a number of whimsical or artificial elements that seem drawn from his Parisian production. These include the wisps of tall grasses on the edge of the cliff, silhouetted against the sea like patterned decorations (see fig. 27), and the oversized boats in the harbour.

The blue frame around the painting is said to be by Seurat, although it was separated from the painting for many decades. The artist initially favoured flat, white frames for his works but began creating bespoke coloured frames around 1889 (some examples can be seen in fig. 13 and 14). He also retroactively fitted some earlier canvases with such frames at that time (fig. 26). The frames are always painted in a darker tone, most often dark blue or purple, but nuanced by the addition of dots of other colours contrasting with the adjacent hues on the canvas. Some aspects of the present frame, however, differ markedly from other known frames by Seurat: it does not share their flat profile and its application of paint is not so nuanced and refined.

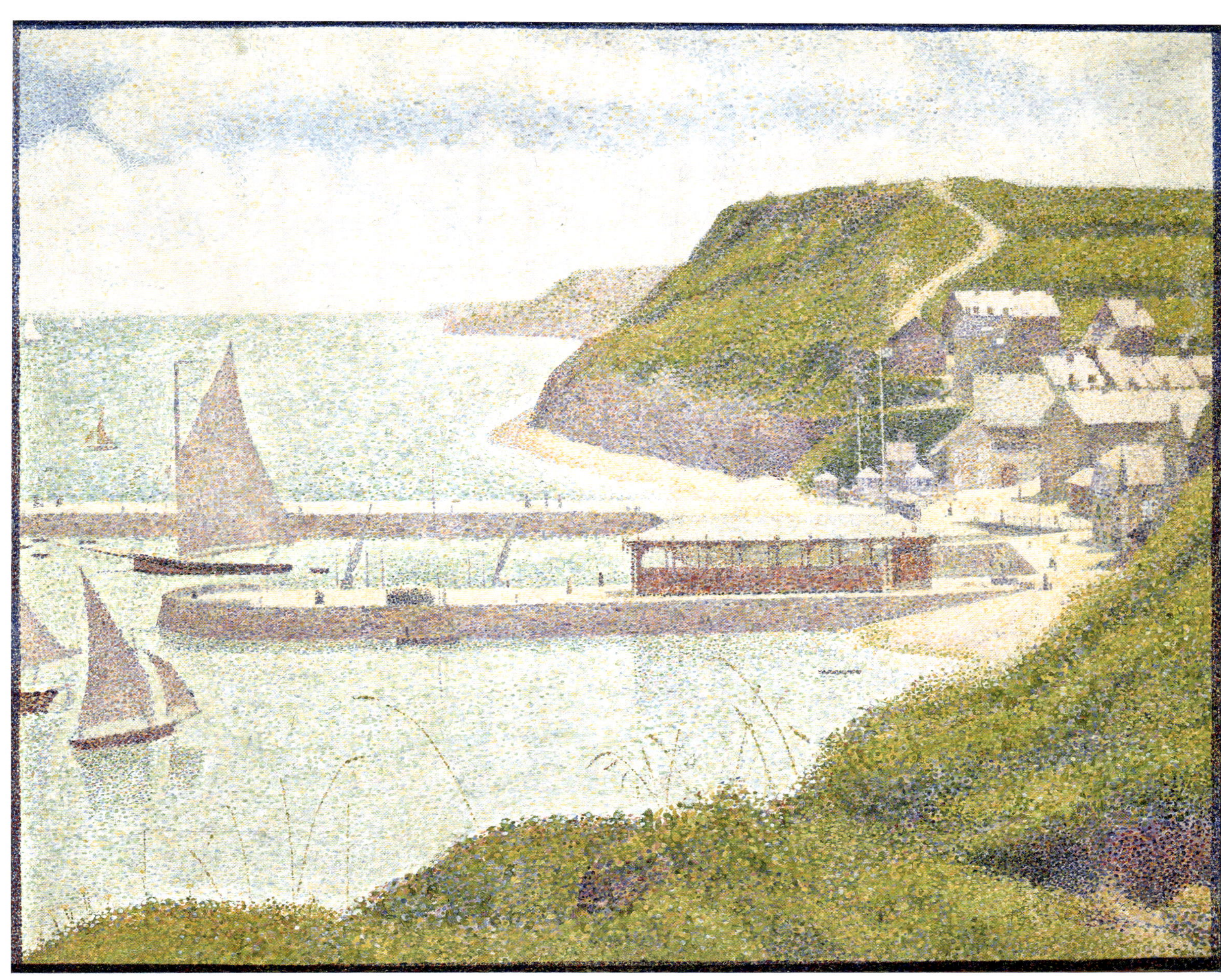

15

Port-en-Bessin, Entrance to the Outer Harbour

1888, reworked c. 1889
Oil on canvas
54.9 × 65.1 cm
The Museum of Modern Art, New York
Lillie P. Bliss Collection

DR 186
H 192

Exhibitions

1889 Brussels (*Port-en-Bessin – Les jetées*)
1890 Paris (*Port-en-Bessin, entrée de l'avant-port*)

Provenance

By inheritance to the artist's mother, Ernestine Seurat
(née Faivre; 1828–1899), Paris, 1891; by descent to her
daughter, Marie-Berthe (1847–1921), and son-in-law, Léon
Appert (1837–1925), Paris, 1899; [Étienne Bignou, Paris];
[Alex. Reid & Lefevre, London] by 1926; jointly owned with
[Knoedler & Co., New York], December 1926; acquired
from the latter by Lillie P. Bliss (1864–1931), New York, July
1927; bequeathed by her to The Museum of Modern Art,
1934

Georges Seurat here captured a fleet of fishing boats leaving the safety of the harbour and heading out to the open sea, already dotted with other white sails. To paint this view, the artist remained in roughly the same spot as the one for *The Outer Harbour (High Tide)* (cat. 14) but rotated north, facing the two large stone jetties of the outer harbour, built in the early 1860s to protect Port-en-Bessin from the tides and currents of the Channel. A contemporary postcard depicts a similar moment but is taken from lower down on the hill (fig. 61). Instead of houses in the foreground, Seurat's painting opens on to a large expanse of sand and low vegetation, rendered in a mix of multicoloured dots of varying sizes and shapes. The surface of the canvas is covered by an initial layer of larger dots and criss-cross strokes, to which smaller points of colour were later added, especially to render the shadows. The patches of green vegetation in the foreground echo the large darker areas on the sea. They are presumably the shadows of passing clouds, as in *The Roadstead of Grandcamp* (cat. 3), rather than changes in the depth of the water. Their strangely regular distribution and their ellipsoidal shape constitute particularly stylised and patterned elements of the composition, like the scalloped cloud and flags in *A Sunday* (cat. 11) and the wisps of tall grass in *The Outer Harbour (High Tide)*. They play a key role in cueing us to Seurat's interest in creating light and shadow through colour. The soft and iridescent atmosphere of the northern coast is perfectly rendered in his nuanced application of varied dots.

In an unprecedented occurrence, Seurat changed the title of this work between its two exhibition displays. Titled *Port-en-Bessin – The Jetties* when it was first shown, with the rest of the group, in Brussels in February 1889, it became known as *Port-en-Bessin, Entrance to the Outer Harbour* when displayed in Paris the following year. The artist may have wanted the work's title to match those of the other representations of the harbour.

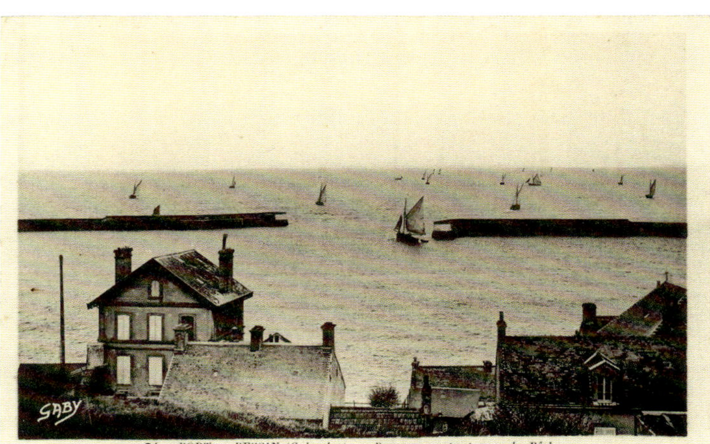

61. Postcard of Port-en-Bessin, 'Boats Leaving on a Fishing Trip', late 19th century, private collection

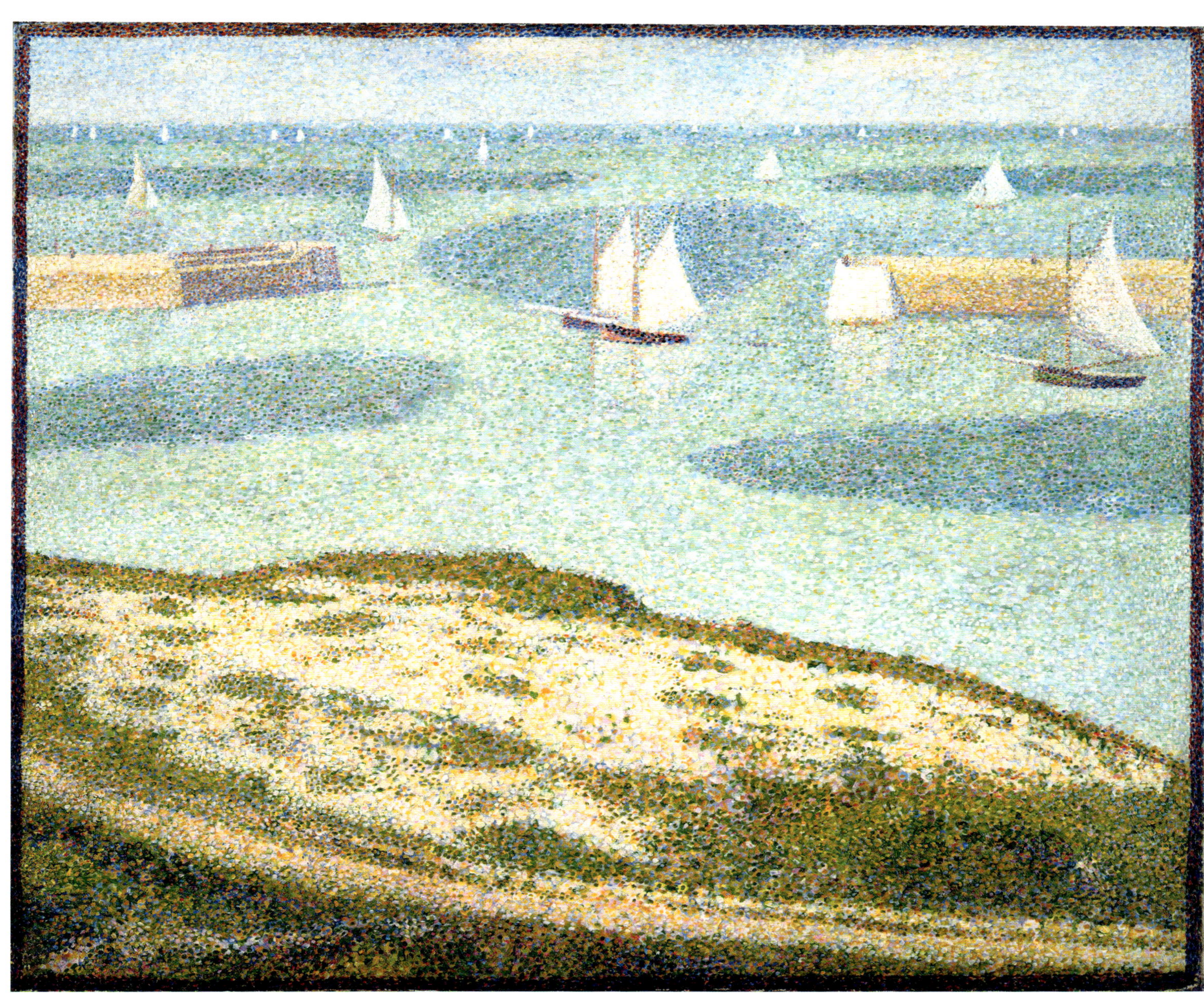

16

The Semaphores and the Cliff

1888, reworked c. 1889
Oil on canvas
65.1 × 80.9 cm
National Gallery of Art, Washington, D.C.
Gift of the W. Averell Harriman Foundation in memory
of Marie N. Harriman

Exhibitions

1889 Brussels (*Les Grues et la Percée*)
1890 Paris

Provenance

By inheritance to the artist's mother, Ernestine Seurat
(née Faivre; 1828–1899), Paris, 1891; by descent to her
daughter, Marie-Berthe (1847–1921), and son-in-law, Léon
Appert (1837–1925), Paris, 1899; acquired from him and his
son Léopold by Félix Fénéon (1861–1944), Paris, probably
March 1924; acquired from him by Marie N. Harriman
(1903–1970), New York, September 1937; by inheritance to
her husband, W. Averell Harriman (1891–1986), New York,
1970; gifted by the W. Averell Harriman Foundation, New
York, to the National Gallery of Art, 1972

The present work is one of three views painted from the cliffs surrounding Port-en-Bessin (see also cat. 14 and 15). Moving away from the port, Georges Seurat made his way to higher ground to depict the town and its coastline. This painting is an outlier amongst the six created that summer as it turns its back to the harbour to focus on the dramatic cliffs and open sea to the west. However, even this view retains signs of human activity with the inclusion on the clifftop in the upper left of the new semaphore inaugurated on 2 September that year and a large buoy out at sea.

The painting's seemingly mysterious French title, *'Les Grues et la percée'* – chosen by Seurat – is in fact very much anchored in its location. *'Les Grues'* (literally 'the cranes') was the name given to a site on the cliffs just west of town since at least the Napoleonic era and probably stems from an early semaphore built there. At that period, semaphores were large structures with moving arms; by pivoting these indicators to predetermined positions, information could be quickly relayed from tower to tower. By Seurat's time, the arms had been replaced with light signals. *'La Percée'* similarly refers to a local landmark, 'la Pointe de la Percée', a slip of land protruding into, or 'piercing', the sea – a prominent feature in the middle distance of Seurat's painting. Like *'Les Grues'*, the area retains that name today, although it has changed dramatically due to multiple landslides of the limestone cliffs over the past century and bombing during the Second World War.[38] For the English title, we have followed the one proposed by Robert L. Herbert for the 1991 Seurat retrospective, although it does not satisfactorily convey Seurat's knowledge of the local topography and his attentiveness to the sites he depicted.[39]

The Port-en-Bessin paintings demonstrate the striking development of Seurat's 'method'. The painter began the present work with the same application of paint in criss-cross strokes or large directional dashes found in the Honfleur paintings two years earlier. This step was crucial to map out the composition and place all the elements. Despite the looser brushstrokes, the approach was slow and methodical. As he had done in earlier canvases and *croquetons*, he also continued to leave the support or white ground visible and used it as a light tone in his overall colour scheme, mostly in the water and sky. This approach reached a new level of refinement and nuance in the Port-en-Bessin paintings, as seen in the surface treatment of the present work. It is only in the top layer that Seurat applied a dusting of thin dots to map out the shadows, sharpen the edge of the cliffs and shape the various elements of the composition. While key to the overall balance, this final pass also shows a certain levity and playfulness in the distribution of the dots of colours across the canvas to ensure that the viewer's eye moves around the image.[40]

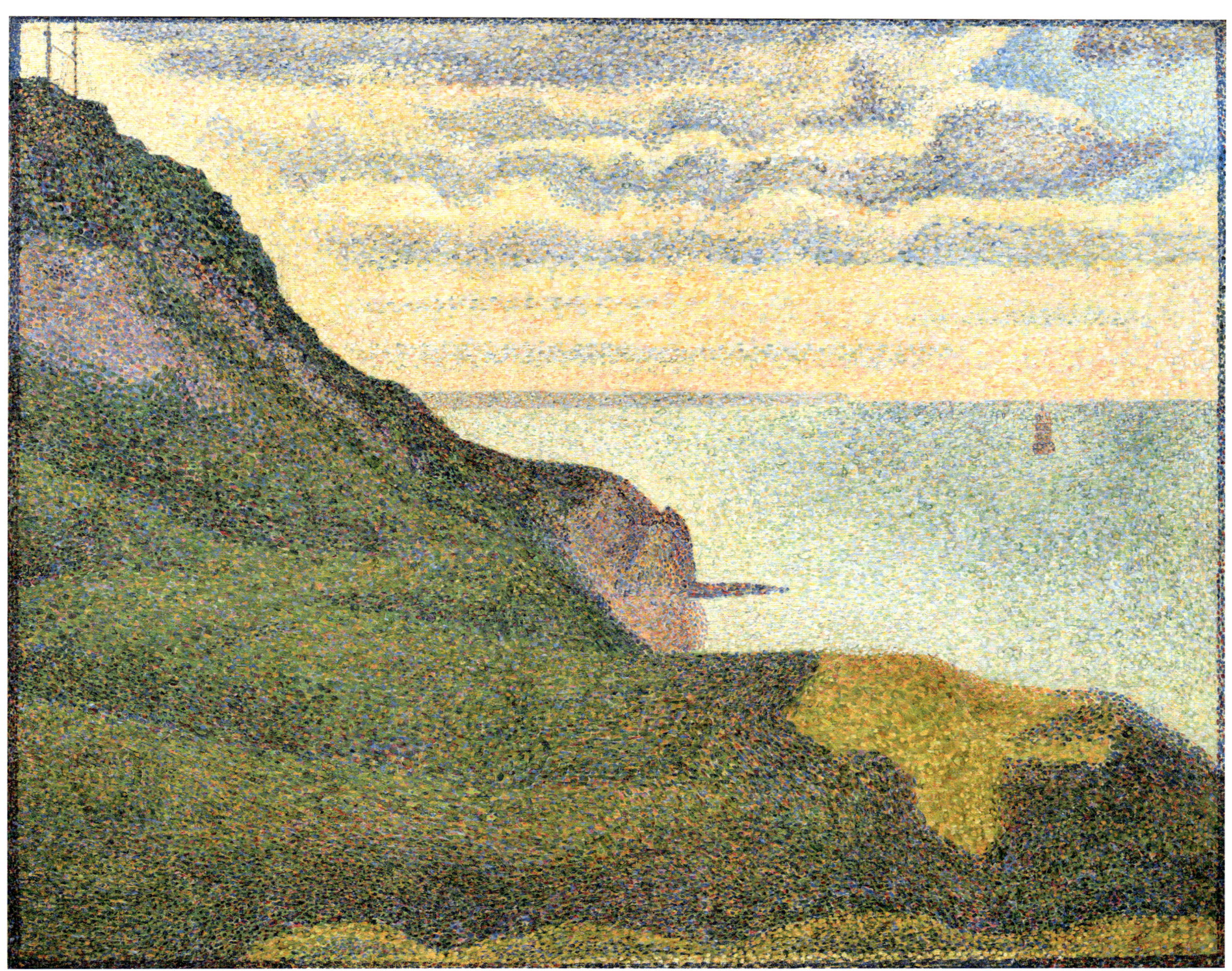

17

Le Crotoy (Downstream)

1889
Oil on canvas
70.5 × 86.4 cm
Private collection

DR 192
H 195

Exhibitions
1889 Paris (*Le Crotoy [aval]*)
1891 Brussels

Provenance
Edmond Picard (1836–1924), Brussels, by 1892; his sale, [Galerie J. & A. Le Roy Frères, Brussels], 26 March 1904, lot 54; perhaps Count Harry Kessler, Weimar, and his sale, [Hôtel Drouot, Paris], 16 May 1908, lot 40; acquired there by [Bernheim-Jeune, Paris], and held until at least 1911; Richard Goetz (1874–1954), Paris, by 1914; his property sequestered by the French state during the First World War; sale of his sequestered property, [Hôtel Drouot, Paris], 23 February 1922, lot 180; acquired there by 'Loewenstein' (perhaps Wilhelm Loewenstein, who probably returned it to Goetz); Richard Goetz, Paris, by 1935; [Galerie Hector Brame, Paris]; acquired jointly by [Knoedler & Co., New York] and [Jacques Seligmann & Co., New York], November 1935; acquired from the latter by Edward G. (1893–1973) and Gladys Lloyd (1895–1971) Robinson, Beverly Hills, February 1938 and held until 1957; acquired from [Knoedler & Co., New York] by Stavros Niarchos, Athens and Paris, February 1957

For his 1889 summer campaign, Georges Seurat eschewed the dramatic coastline of Normandy and moved further north to the town of Le Crotoy, located on the estuary of the river Somme. Instead of cliffs, the region offered low sand dunes, which must have appealed to Seurat's love of depicting large expanses of sand. He made only two paintings that summer, and no *croquetons* or drawings from that time are known. It may be that his time in Le Crotoy was cut short but the paintings he produced – the present work and *Le Crotoy (Upstream)* (fig. 13) – are incredibly intricate and refined. They both demonstrate a certain level of abstraction as forms are smoothed and somewhat subjugated to the decorative patterns created by the tight application of dots of colour.

The two Crotoy paintings see Seurat continue his detailed exploration of a specific site, as he had the previous year in Port-en-Bessin. This approach is attested by the symmetrical titles he gave the paintings – *Upstream* and *Downstream*. While the first canvas looks out from the estuary towards the town, the present work turns back to the mouth of the river, capturing the houses along the beach. It follows Seurat's preferred composition of a diagonal cutting the surface in the foreground and a large expanse beyond, marked by the horizontal bands of the water line and low dunes in the distance. The breadth of the beach is indicated by a few vertical lines representing tiny figures on the sand.

Nevertheless, the Crotoy paintings mark a major shift in Seurat's seascapes. The artist is no longer preoccupied with rendering port activity and eschews the tight and deliberately congested compositions of Honfleur and Port-en-Bessin in favour of more expansive vistas. Even without looking out to sea, Seurat manages, in these works and those made the following year in Gravelines, to create open, sweeping views.

Unusually, the Crotoy paintings were not finished over the winter in Paris but exhibited that September at the *Fifth Salon des Indépendants*. Although a staunch supporter of Seurat, the critic Félix Fénéon was wary of new developments in Seurat's seascapes, most notably the introduction of more decorative patterns reminiscent of the backgrounds of his large figural canvases. He objected to the billowing forms in the sky, noting 'The shell-like clouds of *Crotoy (Morning)* are not very convincing.'[41] Similarly, the flat silhouettes of the two large sailboats, like the one in *The Channel of Gravelines: An Evening* (cat. 22), are, in the words of the art historian Robert L. Herbert, 'more like emblems of the sea coast than active presences'.[42]

The Crotoy paintings were the first of Seurat's seascapes to be given a centimetre-wide border (not visible in this reproduction) conceived at the same time as the composition – a development also found in Seurat's Parisian production. They were complemented by a bespoke wide frame with a flat profile, painted with great delicacy to extend and balance the overall colour

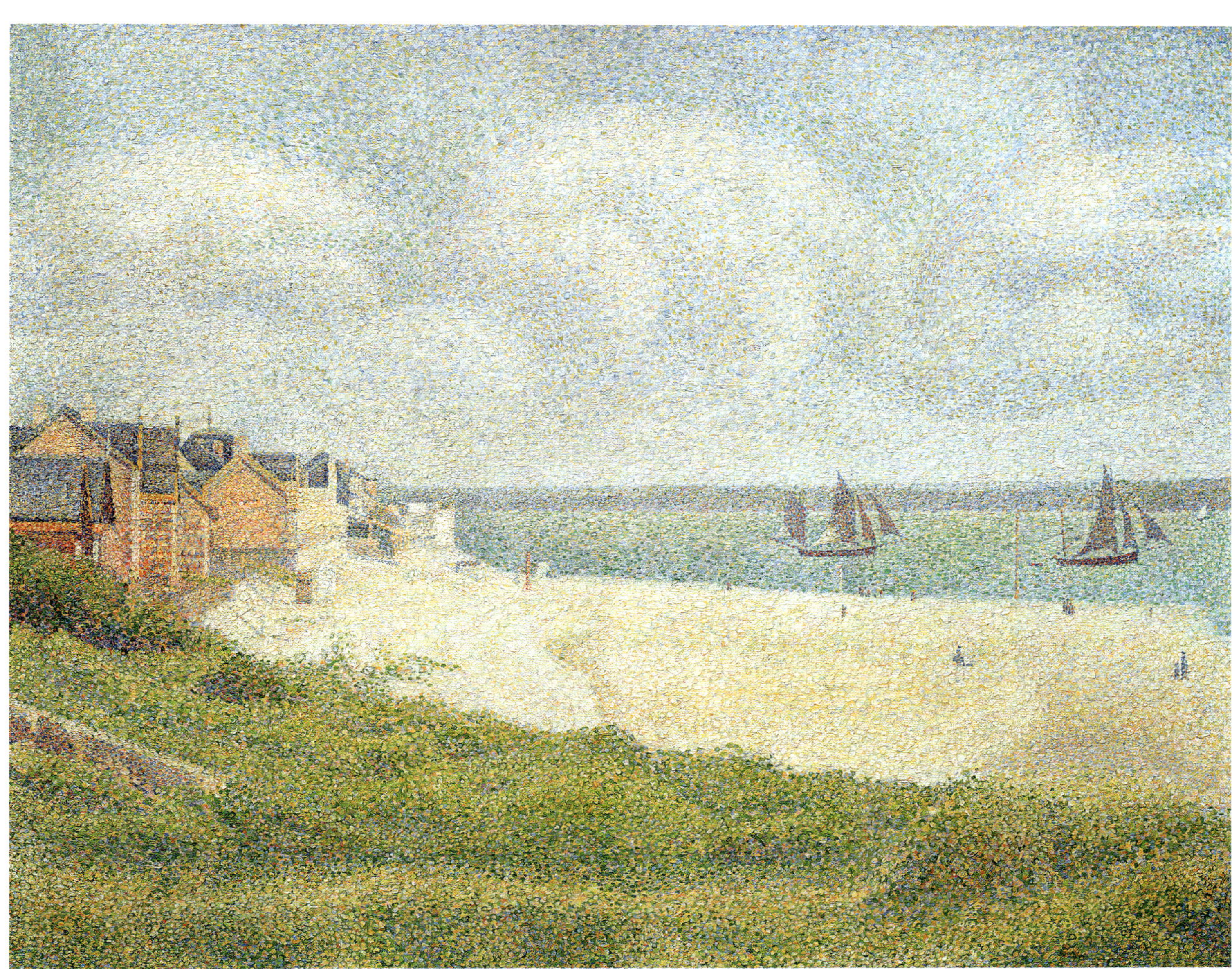

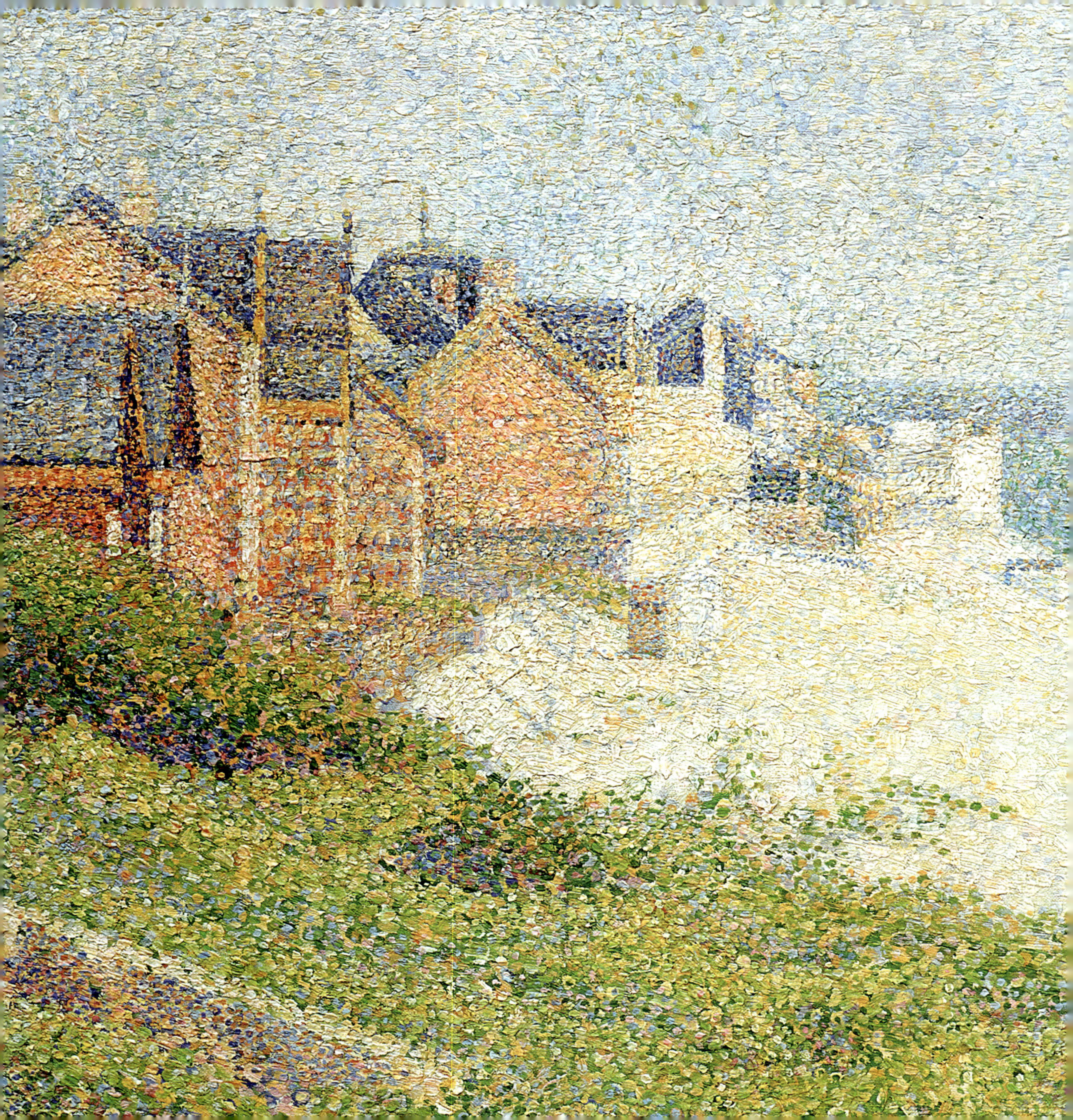

scheme. The frame for *Le Crotoy (Upstream)* survives while the one for the present painting is known only through a rare early photograph (fig. 14).

Le Crotoy (Downstream) was included in the seminal exhibition *Manet and the Post-Impressionists* at the Grafton Galleries in London in 1910. The exhibition aimed to introduce the British public to the work of Paul Cézanne, Vincent van Gogh and Paul Gauguin, artists who had – in the eyes of the organiser of the exhibition, the critic and painter Roger Fry (1866–1934) – taken forward and transformed the lessons of Impressionism. Fry coined the term 'Post-Impressionist' on that occasion. Seurat was represented by only two works, borrowed from Parisian dealers (the other was cat. 5) and had a reticent reception; an anonymous annotation next to the entry for *Le Crotoy (Downstream)* in one of the exhibition booklets reads: 'most people get stuck here'.[43] Fry himself initially had mixed feelings about Neo-Impressionism but would, in the late 1910s and 1920s, come to regard Seurat as one of the two most important figures of Post-Impressionism alongside Cézanne.[44]

18

The Channel of Gravelines: Grand-Fort-Philippe

1890
Oil on canvas
65 × 81 cm
National Gallery, London
Bought with the aid of a grant from the Heritage
Lottery Fund

DR 206
H 205

Exhibitions

1891 Brussels (*Le chenal de Gravelines : Grand Fort Philippe*)
1891 Paris

Provenance

By inheritance to the artist's mother, Ernestine Seurat
(née Faivre; 1828–1899), Paris, 1891; with her son-in-law,
Léon Appert (1837–1925), Paris, by 1900; [Étienne Bignou,
Paris]; acquired from [Alex. Reid & Lefevre, London]
by Samuel Courtauld (1876–1947), London, February
1926; by descent to his daughter, Sydney (1902–1954),
London, 1947; by inheritance to her husband, R.A. Butler
(1902–1982), 1954; by inheritance to his second wife,
Mollie Montgomery (1907–2005), 1982; acquired from her
by Heinz Berggruen (1914–2007), Paris, 1986; acquired
from him by the National Gallery, with the aid of a grant
from the Heritage Lottery Fund, 1995

Georges Seurat spent his last summer in the town of Gravelines, located between the ports of Calais and Dunkerque. In choosing this site, Seurat continued his move away from picturesque Normandy and towards the flatter, more austere – and less touristy – recesses of northern France. In the four large paintings created there (all of which are included in this exhibition), he focused exclusively on the canalised river Aa, which provided the seventeenth-century fortified town, situated slightly inland, with access to the sea. For the present painting, Seurat stationed himself in the hamlet of Petit-Fort-Philippe, where he was lodging, and looked towards the town of Grand-Fort-Philippe located west across the river. The foreground is occupied by an open expanse of sand while mooring posts line the banks of the canal and provide a dark contrast. The port's tall tide signal mast is visible in the distance. The painting is indicative of the increasing refinement of Seurat's technique. Although described by Camille Pissarro as 'a little white and weak in colour',[45] the Gravelines paintings display an incredible mastery of pigments, with the use of a range of tints – in the case of the present painting, yellow mixed with white – to create subtle tonal contrasts. In addition, the applied dots of colour, although never uniformly round, get thinner as they recess, aiding the impression of perspective.

The four Gravelines paintings mark a decisive shift from the works Seurat made in Normandy. In addition to a more restricted colour palette, the works are also much sparer. They inevitably respond to the specificities of the site – no longer a busy port amidst tall cliffs but a canal in a low region – but equally demonstrate a new interest on Seurat's part in capturing sweeping vistas and open skies. This move had begun the previous year in Le Crotoy but finds its fullest expression in the works made in Gravelines.

The 1920s saw an unprecedented interest in Seurat's works on the international art market. It is during that decade that six of his seven large canvases changed hands and were acquired by the private collectors who would eventually donate them to their permanent homes in European and American museums.[46] It was also at that time that the British industrialist and art collector Samuel Courtauld started purchasing works by Seurat, eventually amassing thirteen paintings and drawings for his private collection, in addition to the bold purchase of *Bathing, Asnières* (fig. 2) for the nation in 1924.[47] He acquired *The Channel of Gravelines: Grand-Fort-Philippe* in February 1926 and lent it two months later to the first monographic exhibition on Seurat in Britain, held at the premises of the newly opened commercial gallery Alex. Reid & Lefevre in London. Unlike *Beach at Gravelines* (cat. 26), the painting was not bequeathed to the Courtauld Institute of Art, founded by Courtauld and others in 1932, but to his daughter, Sydney, and later acquired by the National Gallery.

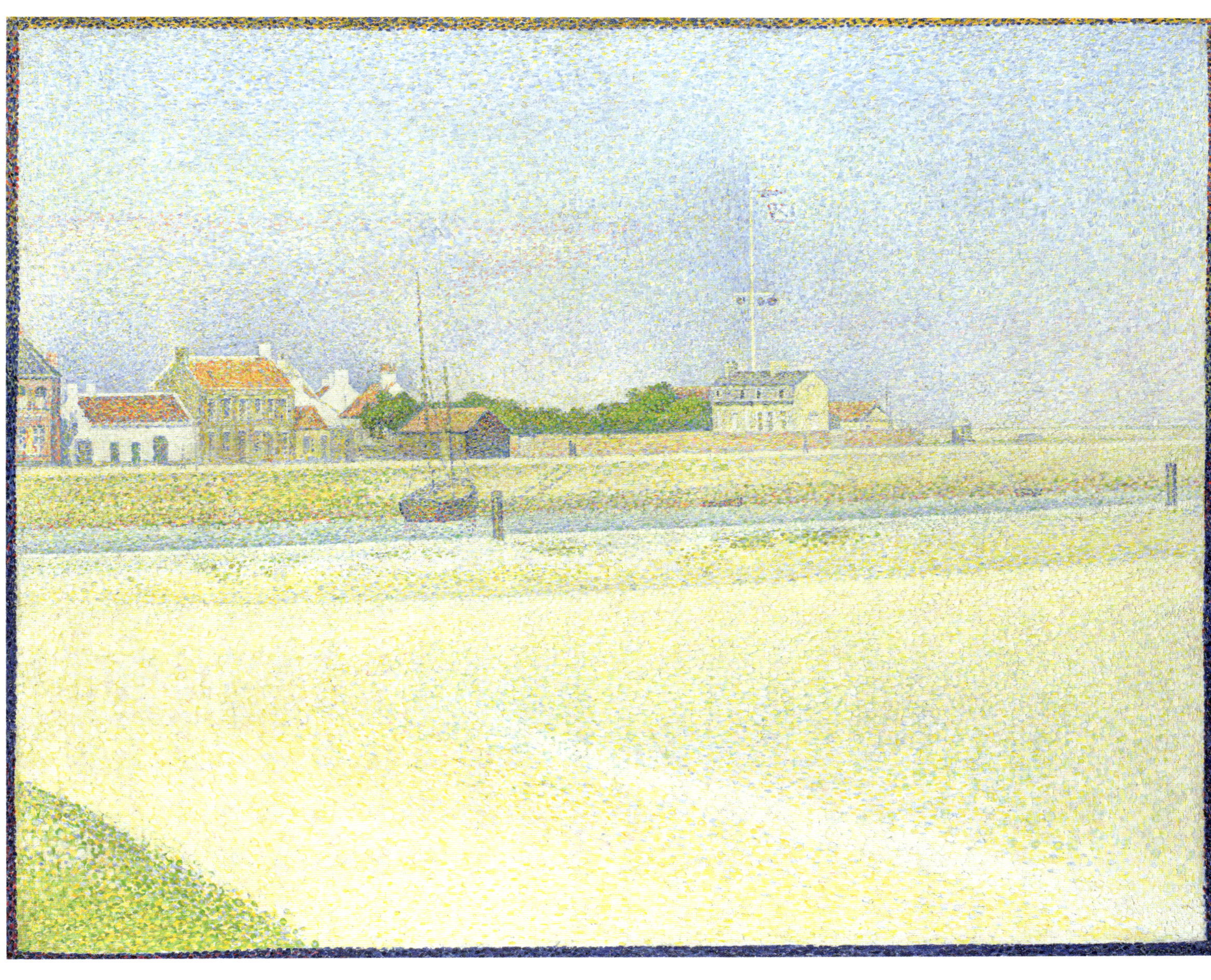

19

The Channel of Gravelines: Direction of the Sea

1890
Oil on canvas
73.5 × 92.3 cm
Kröller-Müller Museum, Otterlo

DR 207
H 206

Exhibitions

1891 Brussels (*Le chenal de Gravelines: direction de la Mer*)
1891 Paris

Provenance:
Probably by inheritance to the artist's partner, Madeleine Knobloch (d. 1903), Paris, 1891; Alexandre Braun (1847–1935), Brussels, by 1892 and at least until 1905; Théo van Rysselberghe (1862–1926), Brussels, by 1908; [Galerie Druet, Paris]; acquired by Helene Kröller-Müller (1869–1939), The Hague; donated by the Kröller-Müller Foundation to the Dutch state, 1935

The recurring motifs found throughout Georges Seurat's four Gravelines paintings attest to the small perimeter in which he was working. His favoured site was the outer harbour, an area where the canalised Aa widens slightly to allow boats to moor. This recess, framed by the hamlets of Grand-Fort-Philippe and Petit-Fort-Philippe on either side, is represented in the present painting. Beyond it, in the middle distance, one recognises the large expanse of yellow sand and mooring posts depicted in *The Channel of Gravelines: Grand-Fort-Philippe* (cat. 18). The same cove is seen from the other side of the river, with the white lighthouse more prominently foregrounded, in *The Channel of Gravelines: Petit-Fort-Philippe* (cat. 20). These deliberately planned and closely related vantage points around a site seem like a natural progression from Seurat's approach in Port-en-Bessin and Le Crotoy.

The thick painted borders that surround the Gravelines paintings were executed at the same time as the rest of the image, unlike those found in the Grandcamp, Honfleur and Port-en-Bessin works, added retroactively. Here, the border is dominated by dark blue but shows a rich and complex interweaving of multiple colours, whose prominence ebbs and flows to match the tones immediately adjacent. For example, orange is heavily present in the top border of the present painting, complementing the blue of the sky, while dark red in the lower section offsets the green vegetation next to it.

This painting is one of five works by Seurat acquired in the 1910s and early 1920s by the major German-born collector Helene Kröller-Müller, whose remarkable collection today forms the core of the Kröller-Müller Museum in Otterlo. Based in Rotterdam and later The Hague following her marriage to the Dutch entrepreneur Anton Kröller in 1888, Kröller-Müller championed modern art and collected widely, most especially the work of Vincent van Gogh (1853–1890). Her holdings of Seurat are equally remarkable, with four seascapes (the present painting, cat. 11, and fig. 18 and 20) and the large-scale canvas *Chahut* (1889–90).[48]

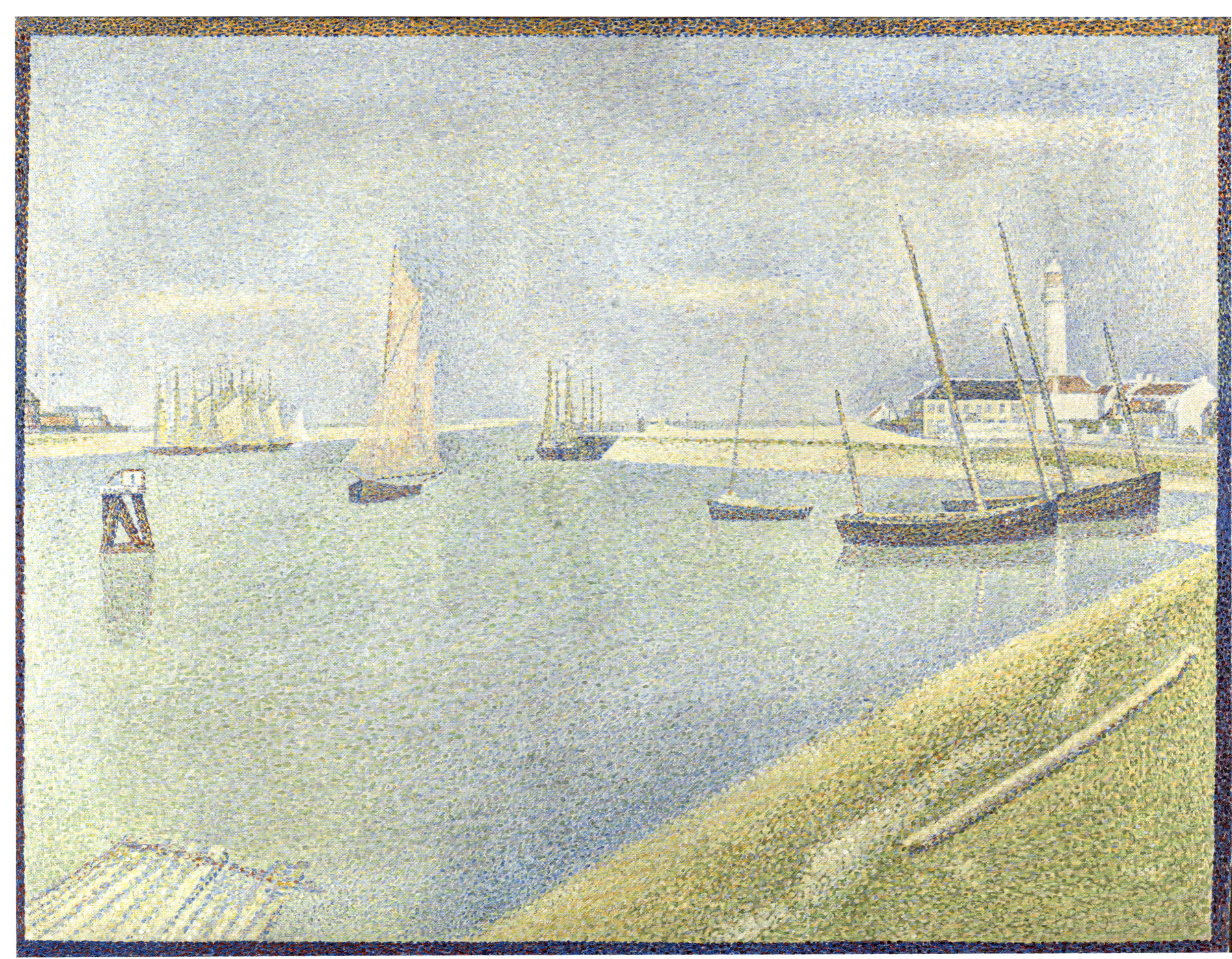

20

The Channel of Gravelines:
Petit-Fort-Philippe

1890
Oil on canvas
73.3 × 92.1 cm
Indianapolis Museum of Art at Newfields
Gift of Mrs. James W. Fesler in memory of Daniel W.
and Elizabeth C. Marmon

DR 205
H 208

Exhibitions

1891 Brussels (*Le chenal de Gravelines : Petit Fort Philippe*)
1891 Paris

Provenance

By inheritance to the artist's mother, Ernestine Seurat
(née Faivre; 1828–1899), Paris, 1891; by descent to her
daughter, Marie-Berthe (1847–1921), and son-in-law,
Léon Appert (1837–1925), 1899; probably by descent to
their son Léopold Appert (1867–1931), 1925; acquired from
him by [Alex. Reid & Lefevre, London], by 1926; D.W.T.
Cargill, Lanark, Scotland, by 1927 and until at least 1935;
[Bignou Gallery, New York] by 1937; on joint account with
[Knoedler & Co., New York], 1942; acquired from the latter
by Caroline Marmon Fesler (1878–1960), Indianapolis,
June 1945; gifted by her to the John Herron Art Institute,
now the Indianapolis Museum of Art at Newfields, 1945

The present painting is the only work out of the four Gravelines canvases to be made from across the river from Petit-Fort-Philippe, where Seurat was staying that summer. The painter has placed himself next to the tide signal station of Grand-Fort-Philippe, looking down the length of the canal towards the town of Gravelines itself, located slightly inland. In the centre of the composition is the small cove that was the subject of *The Channel of Gravelines: Direction of the Sea* (cat. 19).

In the Gravelines paintings, Seurat showed a striking ability to find a sense of space and expansion within the constricted surroundings of a canalised river surrounded by two towns. He uses the sweeping quay, with its receding line of mooring posts, to create a dynamic perspectival line and a feeling of recession absent from earlier seascapes. The single bollard in the foreground, whose upright form echoes the lighthouse in the upper left, grounds the viewer on the quay but also serves to accentuate the openness of the space behind it. Seurat had used a similar device in earlier compositions, most notably *Entrance of the Port of Honfleur* (cat. 8) and *The 'Maria' (Honfleur)* (cat. 10), but it is deployed to greater effect here. The post is a late addition, judging by its absence from the preparatory oil sketch for this painting (cat. 21), whose foreground is occupied by a moored sailing boat.

The shadows cast by the mooring post and the ledge of the quay onto the water indicate that the sun is low in the western sky and that Seurat painted a late afternoon scene. The art historian Ellen Lee suggested that the four Gravelines paintings were meant to render the light at different times of day: *Grand-Fort-Philippe* (cat. 18) has the bright clarity of the morning while the short, straight shadows in *Direction of the Sea* (cat. 19) could indicate noon. Dusk is represented by the pink glow – and title – of *An Evening* (cat. 22).[49] This sequence corresponds to the way the paintings were listed in both catalogues of the exhibitions in which they were presented in Seurat's lifetime.

In addition to the intricate painted borders on the canvases themselves, Seurat also created bespoke frames for the Gravelines paintings, meant to extend their colour harmonies and isolate the images from their immediate surroundings. The loss of these frames inevitably compromises our perception of the works and understanding of Seurat's intention. The wide blue frame on the present painting is a modern addition, created by the Indianapolis Museum of Art in 1982 in an effort to capture some of the contrasts sought by Seurat.

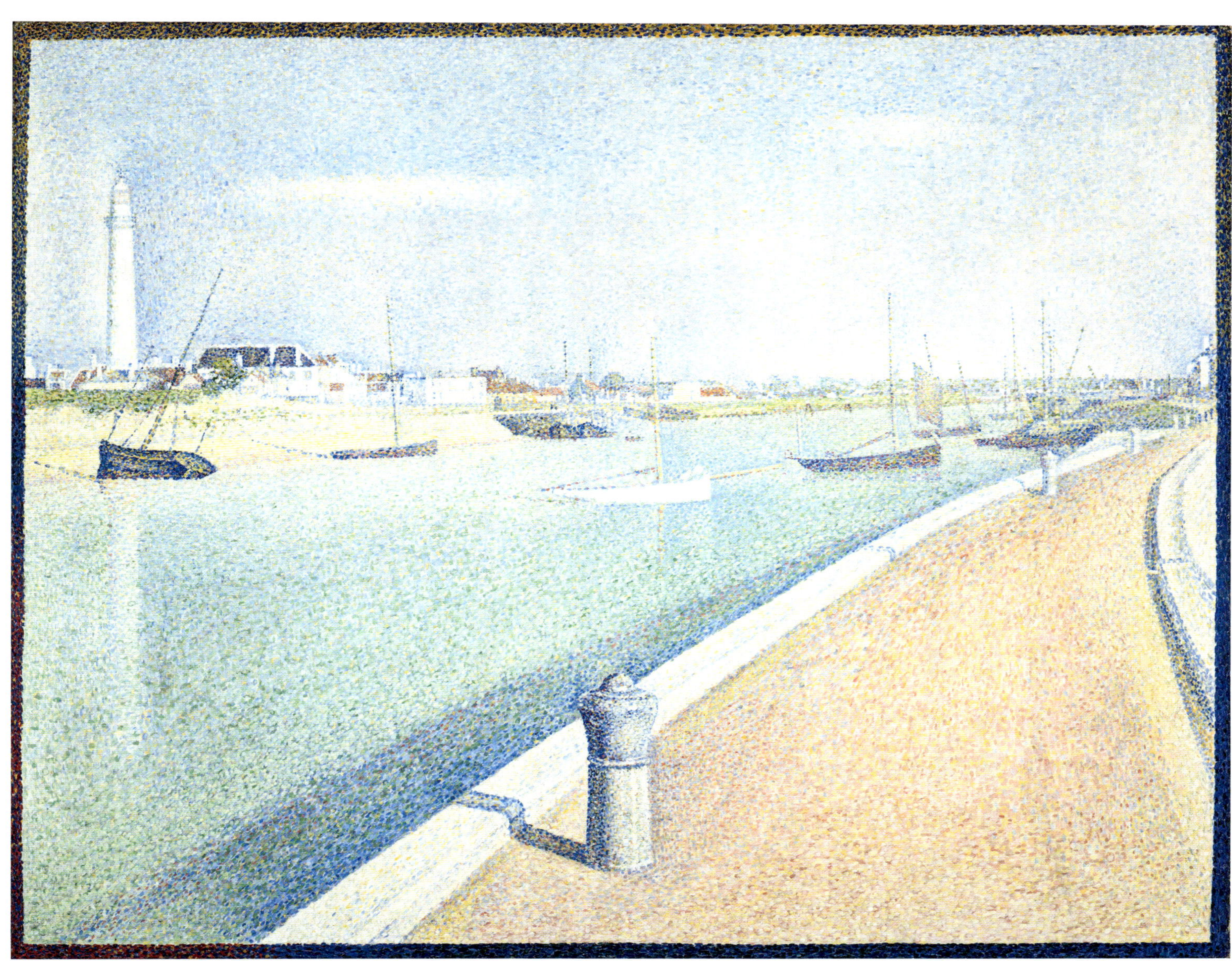

21

Study for The Channel of Gravelines: Petit-Fort-Philippe

1890
Oil on wood panel
15.9 × 25.1 cm
The Nelson-Atkins Museum of Art, Kansas City
Gift of Henry W. and Marion H. Bloch

DR 204
H 207

Provenance

Maximilien Luce (1858–1941), Paris, by 1905 and until at least 1934; probably bequeathed to his nephew, Édouard Alexandre Bouin (1897–1988), Paris and La Celle-Saint-Cloud, 1941 and until no later than December 1978; sale of his son, Jean Bouin-Luce (1920–1999), [Sotheby Parke Bernet, London], 6 December 1978, lot 216; acquired there by Fujii Gallery, Tokyo, and held until at least November 1990; offered for sale at [Sotheby's, New York], 1 May 1996, lot 34; following the withdrawal of the highest bidder, acquired in a private sale from [Sotheby's, New York], through [Richard L. Feigen and Co., New York], by Marion (née Helzberg, 1931–2013) and Henry (1922–2019) Bloch, Shawnee Mission, Kansas, July 1996; gifted by them to The Nelson-Atkins Museum of Art, June 2015

In addition to four canvases, Georges Seurat also brought back four oil sketches from his summer in Gravelines. Two were probably created as stand-alone works (cat. 26 and fig. 15), while the other two relate closely to one of the larger paintings. The present *croqueton* shows the composition of *Petit-Fort-Philippe* (cat. 20) almost already fully worked out. A few changes can be seen in the placement of the lighthouse, which Seurat has moved away from the edge of the composition in the final canvas, and the boat in the foreground, ultimately replaced by a central bollard. As is the case in the other oil sketch, *Study for The Channel of Gravelines: An Evening* (cat. 23), the scene depicted here is spare and empty; the boats that line the canal in the final work have been studied and added separately (see, for example, the drawing for the white clipper in the centre, now in the Guggenheim Museum, New York).

The handling of paint in this sketch is very lively and uses a wide range of colours, apposed in small touches. Many of the short brushstrokes are directional; for example, the dark blue dashes used for the boat in the foreground follow the shape of its hull, while those on the quay (most especially the white brushstrokes of the ledge) are diagonal to emphasise its recession. Technical analysis has shown that the sketch was made over several campaigns as some areas had had time to dry before new paint was applied over them.[50] This demonstrates the care Seurat devoted to his *croquetons*. They remained, however, studies of the motif and the particles of sand found caught in the paint of the present work confirm that it was made out of doors. This was also the case for *The Beach at Gravelines* (cat. 26). The white area of paint on the lower right of the composition, composed solely of vertical white brushstrokes, is surprisingly unarticulated. Seurat may have been covering up a tentative composition. It strikes a jarring note in an otherwise nuanced paint scheme. The perimeter of the sketch is composed of dashes of dark blue pigment, alternating with pine green, khaki and orange, which play off the adjacent colours in the image (sky, water, quay), and anticipates the thick border found in the final canvas. The sketch is recorded in Seurat's posthumous inventory as no. 138, one of 163 that were found in his studio after his death.

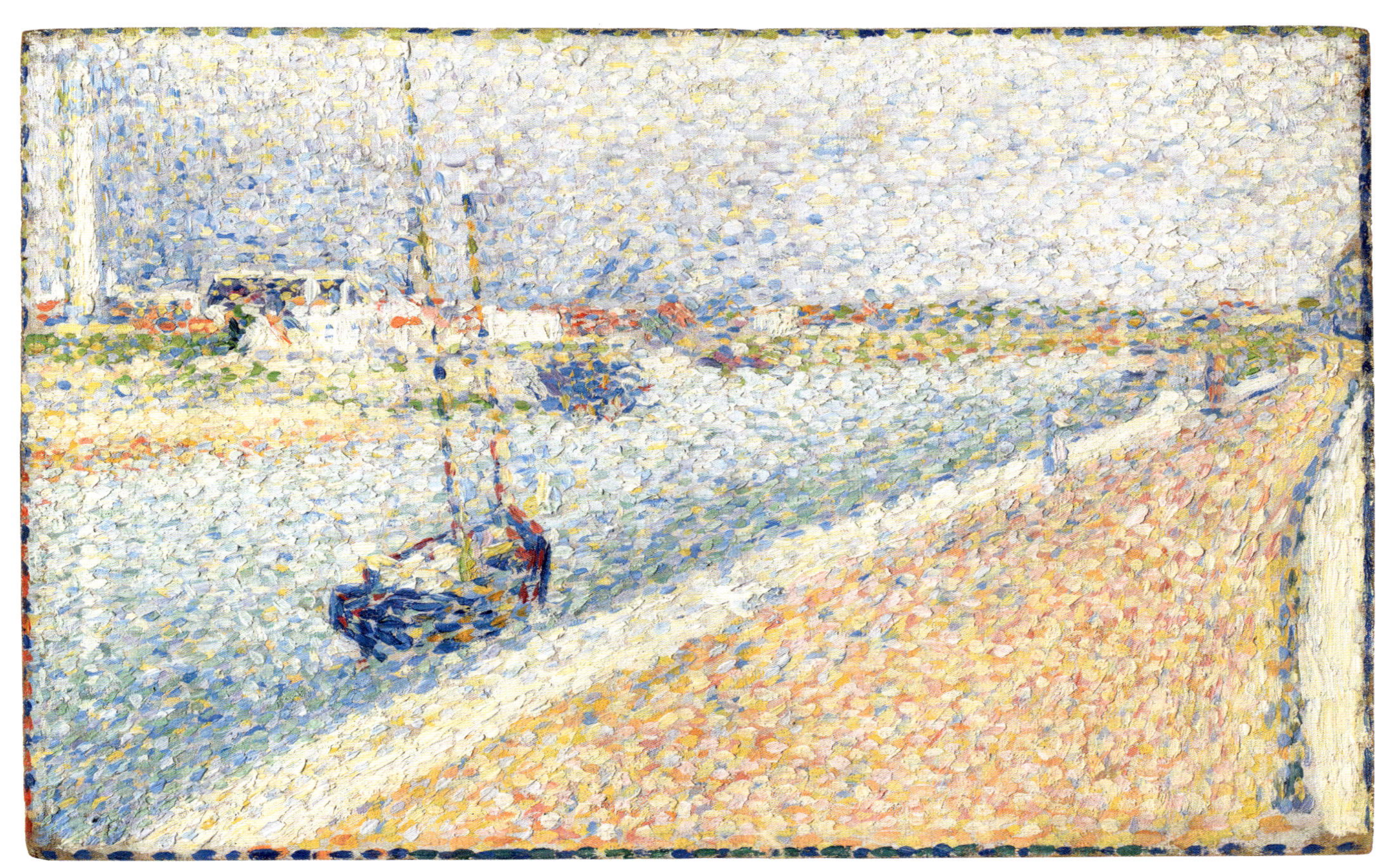

22

The Channel of Gravelines: An Evening

1890
Oil on canvas
65.4 × 81.9 cm
The Museum of Modern Art, New York
Gift of Mr. and Mrs. William A.M. Burden

DR 203
H 210

Exhibitions

1891 Brussels (*Le chenal de Gravelines : un Soir*)
1891 Paris

Provenance

Likely by inheritance to the artist's partner, Madeleine Knobloch (d. 1903), Paris, 1891; acquired by Sylvie Monnom (1836–1921), Brussels, 1892; gifted by her to her daughter Marie (1866–1959) and son-in-law, Théo van Rysselberghe (1862–1926), Brussels, by 1904 and until at least 1909; [Alfred Flechtheim, Düsseldorf]; acquired through [Gustaf (Gösta) Adolf Olson, Stockholm] by Rolf de Maré (1888–1964), Stockholm and Paris, 1918 and held until at least 1936; probably acquired from him by [Paul Rosenberg, Paris]; confiscated from him during the Nazi occupation by the ERR (Einsatzstab Reichsleiter Rosenberg), 1941; traded by Hermann Goering's agent Andreas Hofer with [Hans Wendland and Theodor Fischer, Lucerne], April 1942; turned over by Fischer at the request of the Swiss government to the collecting point at the Kunstmuseum Bern, 1945; returned to [Paul Rosenberg, New York], June 1948; acquired by William A.M. (1906–1984) and Margaret (née Livingston Partridge; 1909–1996) Burden, New York, October 1948; gifted by them to The Museum of Modern Art, 1963

This evocative painting depicts the pink glow of a summer twilight on the northern coast of France. Georges Seurat represented an evening scene in almost all of his summer campaigns (the exception being Le Crotoy, from where he brought back only two works). *Grandcamp (Evening)* (fig. 7), *Mouth of the Seine. Evening* (fig. 26) in Honfleur and *The Semaphores and the Cliff* from Port-en-Bessin (cat. 16) allowed him to change his colour harmonies from the blue and green sea and skies in the daytime to the purple, pink and yellow of sunset. The present composition alternates bands of dark and light colour: darkness is falling on the quays and the lamp post casts a long blue shadow, but the water and sky are still illuminated by the last rays of sun. Seurat stands on the edge of the canal in Petit-Fort-Philippe, looking out towards the tide signal station of Grand-Fort-Philippe across the way. The band of white beyond it is the open sea. The scene is perfectly framed by the lamp post on the left and the docked anchors on the right. In the middle distance, Seurat has added a small boat moored across the river and a passing sailboat, whose form seems to nestle within the left anchor.

The Channel of Gravelines: An Evening is the work for which Seurat left the most studies, both in oil and Conté crayon. One preparatory sketch and at least four drawings relate to this painting. A *croqueton* (cat. 23) and a compositional drawing (cat. 24) show Seurat working out the overall scene in both media. The external elements, such as the anchors and sailboat, were studied and added separately (see cat. 25 and fig. 16), creating, in the words of the art historian Robert L. Herbert, 'a reconstructed landscape'.[51]

In the Gravelines paintings, Seurat conjured a sense of infinity that belies the constricted and highly constructed space in which he worked. He united the port architecture and geometrical structures that so fascinated him in Honfleur and Port-en-Bessin with the open vistas of Le Crotoy. Vast skies now occupy at least half of the scenes. In paring down his compositions, Seurat created a feeling of expansiveness that is particular to this summer campaign.

As with all the Gravelines paintings, the present work had a large flat frame painted by Seurat to complement the tones of his image and the painted border. The frame, which was an integral part of Seurat's scheme, is now lost but can be seen in an early photograph of an exhibition to which it was lent in 1892 (fig. 14).

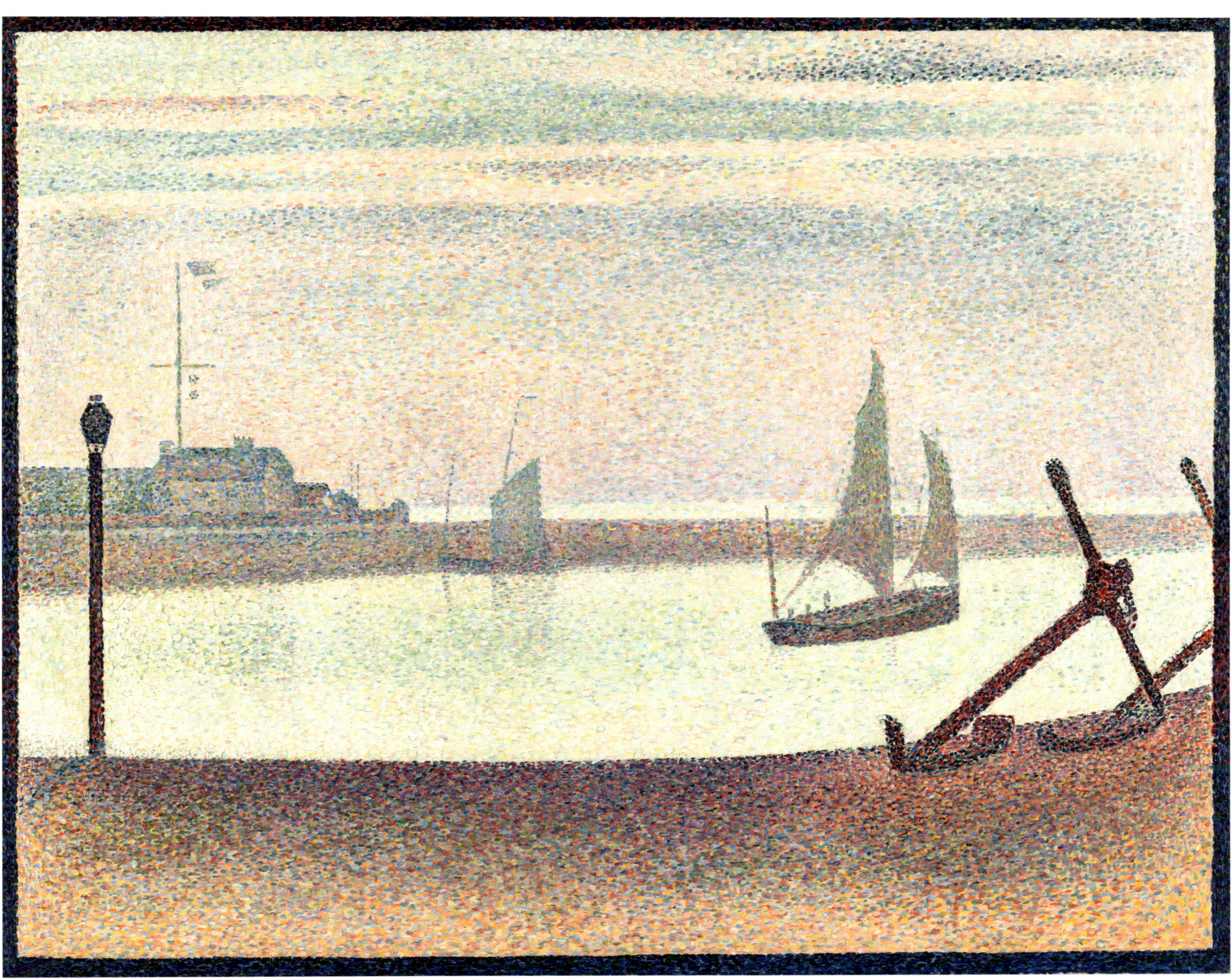

23

Study for The Channel of Gravelines: An Evening

1890
Oil on wood panel
16 × 25.6 cm
Centre Pompidou, Paris
Musée national d'art moderne / Centre de création
industrielle
On long-term loan to Musée de l'Annonciade,
Saint-Tropez
Bequest of George Grammont

DR 202
H 209

Provenance

Paul Signac (1863–1935), Paris, by 1905 and until at least
1908 (but more probably from 1891 to his death in 1935);
by descent to his daughter Ginette Signac (1913–1980),
Paris, 1935; George Grammont, by 1952; bequeathed
by him to the French state for loan to the Musée de
l'Annonciade, Saint-Tropez, 1959

In the inventory of Georges Seurat's studio after his death,[52] the present painting was listed immediately after *Study for The Channel of Gravelines: Petit-Fort-Philippe* (cat. 21) and shares many characteristics with it. Although preparatory for canvases painted during Seurat's summer in Gravelines in 1890, both works are fully realised and carefully painted – miniature worlds in their own right. Their compositions are relatively empty; Seurat only added the 'movable elements', in the words of the art historian Robert L. Herbert, in the final canvas.[53] An important difference is the absence of a border around the work, which would have anticipated the one in *The Channel of Gravelines: An Evening* (cat. 22).

In the present painting, Seurat has already fixed the final scene, buttressed by the dark lamp post on the left and the sweep of the quay in the foreground, where the estuary of the river Aa widens slightly. The balance of the composition is strongly tilted to the left, with the tall tide signal mast and the block of the station below, while the other half is spare, opening up to the channel and the sea beyond. Seurat would adjust this in the final work by the addition of the large anchors and sailing boat to the right.

The wood panel support was first given a light layer of white priming. The uneven application suggests that it was done by the artist himself and is, in some areas, so thin as to let the darker wood tone show through, a feature also found in his other sketches. The intricate application of paint showcases the incredible refinement of Seurat's technique and sense of colour. The work is composed of short touches of paint in a wide array of tones. The marks frequently overlap but each is conferred its own texture by the bristles of the brush. The addition of unexpected colours, such as light green, dusted on the surface in the final stages, demonstrates a level of spontaneity and play that is particularly evident in Seurat's *croquetons*. While the sky in the present preparatory sketch already shows the pink glow found in *The Channel of Gravelines: An Evening*, Seurat further softened and darkened his colours in the final painting.

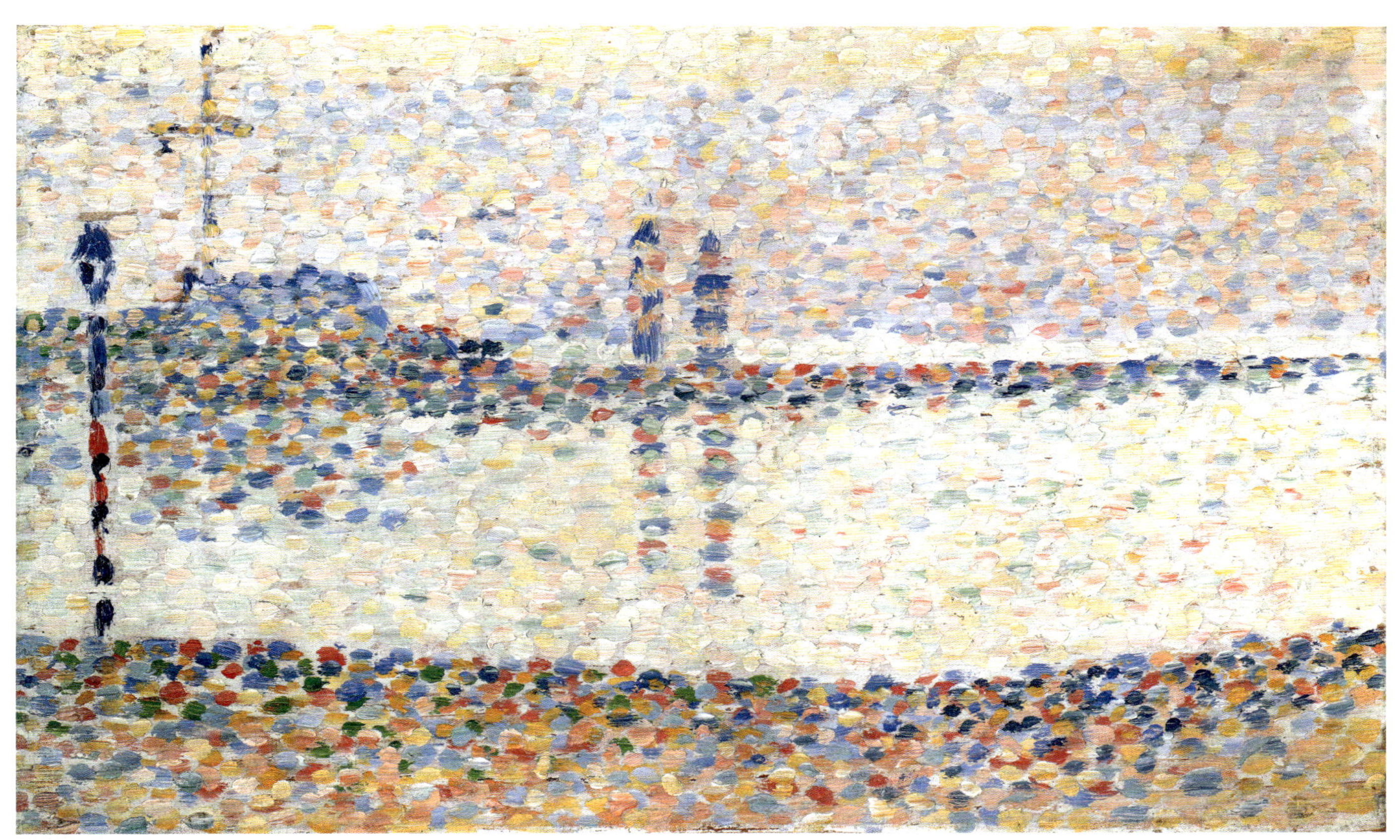

24

Gravelines, An Evening

1890
Conté crayon on laid paper
23.8 × 31.5cm
Jack Shear Collection, New York

DR 202a
H 696

Provenance

By inheritance to the artist's mother, Ernestine Seurat (née Faivre; 1828–1899), Paris, 1891; by descent to her daughter, Marie-Berthe (1847–1921), and son-in-law, Léon Appert (1837–1925), Paris, 1899; by descent to their daughter, Louise Alice Appert (1866–1939), 1925; possibly by descent to one of her sons, Henry or François Roussel, 1939 and until at least 1957; acquired at [Ader Picard Tajan, Paris], 22 June 1988, lot 3, by André Bromberg, Paris, and held until at least 1991; acquired from [Daxer & Marschall, Munich] by the present owner, 2018

Although a prolific draughtsman since his youth, Georges Seurat seems to have begun drawing on the Channel coast only during his second campaign, in Honfleur in 1886 (see cat. 9). Just as he favoured the same size of support for his oil sketches so he remained faithful to the quarter-page Michallet paper for his drawings, as confirmed by this delicate compositional sketch for *The Channel of Gravelines: An Evening* (cat. 22). As he had done earlier, Seurat used different pressures of the Conté crayon, as well as the layering of strokes, to achieve a range of tonal effects. As the medium does not smudge or blend, Seurat used light criss-cross strokes in the background to indicate the darkening sky and long lines for reflections on the water. Darker areas punctuate the composition and draw the viewer's eye across it, from the lamp post on the left and the edge of the quay to the hulls of the boats across the canalised river.

The composition of the drawing is similar to the one found in the related preparatory oil sketch (cat. 23). The two tower-like central elements (possibly masts?) have here been replaced with several moored boats, including one with its sail still hoisted, an element retained in the final canvas. The squarer proportions of the sheet are closer to those of the final composition than the elongated *croqueton*, and the prominence given to the sky in the canvas is already apparent here.

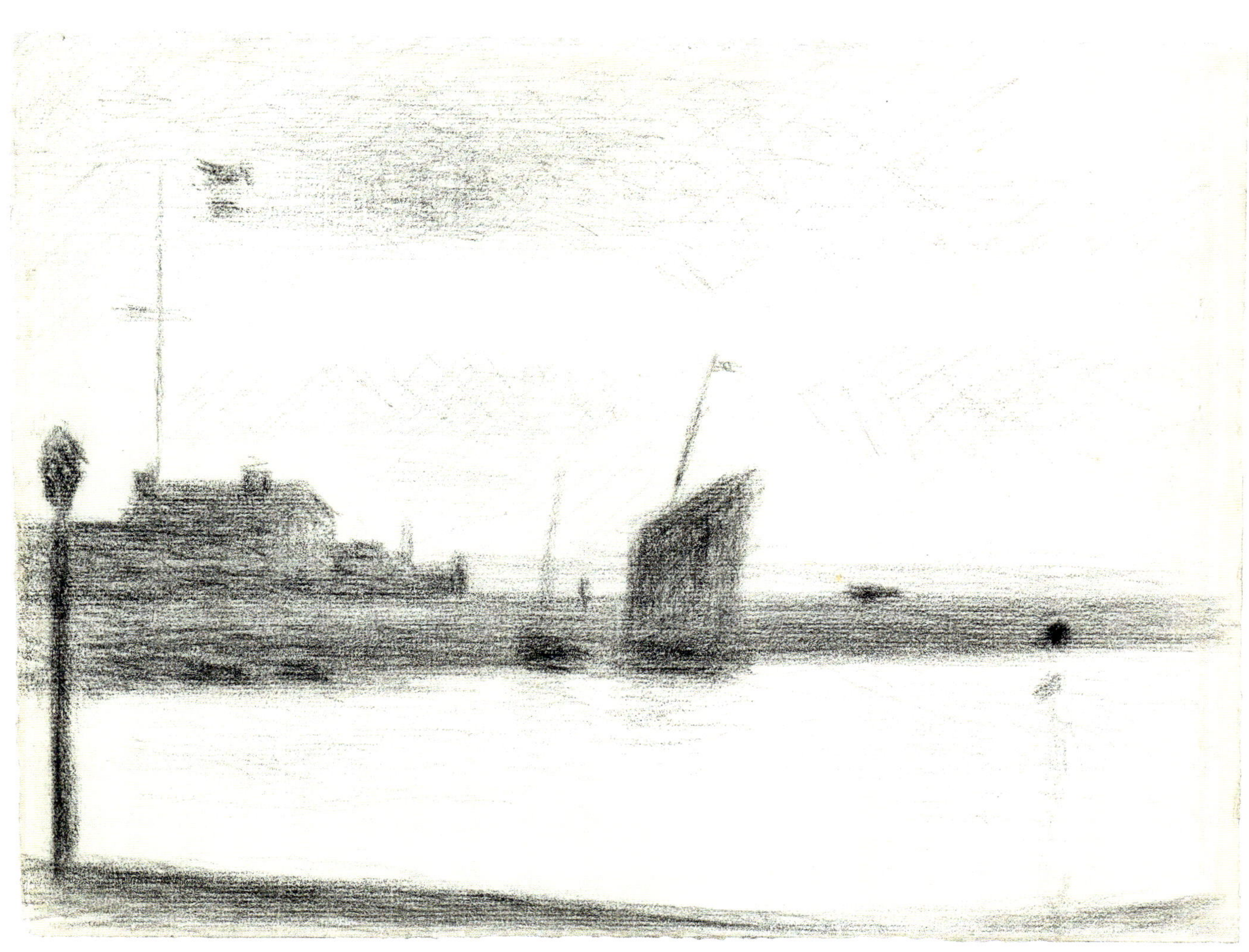

25

Study for The Channel of Gravelines: An Evening

1890
Conté crayon on laid paper
23.8 × 31.5 cm
Victoria and Albert Museum, London

DR 202d
H 698

Provenance
Émile Seurat (1846–1906), Paris; Édouard Vuillard
(1868–1940), Paris, by 1926; possibly by descent to his
nephew, Jacques Roussel (born c. 1900), 1940; possibly by
descent to his nephew, Antoine Salomon (born c. 1926);
acquired from JPL Fine Arts, London, by the Victoria and
Albert Museum, 1982

In addition to two compositional sketches (one in oil and the other in Conté crayon: see cat. 23 and 24), Georges Seurat also made studies of individual elements in preparation for *The Channel of Gravelines: An Evening* (cat. 22). This drawing is one of the most striking and depicts large anchors resting on the quay, with the jetty of Grand-Fort-Philippe and a moored boat in the distance. The arrangement of the anchors is identical to the one used in the final canvas, where they play a key role in creating a balance with the dark lamp-post on the left and in bringing in a diagonal element to counteract the bands of horizontal lines in the composition. It is likely that Seurat observed them somewhere along the quay but changed their location to bring them into his final composition.

The drawing is a particularly fine example of Seurat's mastery of Conté crayon. He managed to achieve a wide tonal range with the medium, from the light lines to evoke the sky and water to the shading of the pier in the middle distance and the darker quay in the foreground, rendered by applying more pressure to the crayon and by layering strokes. The anchors themselves are rendered with nuance; Seurat used the corner of his Conté stick to create finer and darker lines to mark their edges. Although Seurat regularly exhibited preparatory drawings for his larger canvases, the Gravelines drawings were not shown during his lifetime (perhaps because they were made only eight months before his death) but were included in several retrospective exhibitions thereafter.

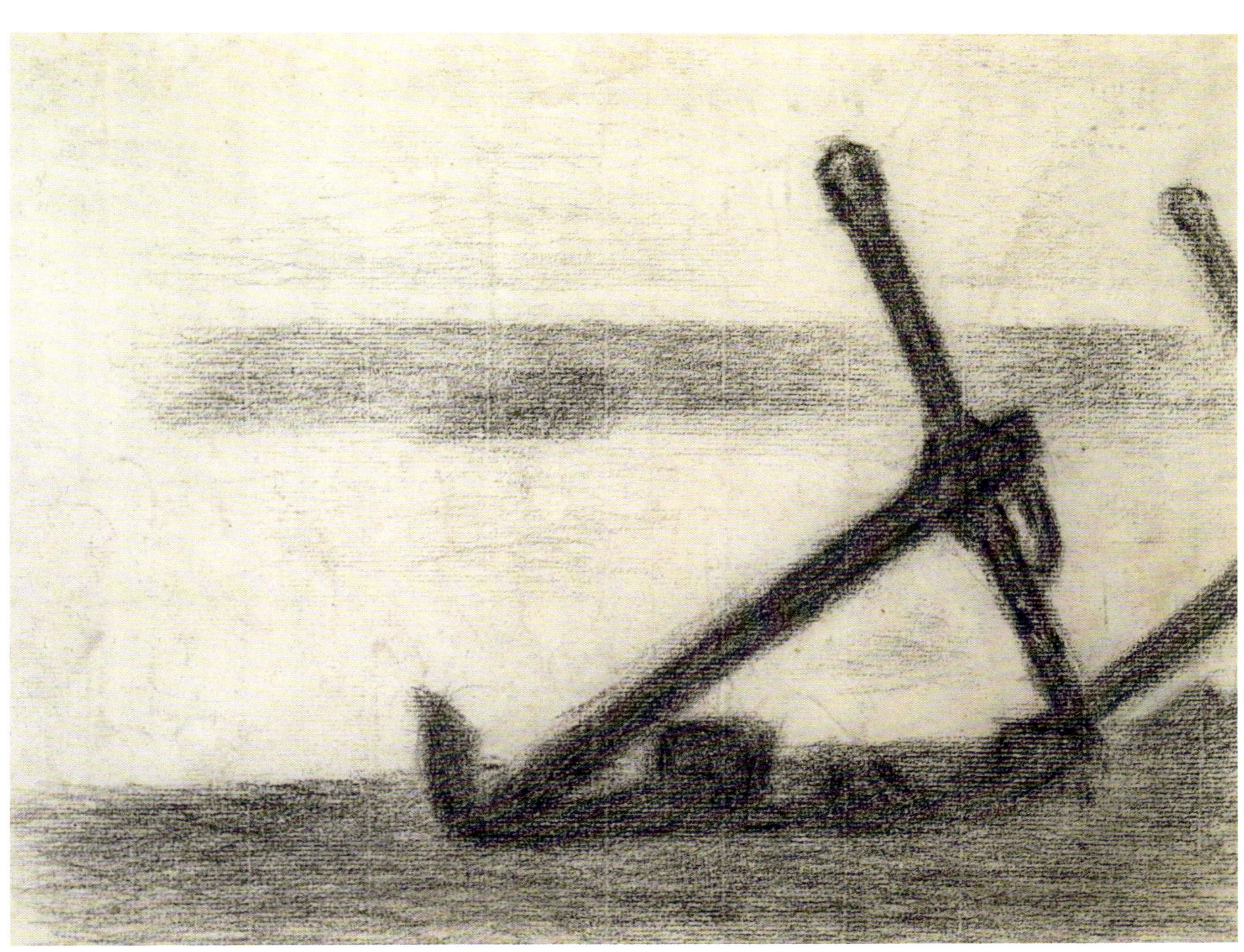

26

The Beach at Gravelines

1890
Oil on wood panel
16 × 24.5 cm
Courtauld Gallery, London (Samuel Courtauld Trust)

DR 201
H 204

Provenance
By inheritance to the artist's mother, Ernestine Seurat (née Faivre; 1828–1899), Paris, 1891; Alfred Tobler, Paris; [Bernheim-Jeune, Paris]; Alphonse Kann (1870–1948), Saint-Germain-en-Laye; acquired from [Alex. Reid & Lefevre, London] by Samuel Courtauld (1876–1947), London, July 1928; bequeathed by him to the Home House Trustees (now Samuel Courtauld Trust), 1948

This view from the beach looking out to sea captures the cloudy radiance of the northern coast of France. Water and sky blur into one another, as the horizon line is barely demarcated by a few orange and blue dots. In the foreground, a pool of water left by the tide provides even more luminosity and reflects the white clouds above. The sketch seems to be an exercise in using a limited palette to turn a prosaic landscape into a poetic vision, pushing the limits of figuration.

The *croqueton* is not preparatory for a larger canvas but done simply for pleasure. Particles of sand found embedded in the wet paint attest to its execution out of doors. Seurat first applied a thin white priming to the wooden panel. He then marked the shoreline with a series of large elongated dots of emerald green and placed other elements with dashes of cobalt blue, later covered by layers of paint.[54] As in Seurat's other sketches, his brush marks do not sit neatly side by side but overlap slightly. The water is rendered with thick white and yellow dots, given texture by the bristles of the brush. The orange and red dots scattered on the sand and on the horizon, added as a final layer, are sharper.

The feeling of melancholy in the present work, depicting an overcast day on the beach, is very different from the other known stand-alone sketch made that summer, *Seascape (Gravelines)* (fig. 15). The narrow colour scheme of *The Beach at Gravelines* gives way in that sketch to a vast array of juxtaposed colours to render the setting sun over the Channel. Like all of Seurat's paintings that summer, light is his true subject matter. Both *croquetons* were given a thin border long after the paint underneath had dried. The dark blue perimeter contains the composition and strikingly sets off its lighter colours.

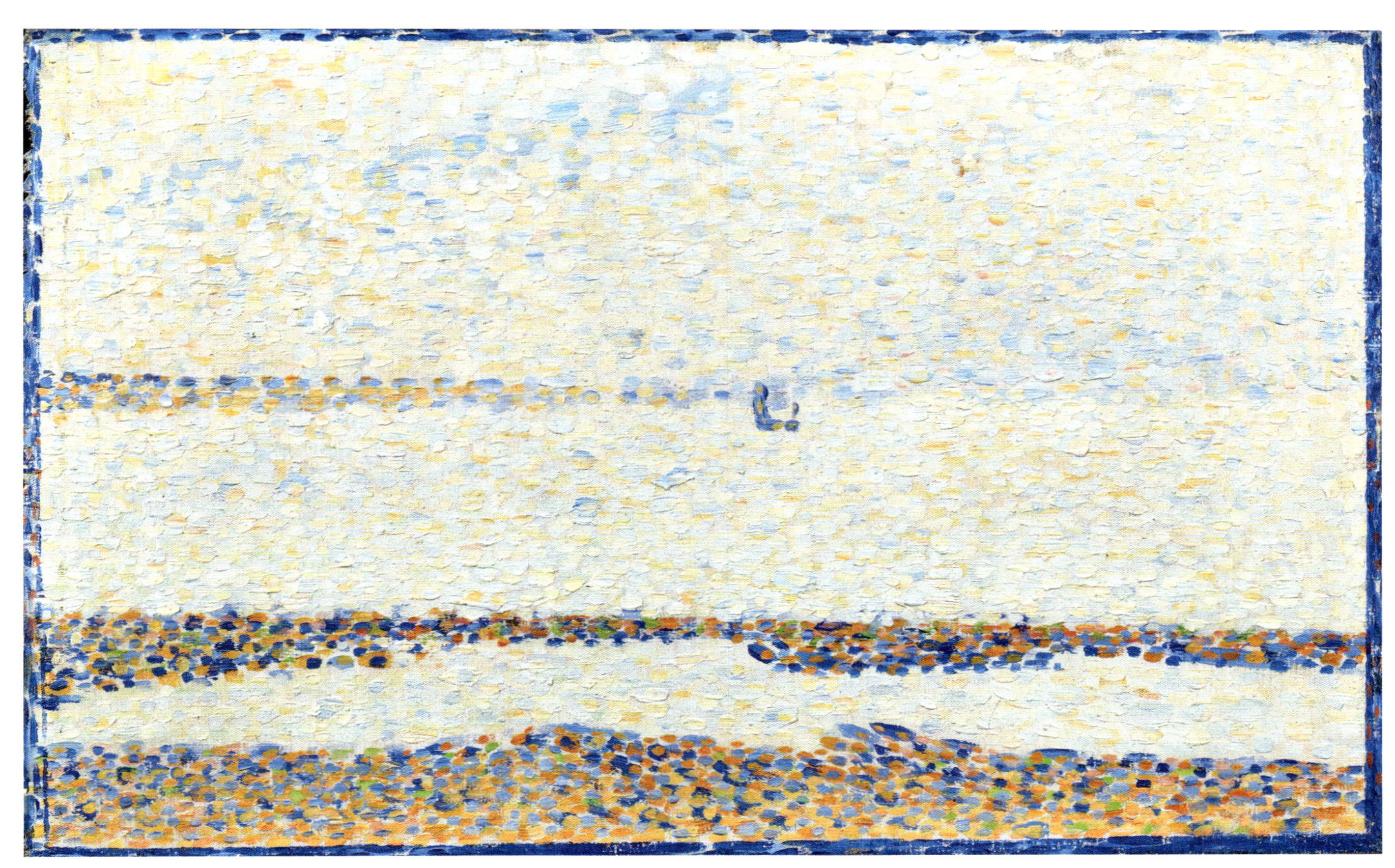

Notes

1   Kirby et al. 2003, p. 28.
2   Gustave Geffroy, 'Salon de 1886. VIII. Hors du Salon. – Les Impressionnistes', *La Justice*, 26 May 1886, pp. 1–2, at p. 1.
3   Letter from Georges Seurat to Paul Signac, 25 June 1886, Honfleur, first published in Rewald 1948, p. 111.
4   Thomson 1985, p. 158.
5   The other sketches in the frame were three studies for *Bathing, Asnières*, three for *A Sunday on La Grande Jatte* and four suburban scenes.
6   Hauke Archives 36/1/2/2.
7   Hauke Archives 36/1/5/2, reproduced in Hauke 1961, vol. 1, p. XXVIII.
8   Fénéon 1886 (Sept.), p. 301.
9   See 'Labruyère', 'Les Impressionnistes. II', *Le Cri du peuple*, 3rd year, no. 942, 28 May 1886, pp. 1–2, at p. 2: 'I was moved by the penetrating melancholy of his Roadstead of Grandcamp'.
10 Quoted in Coquiot 1924, p. 39.
11 Robert L. Herbert, *Seurat's Drawings*, New York: Shorewood Publishers, 1962, p. 179.
12 Herbert 1991, p. 287, noted that it was an abandoned dockyard.
13 Ann Hoenigswald, 'Examination Report and Treatment Proposal', 14 December 2004, National Gallery of Art Conservation Archives, pp. 1–5, at p. 2. I am grateful to Elizabeth Walmsley and Ann Hoenigswald for providing access to this documentation and the x-ray of the painting.
14 Herbert 1959, p. 322.
15 Marcel Fouquier, 'L'Exposition des artistes indépendants', *XIXe siècle*, 28 March 1887, p. 2.
16 Verhaeren 1887, p. 138.
17 Herbert 1959, p. 322.
18 The exhibition ran from 10 October 1886 to 15 January 1887 and included a room of 'Impressionists': see Lévy and Sciama 2018.
19 *Le Phare de la Loire,* 27 November 1886, quoted in Dorra and Rewald 1959, p. LI.
20 Trublot (Paul Alexis), 'À Minuit. L'Exposition des Artistes Indépendants', *Le Cri du peuple*, 26 March 1887, p. 3.
21 Paul Adam, 'Les Artistes indépendants', *La Revue rose: littéraire et artistique*, 3rd year, no. 5, May 1887, pp. 139–45, at pp. 142–43.
22 Signac 1934, p. 58.
23 Cyrille Sciama, '55. Georges Seurat. La Grève du Bas-Butin à Honfleur', in Lévy and Sciama 2018, p. 238.
24 Darragon 1984, p. 276, and the essay by Paul Smith in this publication.

25 See Smith 1984 on the setting of the views of Honfleur.
26 See also the list drawn up by Seurat in late 1886 or early 1887 of owners of his works, in Hauke Archives 36/1/2/2.
27 Hauke 1961, vol. 1, p. 142. This assertion is slightly undermined by the fact that the *croqueton* appears in Seurat's posthumous inventory in 1891. However, Hauke's catalogue is based on Fénéon's own notes and was written in collaboration with him so one must assume the information is correct.
28 *Seurat et ses amis: la suite de l'impressionnisme*, Galerie 'Beaux-Arts', Paris, December 1933–January 1934.
29 Signac 2014, p. 109.
30 Darragon 1984 found that the ship went back and forth between England and France twice weekly. It was therefore present in Honfleur every three days, depending on the tide.
31 See Darragon 1991; Herbert 1991, p. 318; and Foa 2015, pp. 44–50.
32 Darragon 1991, p. 53.
33 Ibid., p. 49.
34 Octave Maus, 'Le Salon des XX, à Bruxelles (VIe Exposition annuelle)', *La Cravache parisienne*, 9th year, no. 417, 16 February 1889, p. 1.
35 Darragon 1991, p. 49. See also Richard Thomson's essay in this publication.
36 Any Allard, 'Port-en-Bessin: le mystère de la Maison des Feux', *Le Pilote*, 2017: https://anystoire.blogspot.com/2018/02/port-en-bessin-le-mystere-de-la-maison.html (accessed 20 June 2025)
37 Fénéon 1889, p. 339.
38 The semaphore Seurat knew collapsed in 1913 with a landslide. I am very grateful to the author and historian of Port-en-Bessin Any Allard for sharing her knowledge with me. See her publications *Port-en-Bessin insolite*, Athis-Val de Rouvre: Éditions Charles Corlet, 2019, and *Vivre sur la falaise*, Port-en-Bessin: Édition La Goélette du Goéland, 2025.
39 Herbert 1991, p. 318.
40 I am greatly indebted to Elizabeth Walmsley and Ann Hoenigswald for discussion of this work and the opportunity to consult technical documentation on the painting: see Ann Hoenigswald, 'Examination Report and Treatment Proposal', 24 February 1992, pp. 1–5, and 'After Treatment Report', 21 December 2004, pp. 1–3, National Gallery of Art Conservation Archives, Washington, D.C.

41 Fénéon 1889, p. 339.
42 Herbert 1991, p. 233.
43 See Anna Gruetzner Robins, '*Manet and the Post-Impressionists*: a Checklist of Exhibits', *The Burlington Magazine*, vol. 152, no. 1293, December 2010, pp. 782–93, at p. 791, note 103.
44 Roger Fry, 'Seurat', *The Dial*, September 1926, pp. 224–32. See also Nancy Ireson, 'The Pointillist and the Past: Three English Views of Seurat', *The Burlington Magazine*, vol. 152, no. 1293, December 2010, pp. 799–803, and Chauffour 2019, p. 81.
45 Letter from Camille to Lucien Pissarro, 30 March 1891, in Pissarro 1950, p. 222.
46 See Chauffour 2019. The exception is *Circus Sideshow* (fig. 11), acquired slightly after that decade, in 1932, by Stephen C. Clark and bequeathed to The Metropolitan Museum of Art, New York.
47 One painting, *Nude with Yellow Hair*, is no longer attributed to Seurat.
48 See, most recently, Marieke Jooren and Suzanne Veldink, 'The Seurats of Helene Kröller-Müller', in Marieke Jooren, Suzanne Veldink and Helewise Berger, eds, *Seurat. Master of Pointillism*, exh. cat. Kröller-Müller Museum, Otterlo, 2014, pp. 132–33, and Julien Domercq, ed., *Radical Harmony. Helene Kröller-Müller's Neo-Impressionists*, exh. cat. The National Gallery, London (London: National Gallery Global Limited), 2025.
49 Ellen W. Lee, 'Seurat at Gravelines: The Last Landscapes', in Lee 1990, pp. 24–59, at p. 27.
50 See Diana M. Jaskierny, 'Georges Seurat, Study for The Channel of Gravelines, Petit Fort Philippe', 1890, technical entry in DeGalan 2023.
51 Herbert 1991, p. 354.
52 There is no established inventory list but the works were numbered on the back by the three executors, Félix Fénéon, Paul Signac and Maximilien Luce: see Hauke 1961, vol. 1, pp. XXIX–XXX.
53 Herbert 1991, p. 354.
54 Aviva Burnstock, 'Report of a Technical Examination of CIA 0293', Department of Conservation, Courtauld Institute of Art, London, June 2025. This has been observed in other sketches: see Kirby et al. 2003 and Diana M. Jaskierny, 'Georges Seurat, Study for The Channel of Gravelines, Petit Fort Philippe', 1890, technical entry in DeGalan 2023.

Sources and Publications Cited

Allard, Any, 'Historique du Port, Port-en-Bessin', 2014: portenbessin-huppain.fr/usp-content/uploads/2014/10/Historique-de-Port.-Allard-définitif.pdf

Baker, Master Asher, *Sailing Directions for the English Channel, Part II. North Coast of France and Channel Islands*, Washington, D.C.: Government Printing Office, 1877

Becker, Christoph, and Julia Burckhardt Bild, eds, *Georges Seurat: Figure in Space*, exh. cat., Kunsthaus Zürich and Schirn Kunsthalle Frankfurt (Ostfildern: Hatje Cantz), 2009

Berson, Ruth, *The New Painting. Impressionism 1874–1886. Documentation*, 2 vols, Fine Arts Museums of San Francisco, 1996

Braddick, Oliver, 'The Many Faces of Motion Perception', in Richard Gregory, John Harris, Priscilla Heard and David Rose, eds, *The Artful Eye*, Oxford: Oxford University Press, 1995, pp. 205–31

Brücke, Ernst, and Hermann von Helmholtz, *Principes scientifiques des beaux-arts : essais et fragments de théorie ; suivis de L'Optique et la peinture*, Paris: Baillère, 1878

Cachin, Françoise, *Signac. Catalogue raisonné de l'œuvre peint*, Paris: Gallimard, 2000

Callen, Anthea, *The Work of Art. Plein-air Painting and Artistic Identity in Nineteenth-Century France*, London: Reaktion Books, 2015

Chauffour, Sébastien, 'Competing for Masterpieces. Seurat in the Collection of Samuel Courtauld', in Karen Serres, ed., *The Courtauld Collection: A Vision for Impressionism*, exh. cat., Fondation Louis Vuitton, Paris (London: Paul Holberton Publishing), 2019, pp. 79–87

Coquiot, Gustave, *Seurat*, Paris: Albin Michel, 1924

Cousturier, Lucie, *Seurat*, Paris: G. Crès & Cie, 1926

Darragon, Éric, 'Seurat, Honfleur et La «Maria» en 1886', *Bulletin de la Société de l'histoire de l'art français*, 1984, pp. 263–80

Darragon, Éric, 'Lumière-Frontière. Remarques sur la série Port-en-Bessin de Seurat', in *L'Art, effacement et surgissement des figures. Hommage à Marc Le Bot*, Paris: Publications de la Sorbonne, 1991, pp. 45–55

DeGalan, Aimee Marcereau, ed., *French Paintings and Pastels, 1600–1945: The Collections of The Nelson-Atkins Museum of Art*, 2023, online catalogue, https://doi.org/10.37764/78973

Dorra, Henri, and John Rewald, *Seurat. L'Œuvre peint. Biographie et catalogue critique*, Paris: Les Beaux-Arts, 1959

Fénéon, Félix, 'Les Impressionnistes', *La Vogue*, no. 8, 15–20 June 1886, pp. 261–75

Fénéon, Félix, 'L'Impressionnisme aux Tuileries', *L'Art moderne* (Brussels), 6th year, no. 38, 19 September 1886, pp. 300–02

Fénéon, Félix, 'Le Néo-impressionnisme', *L'Art moderne* (Brussels), 7th year, no. 18, 1 May 1887, pp. 138–40

Fénéon, Félix, 'Exposition des Artistes-Indépendants à Paris', *L'Art Moderne* (Brussels), 9th year, no. 43, 27 October 1889, pp. 339–41 (revised version of an article first published as 'Tableaux', *La Vogue*, September 1889)

Fénéon, Félix, *Œuvres plus que complètes*, 2 vols, ed. Joan U. Halperin, Geneva: Librairie Droz, 1970

Figuier, Louis, *Les Merveilles de la science, ou description populaire des inventions modernes*, vol. 4, Paris: Librairie Furne, Éditeurs Jouvet et Cie, 1870

Foa, Michelle, *Georges Seurat: The Art of Vision*, New Haven and London: Yale University Press, 2015

Gombrich, Ernst, 'Moment and Movement in Art', in *The Image and the Eye: Further Studies in the Psychology of Pictorial Representation*, Oxford: Phaidon, 1982, pp. 45–62

Hauke Archives (archives of the dealer César Mange de Hauke [1900–1965], incorporating those of Félix Fénéon and largely related to the preparation of his catalogue raisonné on Seurat): no. 36, 'Acteurs du marché de l'art', Archives, autographes, manuscrits, dessins, objets et photographies, Bibliothèque de l'Institut national d'histoire de l'art, Paris

Hauke, César Mange de, *Seurat et son œuvre*, 2 vols, Paris: Gründ, 1961

Hauptman, Jodi, ed., *Georges Seurat: The Drawings*, exh. cat. Museum of Modern Art, New York, 2007

Herbert, Robert L., 'Seurat and Émile Verhaeren: Unpublished Letters', *Gazette des beaux-arts*, vol. LIV, no. 1091, December 1959, pp. 315–28

Herbert, Robert L., ed., *Georges Seurat 1859–1891*, exh. cat., Galeries nationales du Grand Palais, Paris, and The Metropolitan Museum of Art, New York (English edition: New York: The Metropolitan Museum of Art), 1991

Herbert, Robert L., ed., *Seurat and the Making of La Grande Jatte*, exh. cat., The Art Institute of Chicago (Berkeley and Los Angeles: University of California Press), 2004

Homburg, Cornelia, ed., *Neo-Impressionism and the Dream of Realities. Painting, Poetry, Music*, exh. cat., The Phillips Collection, Washington, D.C. (New Haven and London: Yale University Press), 2014

Hubbard, Timothy L., 'Extending Prägnantz: Dynamic Aspects of Mental Representation and Gestalt Principles', in Liliana Albertazzi et al., eds, *Perception Beyond Inference: The Information Content of Visual Processes*, Cambridge, Mass. and London: MIT Press, 2010, pp. 75–108

Huysmans, Joris-Karl, 'Chronique d'art. Les Indépendants', *La Revue indépendante*, vol. III, no. 6, April 1887, pp. 51–57

Kahn, Gustave, 'La Vie artistique', *La Vie moderne*, 9th year, no. 15, 9 April 1887, pp. 229–33

Kahn, Gustave, 'Seurat', *L'Art moderne*, 11th year, no. 14, 5 April 1891, pp. 107–10

Kirby, Jo, Kate Stonor, Ashok Roy, Aviva Burnstock, Rachel Grout and Raymond White, 'Seurat's Painting Practice: Theory, Development and Technology', *National Gallery Technical Bulletin*, vol. 24, 2003, pp. 4–37

Lee, Ellen Wardwell, ed., *Seurat at Gravelines. The Last Landscapes*, exh. cat., Indianapolis Museum of Art (Bloomington: Indiana University Press), 1990

Lévy, Sophie, and Cyrille Sciama, eds, *Nantes, 1886: le scandale impressionniste*, exh. cat., Musée d'arts de Nantes (Le Passage Paris–New York Éditions), 2018

Michelet, Jules, *La Mer*, ed. Marie-Claude Chemin and Paul Viallaneix, Paris: L'Âge d'homme, 1980 (first published 1861)

Pissarro, Camille, *Camille Pissarro. Lettres à son fils Lucien*, Paris: Albin Michel, 1950

Podro, Michael, 'Depiction and the Golden Calf', in Norman Bryson, Michael Ann Holly and Keith Moxey, eds, *Visual Theory: Painting and Interpretation*, Cambridge: Polity, 1991, pp. 163–89

Rewald, John, *Georges Seurat*, Paris: Albin Michel, 1948

Rewald, John, 'Extraits du journal inédit de Paul Signac, I. 1894–1895', *Gazette des beaux-arts*, vol. 36, no. 989–91, July–September 1949, pp. 97–128

Rey, Robert, *La Peinture française à la fin du XIXe siècle. La Renaissance du sentiment classique. Degas, Renoir, Gauguin, Cézanne, Seurat*, Paris: Les Beaux-Arts, 1921

Signac, Paul, 'Le Néo-Impressionnisme. Documents', *Gazette des Beaux-Arts*, vol. XI, January 1934, pp. 49–59 (first published as the introduction to the catalogue of the exhibition *Seurat et ses amis : la suite de l'impressionnisme*, Galerie 'Beaux-Arts', Paris, December 1933–January 1934)

Signac, Paul, *D'Eugène Delacroix au néo-impressionnisme. Écrits et propos sur l'art*, intr. Françoise Cachin, Paris: Editions Hermann, 2014 (3rd edition; first published Paris: La Revue blanche, 1899)

Smith, Paul, 'Seurat and the Port of Honfleur', *The Burlington Magazine*, vol. 126, no. 978, September 1984, pp. 562–69

Smith, Paul, *Seurat and the Avant-Garde*, New Haven and London: Yale University Press, 1997

Stonor, Kate, 'Seurat and the Evolution of Impressionism: an Examination of the Artist's Materials and Techniques in the Works of the Courtauld Collection', Final Year Research Project, Diploma in the Conservation of Easel Paintings, The Courtauld Institute of Art, London, 2001

Sutter, David, 'Les Phénomènes de la vision', *L'Art*, vol. XX, 1880, pp. 74–75, 124–25, 147–49, 195–97, 216–20 and 268–69

Thomson, Richard, *Seurat*, Oxford: Phaidon, 1985

Thomson, Richard, 'Jean-Charles Cazin, 1881–83: Naturalism and Networking, Regionalism and Republicanism', *The Burlington Magazine*, vol. 166, no. 1452, March 2024, pp. 278–85

Veldink, Suzanne, '"A Nearly Indefinable Grey Sea". Georges Seurat and the North French Coast', in Marieke Jooren, Suzanne Veldink and Helewise Berger, eds, *Seurat. Master of Pointillism*, exh. cat., Kröller-Müller Museum, Otterlo, 2014, pp. 99–118

Verhaeren, Émile, 'Le Salon des *Vingt* à Bruxelles', *La Vie moderne*, 9th year, no. 9, 26 February 1887, pp. 135–39

Verhaeren, Émile, 'Georges Seurat', *La Société nouvelle. Revue internationale*, 7th year, vol. 1, LXXVI, April 1891, pp. 429–38

Willats, John, *Art and Representation: New Principles in the Analysis of Pictures*, Princeton: Princeton University Press, 1997

Willats, John, and Fredo Durand, 'Defining Pictorial Style: Lessons from Linguistics and Computer Graphics', *Axiomathes*, vol. XV, no. 3, September 2005, pp. 319–51

Wollheim, Richard, 'Giovanni Morelli and the Origins of Scientific Connoisseurship', in *On Art and the Mind: Essays and Lectures*, London: Allen Lane, 1973, pp. 177–201

Wollheim, Richard, *Painting as an Art*, London: Thames & Hudson, 1987

Woloshyn, Tania, and Anne Dymond, eds, 'New Directions in Neo-Impressionism', *RIHA Journal (Journal of the International Association of Research Institutes in the History of Art)*, Special Issue no. 1, 14 July 2012: https://doi.org/10.11588/riha.2012.1

Zimmermann, Michael F., *Les Mondes de Seurat. Son œuvre et le débat artistique de son temps*, Antwerp: Fonds Mercator and Paris: Albin Michel, 1991

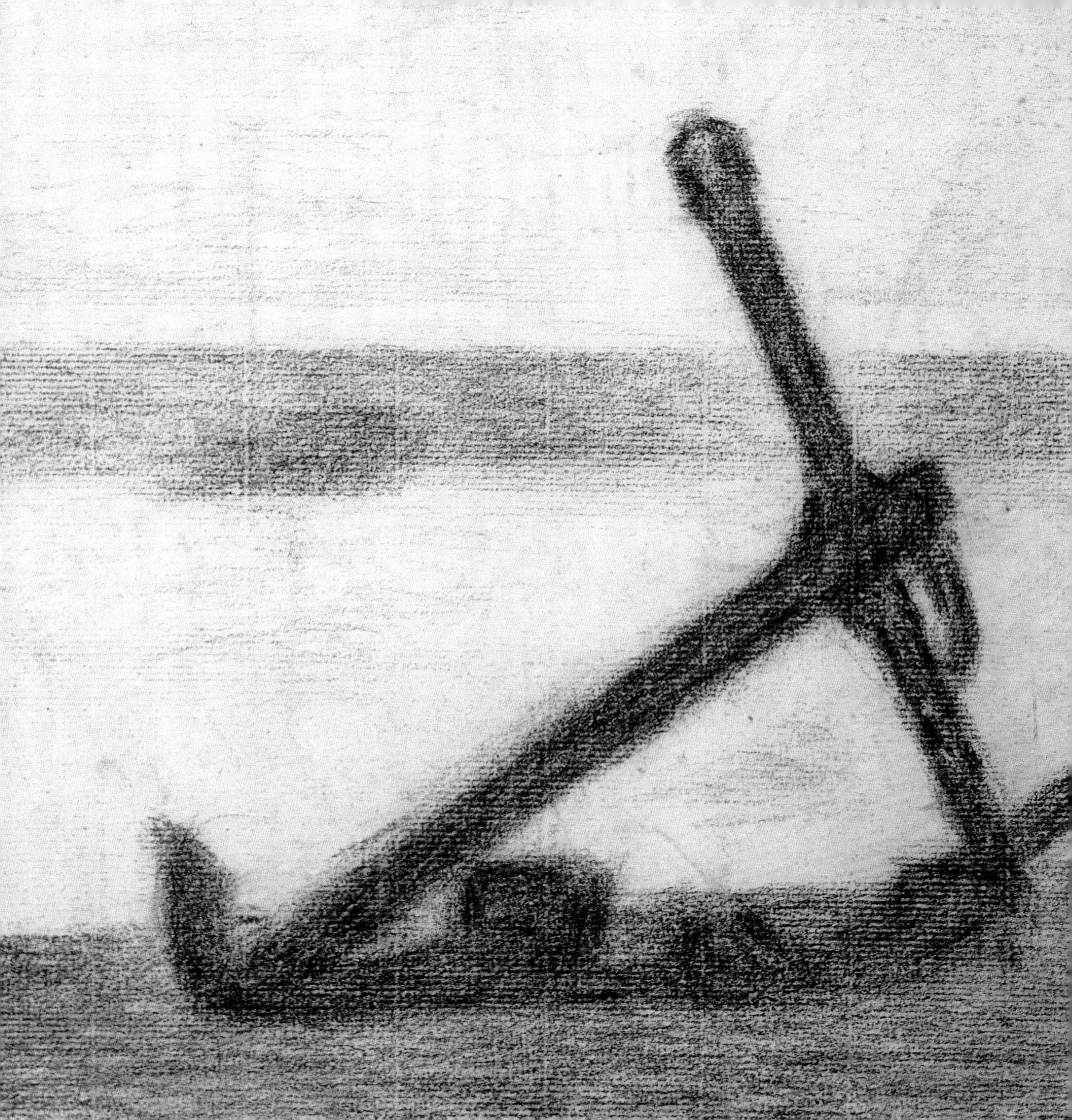

Photographic Credits